A Chicano Manual on How to Handle Gringos

Also by José Angel Gutiérrez

A Gringo Manual on How to Handle Chicanos

They Called Me "King Tiger": My Struggle for the Land and Our Rights, editor and translator

A Chicano Manual on How to Handle Gringos

José Angel Gutiérrez

Foreword by Henry A. J. Ramos

Arte Público Press
Houston, Texas

This volume is made possible through grants from the Charles Stewart Mott Foundation, the City of Houston through The Cultural Arts Council of Houston, Harris County, the Ewing Marion Kauffman Foundation, and the Rockefeller Foundation.

Recovering the past, creating the future

Arte Público Press
University of Houston
452 Cullen Performance Hall
Houston, Texas 77204-2004

Cover art and design by James F. Brisson

Gutiérrez, José Angel.
   A Chicano Manual on How to Handle Gringos /
José Angel Gutiérrez; foreword by Henry A. J. Ramos
      p.   cm. — (The Hispanic Civil Rights Series)
   ISBN 1-55885-396-0 (pbk. : alk. paper)
      1. Mexican Americans—Civil rights—Handbooks, manuals,
etc.   2. Civil rights movements—United States—Handbooks,
manuals, etc.   3. Mexican Americans—Civil rights—Anecdotes.
4. Civil rights movements—United States—Anecdotes.
5. United States—Ethnic relations—Handbooks, manuals, etc.
6. United States—Ethnic relations—Anecdotes.   I. Title
II. Series.
E184.M5G868 2003
323.1′16872073—dc21   2003044429
                                                                        CIP

♾ The paper used in this publication meets the requirements of the American National Standard for Information Sciences—Permanence of Paper for Printed Library Materials, ANSI Z39.48-1984.

3 4 5 6 7 8 9 0 1 2   10 9 8 7 6 5 4 3 2 1

Table of Contents

My Chicano generation uncovered our potential power.
Your generation will realize power.
Together, let's paint the White House Brown!

To my last daughters:
Andrea Lucía Gutiérrez
Clavel Amariz Gutiérrez

To my grandchildren:
Adrián Davison Gutiérrez
Che Nicolás Gutiérrez
Juan Marcel Tijerina
y la Jackie Brown.

In memoriam
Gary Bigger, artist/activist
Warren Burnet, attorney
Roberto "Bob" Cruz, educator
Robert Donley, Chicano activist
Ignacio Fuentes, mi tío
Tony Martínez, boricua actor/musician
Maury Maverick, Jr., activist lawyer
Ruben Munguia, printer/politico
Jesús "Chuy" de la O, barrio activist
Irma Rangel, politician
Frank Trejo, journalist
Raul Villarreal, Chicano militant
Guadalupe Youngblood, Raza Unida Party and MAYO militant

R.I.P. 2002

Foreword

The 1960s and 1970s spawned some of the most significant Hispanic civil rights and social justice activities in U.S. history. During these years, Americans gained unprecedented exposure to the plight of Spanish-speaking people in the United States, through the organizing activities of Latino workers, students, artists, and community activists. The struggles for justice among Mexican Americans across the Southwest, who proudly called themselves Chicanos, were especially intense and significant. One of the leading figures of the Chicano movement of this period was José Angel Gutiérrez. Gutiérrez, then a young community and political organizer from Southwest Texas, spearheaded a new vehicle to radically alter Mexican-American political participation in the region, called the Raza Unida ("United People's") Party. By the early 1970s, the Raza Unida Party succeeded against overwhelming odds to win key elected offices in Texas (Crystal City at the Winter Garden Area, San Antonio, Rio Grande Valley, El Paso), and Washington D.C.'s Adams-Morgan Area. These victories helped to change the face of U.S. Hispanic politics in important ways.

Gutiérrez's many political activities, including school protests, farm worker, marches, and student political organizing, through the Mexican-American Youth Organization (MAYO) produced a substantial body of FBI surveillance and disapproving establishment scrutiny. The electoral movement that he helped to forge ultimately waned, as so many modern American third party efforts have. Gutiérrez persevered in the aftermath of the Raza Unida Party's demise, to pursue a career in progressive scholarship. He remained active in community affairs and organizing activities, developing a widely read underground book called *A Gringo Manual on How to Handle Mexicans*, which he self-published in the mid-1970s. Arte Público Press reproduced the volume in 2001 in updated form, following substantial efforts by Gutiérrez to advance and expand the quality, currency, and relevance of the *Manual* (through constant editing, updating over the years, and one hundred new anecdotes of powerlessness).

Now the former radical activist, still a strong progressive voice in his own right, has produced an important new analogue edition, called *A Chicano Manual on How to Handle Gringos*. This book, presented here by Arte Público as part of its Hispanic Civil Rights Series, provides a roadmap to minority empowerment through an effective use of analysis, practical experience, and anecdote. In an incisive introduction, Gutiérrez analyses various types of power and evaluates Chicano and Latino access to it at various levels of U.S. society. Using very plain, down to earth language and examples, Gutiérrez takes pains to make his broad knowledge and experience available to everyone, but especially to those who want to be activists for themselves and their communities. Quite often, Gutiérrez's voice is not only the seasoned voice of reason, but also that of humor, wry wit, and satire.

We are pleased to feature this key figure of the Chicano Movement years as a leading contributor to Arte Público Press's Hispanic Civil Rights Series. The series seeks to increase public knowledge and appreciation concerning Hispanic contributions to U.S. civil rights advancement in the post World War II era. With generous support from the Charles Stewart Mott Foundation, the Ewing Marion Kauffman Foundation, and the Rockefeller Foundation, the series is supporting the public dissemination and discussion of important new and revised works covering the key organizations, leaders, and movements that have shaped contemporary Hispanic social justice gains. By pointing out the many public achievements of these groups and individuals, even in the face of substantial mainstream resistance, the series aims to expand national comprehension of the strength and vitality of U.S. democratic institutions, and of the promise of our nation's dramatically increasing cultural diversity.

As Hispanic Americans emerge to become the nation's most populous minority group at the outset of the 21st century, many of the injustices first chronicled in Gutiérrez's *A Gringo Manual* sadly are on the rise. Mexican origin and other Hispanic Americans suffer continuing indignities at the hands of politicians, law enforcement officials, employers, universities, the media, philanthropic grant-making organizations, and other leading institutions. Hispanics and especially newer immigrants are also increasingly subject to the nation's growing incidence of racially motivated hate crime. Gutiérrez's entries in *A Chicano Manual* bring forward in full-blown color the ways Mexican Americans (and by extension other Latino groups) have found to combat the pettiness of contemporary anti-Latino racism, xenophobia, and institutional bias. They focus on examples of Hispanic power, rather than powerlessness. They amplify the fact that notwithstanding continuing resistance to Latino ascendance among many in the mainstream culture, Mexican and other Latino people in the U.S. are bound to be a significant force in the American future.

Quite importantly, Gutiérrez's introductory remarks in his earlier work, *A Gringo Manual*, make clear that to be a "Gringo" is not a condition of racial or ethnic assignment. Instead, he observes, to be Gringo speaks to a state of mind; that is, a mind to be anti-Hispanic. Hence, in Gutiérrez's comprehension of the term, Mexican Americans and other Hispanics can also be Gringos; and indeed many regrettably are. Conversely, not all European (or other non-Hispanic) Americans are Gringos. The same logic applies by extension to his current work.

In effect, what Gutiérrez is suggesting here is that the continuing persistence of Gringo-mindedness and Gringo practice in America is neither pre-ordained nor immune from the powerful influences of reason and social evolution. Latino Americans and other Americans of all backgrounds have the power and the opportunity to overcome our sad Gringo legacy. We have the intellectual capacities to place our common humanity before our worst instincts and our darkest historical biases. The remaining unanswered question, however, is whether we finally have the vision and the will to do so.

José Angel Gutiérrez's life's work, and the contents that follow here, challenge us to address these fundamental issues. A leading protagonist of the Chicano Movement's heyday, Gutiérrez remains today a fiercely committed, galvanizing community advocate. His large contributions to the political and intellectual struggle for Hispanic equality in America, however, will have long-enduring impacts. His place in the pantheon of progressive change agents in U.S. Latino history is secure. The work that follows reflects the reasons for this and Arte Público Press is privileged indeed to expand this important leader's contributions to the public record.

Henry A. J. Ramos
Executive Editor
Arte Público Press Hispanic Civil Rights Book Series

Acknowledgments

There are so many persons to thank and acknowledge as having a role in the finalization of this book. First and foremost are all of you who kept asking me when the sequel to the *A Gringo Manual on How to Handle Mexicans* would come out. Second are the countless persons that told me stories fitting for inclusion in this manuscript. Some of those stories are included, others are still in my memory or file box because of space and time limitations. Research has to end sometime, and writing has to begin in order to finish and submit your manuscript on time. But thank you all—you know who you are. Third are my immediate family members who, again, had to walk softly, talk quietly, keep the TV, DVD, and CD noise down, and call me repeatedly for meals when they were cooked. Gloria, Andrea, and Clavel, thank you very much. Fourth, Cecilia Lugo, Gloria Carrillo, Diana Morales, and Joel Vera, thank you for keeping the law office running without me. You have no idea how much the load you carry for me helps. Lastly, Karen McGee, thank you for typing interviews from which portions were gleaned for this work. Thanks, Diana Flores, Gloria Gutiérrez, Irma Mireles, and reviewers, for reading this manuscript and making suggestions for improvement. And, *gracias mil* to my partners and publishers/editors, Nicolás Kanellos, Henry A. J. Ramos, Gabi Baeza Ventura, Marina Tristán, and Mónica Parle of Arte Público Press. Your patience and gentle nudging are appreciated, but more importantly, your willingness to see this book to completion.

Preface

In my prior work in this area, *A Gringo Manual on How to Handle Mexicans,* both editions, I focused on the powerlessness of our ethnic community. I inventoried anecdotes of situations in various fields in which power was used against our community members, to tease out of the story, a lesson on power relations.

In the opening essay in the *A Gringo Manual,* 2nd edition, I posed three fundamental questions. The answers to these questions are the path out of powerlessness. The questions are straightforward:

- How does the world work?
- How do I make the world work for me?
- How do I make the world?

The first question is foundation building. The answer a person finds to this question is what guides him or her the rest of his or her life in given situations. The answer also becomes the power structure for that individual, his or her source of power. This is what the person knows his power to be: skills, potential, ability, reach, range, and level. The question and answer are proscribed primarily by geography, the geography of what a person knows and recognizes as his world. A person's world could be his family, barrio, city, county, state, region, work, imagination, travels, dreams. The overwhelming number of people in the world, not just our Raza, are at this stage of awareness of power, and remain locked in this personal structure and level of power.

The second question is framed by education and skills acquired once a person begins to expand his horizons beyond the family, home, local school, first jobs, barrio, and immediate area of travel.

Most college graduates, skilled workers, and former military soldiers, regardless of years of formal education, are at this question-and-answer stage. In fact, I would argue that most of us who go beyond high school and learn greater skills do so because we have been in the first average state of power and want more personal power. We want a greater power structure. We want the world, as we know it, to work in our favor. When we succeed in college, at work, within a career, and start a family of our own, we are happy. Most of us at this mid-range level of power are comfortable with the power structure we have built. We do not make any more great efforts to further change the way the world works. It works for us, and that was the ultimate goal. That the world does not work for others is not a moving force within us anymore. The degree of purpose, the commitment, *las ganas*, the solidarity with others, and the struggle for the greater good are diminished. We will donate money to causes. We will volunteer some time in an effort and empathize with those not as fortunate, and otherwise lend moral support, but little else. We might even join a civil rights organization. Because we are in the mid-range level of power, our view is upward, not downward. Those below, we begin to believe, must face and deal with that situation. It is *their* problem. We disengage and disinvolve ourselves from direct action with them. Group cohesion is still important, but we now have a new group. We seek to engage and involve ourselves with those above us with greater power.

The third question is posed and pondered by activists. We want to re-make the world to our likeness. We want our interests promoted and protected. Unfortunately, there are not many activists, usually a tiny minority of any given group in any location without regard to age, ethnicity, gender, race, or national origin. These are the doers in any setting. These are the people that bring about change for themselves and for others. For some persons, bringing about change for themselves and others is a package of one ultimate goal; to others the two tracks of change for themselves and change for others are mutually exclusive goals. I have observed that those of us from the Chicano Generation were intent on bringing about an entire package of change for all, one goal. I now observe that the subsequent generation, our children, the Hispanic Generation, are not activists and doers. They do work for change for themselves. They seldom work for change for others. I believe that as mentors and parents of the Hispanic Generation, we are partly to blame for this attitudinal demarcation line. Because of our work in the area of civil rights, we corrected wrongs and obtained remedies to social ills. In so doing, we also produced a generation of beneficiaries who know not how to fight and struggle. They have paid no price for their benefits; hence, they don't know why they should struggle and fight. And, they don't. Rather than identify and confront an enemy, they want to embrace and include the opposition as potential friends and allies.

In this work, I shift the focus, as implied in the title, *A Chicano Manual on How to Handle Gringos*. This sequel is about power, not powerlessness. By 2020, Latinos in the United States will become a majority of the population in most states and urban centers. By that decade we will also become the largest voting bloc in those states and cities.

Over the next 18 years, our power condition will grow from potential power to realized power. We will become the governors and the governed. We will have established political sovereignty over much of the United States. The White House, the various state houses, the numerous city halls, the many school administration buildings, and scores of community college presidents and chancellors will be positions held by Latinas and Latinos. The economy will be led by us as producers, consumers, and owners of business. Our middle class will grow in direct relation to how effectively we pull underclass members into the Latino fold via education, housing ownership, health status, labor organization, and integration of major institutions.

Central to the success of my forecast is the need for group solidarity and identity. We can build group solidarity. But first we must forge new identities as, for example, Latinos of Mexican ancestry or Hispanics of Salvadoran background, or we can retain our existing political identities, as we do *en español: somos hondureños, panameños, guatemaltecos, mexicanos, chilenos, cubanos, dominicanos,* etc. Regional political identities as *tejanos, chilangos, regiomontanos, costeños, manitos*, and the like, will not empower group cohesion or solidarity. These regional attachments only divide us. The U.S. Census Bureau will continue to label us as Hispanics. The U.S. Census Bureau will continue to classify us by ethnicity AND race, and insist we do the same. These are nothing more than methods of social control. We are divided within ourselves as a group by ethnicity and are divided outside ourselves by race. We are all *mestizos*. We are all mixed bloods. The mestizo-group banner will fly before any flag of indigenous purity or European lineage will. We are transnational *mestizo* migrants.

We will realize great electoral power if we renew and/or develop organizational leadership. Our current leaders of organizations, formed during the Chicano Movement, have grown old. They have held office too long and must make immediate plans for succession. They probably won't. They have become addicted to the power inherent in their jobs. It is our group power and the organizational power that created them, but they have taken it as their own. And they cannot do without it.

Current programs for leadership development must include strategic planning, global visioning, and leadership renewal. We must all build within all our organizations second, third, and fourth levels of successors to power. We will realize great electoral power in the nation by 2020 if we maintain group cohesion, practice solidarity, have commonality of purpose and agenda, and renew our organizational leadership.

I will outline the structure and three levels of power held by persons within the U.S. in this work. The purpose is to begin gaining insight into the pressure points of the system of power relations. By illustrating with simple stories how some Chicanas and Chicanos, Latinas and Latinos have realized power, I shall provide the reader at once with a glimpse of the overall structure of personal power and the various levels of power at play.

I use the generic terms Chicano and Latino mostly, and sometimes Latina and Chicana when appropriate. I make no use of the politically correct slash (/) *o/a* for some to designate gender and be inclusive. We are all one and the same in English. I use Raza to include us all. And, lest we forget, Chicano is a political activist, a child born in the U.S. of Mexican parentage; and *gringo* is a normally bad Anglo, but in every case a racist. Not all Anglos are *grin-*

gos, and not all *gringos* are Anglos. We have some black *gringos,* brown *gringos,* yellow *gringos,* red *gringos,* and mixed-blood *gringos. Gringas* are just as bad as the male *gringos.* Being a *gringo* is an attitude, not a nationality, gender, race, or ethnicity.

This book is about the emerging Chicano and Latino power in the United States. The title suggests that new experience for Chicanos and Latinos in this country. It was not long ago that we had virtually no power in any sphere, except maybe along the border with Mexico, where our numbers have exceeded those of Anglos for decades and we managed to elect a handful of *políticos.* That emerging power began in that geographic area in the late 1940s, when our focus on politics turned away from Mexico and into the United States. During the Chicano Movement of the 1960s and into the '80s, we began to expand that emerging power into the heartland of the U.S. The Raza Unida Party, which I founded with the support and help of so many others, had organizations in nineteen states plus the District of Columbia. We had a presence and captured the imagination of many, many voters, but were short-lived. This was and is a country with a two-party political dictatorship, still firmly in place in 2002. Ask Ralph Nader if you doubt me. Ask Ross Perot if you doubt me. Ask Roberto Mondragón or Russell Means, if you doubt me. All of them tried to take on the two-headed political system by running for public office after we did as candidates of La Raza Unida. These other persons also had presence and captured the imagination of voters, but were short-lived. Jesse Ventura in Minnesota was an exception. Barry Sanders of Vermont is an exception. These exceptions are not the beginning of a trend, I assure you.

The Chicano Movement uncovered potential power. We recruited and propelled young people, mostly males and some females, into leadership roles. We founded organizations as we engaged in the serious business of nation building. Aztlán, the building of a Chicano nation, was a very real goal to us. The very organizations founded during the Chicano Movement remain. The founding purpose of helping to build Aztlán does not. Annually, these organizations hold great gatherings in big cities in expensive hotels and give awards to each other and to the white politicians and corporate leaders that give them money: MALDEF, SVREP, NALEO, Project SER, IMAGE,

TAMACC, NOSOTROS, MANA, TELACU, NCLR, Hispanic Scholarship Fund, Spanish Speaking Unity Council, and Latin American Civic Association. There are scores of regional and local organizations, such as Siete del Norte (NM), Chicanos Por La Causa (AZ), Colonias del Valle (TX), Mexican American Opportunity Foundation (CA), TACHE (TX), FLOC (OH), TFW (TX), Casa Aztlán (IL), Centro Aztlán (TX), and Centro de la Raza (WA). These organizations have endured because organizational survival as the primary goal has replaced group ascendancy and the building of Aztlán.

There is pressing need for organizational leadership renewal, particularly at the top.

There is need for even more organizations to form and share the labor of building Aztlán. Aztlán, regrettably, remains a viable goal only to aging Chicanos. The new development in this century is the continuing and expanding Mexican influence and the presence of other Latinos, particularly Central Americans. Neither Mexicanos nor Centro Americanos know about Aztlán or agree to such a group goal. We will become one Mexico sooner than one Central America or Aztlán.

Our power has grown immensely in a short time because of three factors: (1) geography, our spatial presence along the U.S.-Mexico border and in large urban centers; (2) demography, our growing numbers and the decline of other groups; and, (3) economic power, our labor readiness, and consumer power. These three factors produce a fourth reality: political and voting power. Our physical presence in large numbers gives rise to critical mass. Critical mass and money make us the target of politicians, media marketers, corporations, labor unions, churches, criminals, other ethnic and racial groups, and nonprofit organizations. They want us to be part of their strategy of continued growth and success. They want to lead us in the right direction, their direction.

This is not to say there are no problems plaguing us that remain from the days of the Chicano Movement and before. There are. There are too many of our children pushed out of school by white adults and their system of education. There are too many of our kids in the judicial system, at both ends, entering the process of administration of justice as an accused or the tail end on probation or parole.

There are more of our kids in that system than in the system of higher education. Too many of our kids have no health insurance or immunizations. Too many of our kids and their moms live in poverty. Too many of our kids are having kids. Factor in the problems when individually or as a group we arrive at the various intersections of racism, gender discrimination, class distinctions, religious intolerance, sexual preference, and bigotry of varying types. We have many problems. Factor in the problems of conflicting ideologies and cultural loyalties, rising expectations, low levels of gratification, cynicism, apathy, illness, psychological mutilation, and bad environments, especially air and water and neighborhood, and these become formidable pyramids of problems, bad structures.

To overcome and prevail over these problem pyramids, we need to acquire personal power. We need a personal power structure to climb up the steps of the problem pyramid to greater and greater levels of power.

Communication between our various groups, for example, remains a big problem. We do not know each other. We do not look like each other. We have different histories. Communication in a language is essential for a people to dialogue not only amongst themselves but also with others. Language is the transmitter of culture. Language is the transmitter of information and instruction. Language can be spoken, written or signed. It is learned from elders. Words, sounds, hand gestures of the language must be heard, read, seen, and broadcast over distance to be maintained. A maintained language is the key to building community; it promotes the unity of people and solidarity of purpose.

Our problem as Raza residing in the United States was, then and now, that the practice of our Spanish language is threatening to the dominant population groups: blacks and whites. In the public schools during the twentieth century, our children were beaten for speaking Spanish in school. At the job site, our people were reprimanded and fired for speaking Spanish to each other during working hours. In the U.S. military, some English-speaking commanders in Europe banned the speaking of Spanish among the troops because they believed the practice of a foreign language posed a national security problem. In business, Spanish was not valued as a sales tool;

it was only to be spoken as a last resort to a customer.

We did not learn to read in Spanish or speak and write it with any proficiency. Consequently, books written in Spanish could not find a publisher in the United States. Books written about us could find no general market buyers, with only a few of us willing to buy the book. I had to self-publish my book *A Gringo Manual on How to Handle Mexicans* in Mexico for these very reasons in 1974. This anecdote should be the first trick in this sequel. The second trick ought to be that by 2001 the revised edition of *A Gringo Manual was* published by a university press, Arte Público Press of the University of Houston. We learn how to work the system; unfortunately, learning takes time, the infamous learning curve.

This book is divided into three parts. Each part is supported in description and explanation by several anecdotes. There are close to 220 true stories in this book. The anecdotes or stories each help us understand how that power piece fits into the larger personal power structure. The first part, the Average Power Structure and Level of Power, is described and explained by 75 stories. The second part, the Mid-Range Power Structure and Level of Power, is described and explained by some 73 stories. The third part, the Complex Power Structure and Level of Power, is supported by 81 stories. A Post-script closes the book of Power sharing my vision of the world to come. In the world of my grandchildren, when they will be middle-aged, I may not be any longer here. But since I can see it now, I've already been there and know that we did this together. Each generation is a chain link. Each generation makes a contribution to the struggle. The work that follows is one more attempt on my part to advance that struggle.

Introduction

The Structure of Power and the Three Levels of Power

In this work, I describe three levels of personal power wielded by persons. The description and analysis of the structure of personal power becomes the level of power for the person at that level. In other words, a person with power in the first level is limited to those available resources. That is that person's structure of power. That is what that person looks for and believes to be representative of power in others at that level. That is all a person in that level knows about power. Every person in every level usually believes he belongs and is limited to that level; only the ambitious militants and change agents, doers, strive to reach into the higher levels of the structure of power and want more personal power. Those who inherit power, the rich, and those that become instantly famous, the entertainers and lottery winners, often cannot handle their personal power or power structure. It overwhelms them because the learning curve of how to handle power came too fast with too much.

Power emanates from the personal, environmental, organizational, and the implementation or exercise of power. Power is promiscuous and will go with anyone, especially the person who is comfortable with power and uses power. Power accrues to power; it runs away from stagnation and vacuums. Power wants and needs suitors. Power demands a workout regularly. It is insatiable.

Part I: Average Power Structure and Level of Power

I once attended an annual conference of the Texas Association of Chicanos in Higher Education (TACHE), an organization that has been in existence since the Chicano Movement era. At this conference held in November 2001, one of the keynote speakers was Alfredo de los Santos, an academic held in high regard by many Chicanos for his ability, leadership, skill, and intellect, not to mention his longevity. He spoke of power. He said power consisted of having, in order of importance, money, votes, and education. I generally agreed with that assessment and description of the structure of power. That is a good beginning, but there is more to it than that. In this country, those with money have power. There is in current practice the crude and corrupted adage of the Golden Rule. Those with the most gold, rule. Those with money rule because in the United States, a monopoly capitalist system, a person can buy another's talent and creativity. Labor can be had for a price, and usually a cheap one. Intellectuals can be contracted. Services can be had on demand, and usually for a cheap price. Entertainment and pleasure are negotiable anywhere, anytime, at any price. Vice and addiction can be satisfied at a price. Money can buy votes and media time to get votes and lawyers to protect votes obtained. And the reality is that few Chicanos or Latinos have ample sources of money. *Hispanic Business* magazine in its September 2002 issue profiles "75 of the Wealthiest Hispanics in America." Some of us have enough to get by comfortably and most of us, not enough. I personally know a few who have plenty, but I can count them on one hand.

We do have an increasing number of Raza eligible to register to vote. We have an increasing number of persons obtaining U.S. citizenship, mostly because of immigration reform and changes in the law affecting nationality. A Mexican citizen can now retain her or his nationality while in pursuit of legalization in the United States. Citizenship drives coupled with voter registration incentives are also becoming the staples of political campaigns. While we continue to be the minority group with the youngest median age, we also continue to become the largest minority group of all. In other words, we are becoming the majority minority. Conversely, the number of whites continues to decline dramatically. The Baby Boom generation has begun to die, and it is overwhelmingly white. I am in that generation, but most Latinos are not. The number of blacks in America is not growing in any significant way. Because of low growth rate, they are seriously going downward as a percentage of the whole. Black America has seen its better days. Let me give an example: In 1850 the population of Texas was comprised of African slaves and whites; most Mexicans had been run out of the area into Mexico. The families of Lorenzo de Zavala, Juan Seguín, Ignacio Zaragoza, José Antonio Navarro, and the Benavides brothers were no longer needed by Anglos. The percentage of Africans in Texas in 1850 stood at 28 percent of the whole. By 2002, the black share had dropped to 11 percent. (See John Sharp, *The Changing Face of Texas,* Austin: Comptroller of Public Accounts, 1992, p. 10.)

There is another trend among black Americans, which is to relocate from the West (read Los Angeles, California) and the North (read Detroit, Chicago, Gary, Philadelphia, and Baltimore) to the Southeast, the traditional, domestic, black homeland. If this trend continues, then the numbers and percentages of Latinos will increase even more dramatically in those areas vacated by blacks.

The number of Latino elected officials continues to increase. This is a double-gain because the number of elected officials is finite. Every one we gain means someone from another group lost the seat. They are no longer at the table. They are no longer viable players in the political arena. They might remain in the political mix, but not as viable players.

We live in states, primarily, that are necessary for presidential aspirants. Our Raza live in the big cities and in the big states. We are no longer a rural, southwestern states phenomenon. Latinos are as ubiquitous as sunshine. There are more Mexicans in some places than others, but we are ever present. Latinos and Mexicans are found in every county in every state of the union. Our vote in ten of these important, "must-have" states for the presidency is extremely important and growing in importance by the election. We comprised a significant share of the states representing 80 percent of the electoral vote necessary to win the presidency in 2000.

Latinos, with some exception made for geography and national origin, are inclined to support Democratic Party candidates over those of the Republican, Libertarian, Green, Constitutional, Reform, Socialist Workers, or even the Raza Unida Party, should it be revived. Florida Cubans will vote Republican more often than vote Democrat, but they are not the only Latinos in Florida anymore. Northern New Mexico *Hispanos* will vote Republican. Wealthy Raza will vote Republican more often than not. But these are minorities within a minority, and their numbers are not significant at this time.

We are lacking in formal and advanced education as a group. This is a serious drawback to the growing power of our voting numbers and growing middle-class status. It is serious because it retards our realization of power; we remain, therefore, with considerable, untapped power. Our parents and grandparents did not have much formal education or many professional training. But those generations did not need education as much as the current times demand. Our ancestors had life experience, they had common sense, they had high intuitive skills, they had political courage, they had firm and strong values, and they had perseverance. While they had little wealth, they did fund our education. Our ancestors also began the struggle for civil rights; they fought for us to be free from social stigma and oppression as Mexicans in the United States. The Chicano Generation took up the mantle and finished that job. The Latinos that came after the Chicano Movement owe us that social and political debt with interest. We have to tell other Mexicanos and Latinos that, because they are unaware of our history of struggle on their behalf. If you don't tell them our Chicano story of struggle, they will be forced to believe that blacks started the civil rights movement and we watched; or they will believe the whites when they tell them we have no history other than that of being illegal aliens who just arrived last night.

The less educated Latino will continue to tread water, but more probably sink into the underclass with the first catastrophe that hits: a serious illness, tragic accident, gang membership, early pregnancy, deportation, jail sentence, unemployment, no G.E.D. or diploma. In this present world, not even the U.S. military will take a person without a high school education. Some turn to crime or a scam or two or at least a shortcut to perceived success. They want instant gratification without the sweat of earned reward.

The less educated Latino will also not vote or be recruited into an activity that promotes the building of social capital. The less educated Latino will also be short on skills. If, by chance, they can get access to a computer, they will not know how to work it or be able to afford the Internet connection, much less the repairs and upgrades. Writing, spelling, computation, presentation, and appearance will all be areas of shortcoming. Poor people cannot afford to dress well or look like fashion models. Haircuts are once a month or homemade. Work becomes more attractive than schooling. Money over knowledge is the mantra.

Dropping out of school can lead to a low life and the accumulation of a police record. Crime becomes a way of life and conviction a permanent stigma. The gang becomes the family. The Latino gangster or wanna-be-gangster will kill you for your Nike shoes, DVD player, or gold-plated rims while you try to explain *Chicanismo*. Wanting what they see on TV and billboards and movies becomes a need. And the poor will gratify a need with whatever it takes, usually a crime. Crime among our Raza makes them as useless as non-citizens. While a criminal conviction does not preclude a person from voting in Texas automatically, as in prior times, it does preclude a felon from running for public office. You can vote after parole or after probation conditions have been met, but not for yourself. A conviction also precludes you from many good jobs with benefits, particularly with the government. Our poor flock to the jobs for the poor and unskilled, service-related jobs. They see so many others just like them; they begin to assume that is normal and the way life is for Latinos. This is certainly true in the whole of Central and South America and becoming more so in Mexico and the Southern United States.

The majority of our Raza is at this average level of power.

Part II: Mid-Range Power Structure and Level of Power

A high school diploma or an advanced degree does not by definition provide you with power. A graduate has to put to work what he or she learned. You have to practice what skills you have to make them better and get more. In so doing, you get power because others see you as more able, smarter, tougher, better than they, more powerful. You can also be a high school or college graduate in a position of power. An important position will get you many trips to the bank. Position will also get you to the front of the group. Position, then, within an institution, community, program, political group, organization, and religious grouping can be very powerful, particularly if those involved view your position as such. There are three kinds of positions: the one you are working to get to from where you are, the powerful one you have, and a position next to the powerful one someone else has. All three positions are good to have because the first one is a goal you've met, and you are preparing and planning on how to get to a better one. An improved position becomes powerful in the eyes of those below in the organization and society. It is also powerful in the eyes of colleagues if you use the power that comes with the position. The power of a position comes from the job description for that position, what you say it is, and what you do in that position. These are not the same thing. Access and proximity to the holder of a powerful position is strategically a good place to reach and hold. In all major institutions this is certainly true. In the U.S. military, for example, there are careerists. In the public schools and universities, there are careerists. In every institution, there are careerists. In any institution, the leadership mantle is by position, rank, appointment, if you will. Upward mobility is not just dependent on tenure but on politics within the group of present job-holders and those above them.

The title of a position commands respect. This is a top-down structure where you do as you are told when you are told by someone above you. You move up by working up horizontally, not laterally or vertically. You work with peers but not for them; you work for higher-ups and hope to be noticed. This is teamwork and individual effort at the same time. The folks within an institution, at whatever level, are in it for the long haul, until retirement. Once in, they stop being the brightest bulbs in the box. They become the most consistent troopers on the march to the parachute of retirement. They know their jobs, they do them well, and they protect their turf. Change is not of interest to them usually; they like things the way they are. These are the major keepers of the status quo inside organizations, institutions, programs, labor unions, religious groups, and political parties. They seek out others like them to form their network and interest group. They know the rules and they know the game. They know where to look and find the resources needed for their jobs. Change is a threat to the status quo. Ideas are not rewarded if perceived to lead to change.

Mid-range wielders of power are middle-class, well-groomed, effective communicators who have contacts within and without the institution. They have social capital as well as access to human and financial capital to get what they need. Generally, every advanced degree increases personal income by a million dollars over a lifetime. That is to say, a person with a bachelor's degree can expect to earn a million dollars in a lifetime. If she also gets a master's degree, she could earn two million dollars in the course of a lifetime. A Ph.D. or professional degree such as lawyer, doctor, veterinarian, optometrist, pharmacist, or dentist, will get a person within reach of three million or more dollars in a lifetime. This is plenty of pocket change, enough to donate money to causes, accumulate real wealth, acquire more assets, and provide inheritance to offspring. Both the educated, professional Latina and her children will spiral upward into economic well-being from that generation on into the future.

The formally educated and middle-class Raza member will also be a joiner, a doer, and a volunteer of sorts, usually when her children need her to join, support, or do on behalf of the Little League, the Girl Scouts, the *quinceañera*, the homecoming game, the prom, the volleyball team, and the like. But the kids grow up, and this volunteerism stops along with the joining and doing. The middle-class Raza have hobbies. They vacation with their kids. They send their kids to college. They make a will and transfer wealth. They have retirement income and benefits beyond Social Security. They will live longer than any other generation of Latinos. And they probably were involved in some aspect of the Chicano Movement and *la causa* in their youth. They have a memory bank. They may even attend reunions of activists or awards banquets honoring heroines and heroes, and still have unfinished ideas and projects. But they may have reached senior-citizen status and are tired and slower. They are planning retirement.

The middle class today has credit cards with manageable debt. They eat and dress well. They are groomed. They are articulate.

They have skills and keep up with technology. They have a personal computer and are connected. Raza are the fastest-growing U.S. population segment that is hooking up to the Internet. And, the rest of those in Spanish-speaking America are waiting in the wings.

Approximately 25 percent of our Raza is at this mid-range level of power.

Part III: Complex Power Structure and Level of Power

G. William Domhoff, an economic theorist, propounds the notion that in the United States there exists a governing class of wealthy Anglos, who make up the higher circles. He wrote a book by that title in 1970 (NY: Vintage Books). They govern us largely because they subscribe to three C's: class, culture, and consciousness. They know who they are (consciousness), they live the life they are (culture), and they protect the interests of those they are (class). That is the main difference between the middle-range powerful and the complex powerful. The former also have the three C's, but they put them to practice within their world, the institution, the organization, the religion, etc., behind closed doors, to protect turf and property. The latter practice the three C's in the public arena, out in the open because we are their turf and their property. They think they own the world, or at least, think they should. Complex power wielders have long tentacles (corporate and personal networks) that reach beyond borders. They have plans, both short-term and long. They train themselves to have vision, to see the world as they would like it to be and not as it is. They work daily on their agenda, not sporadically like the average power wielder or during their spare time, like the mid-range powerful. Given money, the complex powerful will hire people to attend to the details of their plans and agenda. These managers who stand in for their bosses are very powerful. Most CEOs, CFOs, COOs, and presidents of corporations and businesses are stand-ins, but wealthy stand-ins.

The top-of-the-line powerful stand-ins and owners do not pick sides; they back all sides. They hedge their bets and seldom gamble. The average powerful gambles all the time. And why not? There is little to lose and much to gain, if successful, when you are at the bottom. The truly powerful need not gamble; they can control the environment of those not as powerful. The truly powerful do not fight one another; they collaborate and they share. Everybody wins in the schemes they cook up. This is not to say that the very powerful do not fight. They will, but only to fill a vacuum, seize an opportunity, make space, and establish hegemony. They do compete with one another but would rather allocate to each his own sphere of influence and control. The truly wealthy pass on the power of wealth by inheritance. It will be a long time before we are wealthy enough to pass on significant inheritance to our offspring. It will be sooner if we meet the wealthy or their stand-ins. They need us.

I first realized our strategic position in Texan society in 1990 with the release of the new census data and a subsequent analysis by a top elected official. I quickly sized up our potential, our future power, by looking at the numbers and started thinking about when we could make a move for real power. Let me review what I read in John Sharp's *The Changing Face of Texas* (20). In 1990, he reported that of the 3.4 million Texans under the age of 17 years, Hispanics were 1.6 million and blacks were not even 700,000. Whites under the age of 17 were 2.4 million. In other words, the young Latinos poised to take over the reins of responsibility and governance in Texas from Anglos are already born and in training. Blacks are in serious population decline in this age bracket. The white youth that exist are all there is. There are no white replacements to speak of because within the under-17-years-of-age category, those white children under five years of age are only 716,830, a drop of 1 million whites from those in the next population bracket of 5 to 17 years of age. This is but one part of the population picture of the future.

The other end of the population picture in Texas is the elderly. These figures, in terms of potential power, future power, when Latinos may take over, are very dramatic! In 1990, there were 1.3 million whites over the age of 64 and only 228,631 Hispanics. In other words, over the normal course of aging, five of every six white Texans will die before one Hispanic does. There are no white replacements. This is the beginning of the end of white power in Texas. The world can see this now. In 2000, the census figures released validated the analysis of data from demographers that predicted a quicker rate for the browning of Texas and the United States. By 2000, every major city in Texas, except Dallas, was led by a minority person as mayor. The mayor of Dallas is a white woman, Laura Miller.

The ultimate quest for Latinos in the twenty-first century is to brown America from coast to coast and pole to pole. Latinos will become the next governors of Texas and other states. Hispanics will inherit the White House plus many state houses. Raza will sit with other heads of state and speak Spanish and English, as a first language. We are the future of the United States, of that I am convinced. This is so because the last of the white governing circle needs us. Even if some of them, the *gringos*, are still anti-Mexican, anti-immigrant, anti-everything in their hearts and minds, many are not. Those enlightened Anglos will invest in us. They also know we are their future. They need us to care for them and their children, work for them, pay taxes, carry on their traditions, maintain their institutions, contribute to their pension plans, pay taxes, buy things and products they own, and vote. Individual Anglos may die but their corporations do not. Enlightened Anglos may die but not their legacy. Even the racist *gringos* will die before we do.

The white wealthy and their stand-ins are approachable. They have wealth they want to share with us, not only values and ethics, but money. They have foundations and corporate giving programs. In order to do their philanthropic work and control stock held in foundation portfolios, the rich must give away lots of their money. Ask for it. Someone has to get it and does, annually.

The opportunity is ours to lose. This is all inevitable, and I am not being prophetic, but realistic and pragmatic. We are the future.

There are many among us with a similar vision to mine. There are some among us working on such an eventuality. Latinos must be ready to take responsibility and govern. Power waits on no one. Each of us makes a plan for tomorrow and another for five years down the road, and another for ten, and another for twenty years. Each of us must clone another as best we can by mentoring, networking, sharing, helping, supporting, funding, joining, asserting, talking, recommending, seeking, and engaging with others in the implementation of our plans. Some among us only have individual plans. Others have group plans. It is all good at this point, because what Latinos need are plans.

Very few of our Raza are at this complex level of power. But those numbers are growing.

If you agree, read on . . .

If you agree, study these anecdotes.

If you agree, convene a group, formulate your plan to govern, and implement.

If you agree, make contacts in another country and go visit. Later, invite them here when you are governing.

If you agree, believe you are one in the making and start acting like a complex powerful person. Dress, talk, think, plan, and carry yourself like one.

If you agree, dream of what the world should be like and work toward that.

If you agree, buy a second copy of this book and give it to a potential recruit to help realize your plan, goal, and dream.

When you reach a level of complex power, write a book and explain how you made the world.

PART I

AVERAGE POWER STRUCTURE AND LEVEL OF POWER

1. Bilingual Education

The purpose of the U.S. educational program is to make Anglos out of all of us. That is why we must learn their language, heritage, culture, values, and politics in order to succeed in their world. And personal success is directly related to how Anglo we become. Some of us resisted and forgot Spanish and did not learn English. A few of us have learned to master both languages.

Early on in the 1920s, one of our first national advocacy organizations, the League of United Latin American Citizens (LULAC), recognized the problem and began an early childhood education program, the "Little School of 400." This program was aimed at teaching our young the 400 basic words of the English language. The LULAC program was implemented in the barrio schools that we attended during the era of segregation. Then, with integration in the late 1940s and early 1950s, LULAC stopped the program as unnecessary. And, some of our parents began to stress the learning of English and produced a generation of non-Spanish-speaking Chicanos and Chicanas.

Other parents tried to teach their children both languages. The Chicano Generation changed education policy during the height of the Chicano Movement, beginning in the early 1960s. We demanded the right to be ourselves and speak Spanish. We demanded that the entrance criteria to the U.S. educational system not be our ability to speak English, rather that it be Spanish. We argued for the need to develop cognitive skills in our native tongue as we developed English language skills. English competency, we insisted, should be exit criteria not entrance criteria to the world of learning and knowledge. We called it bilingual education.

We got some programs accepted and adopted across the country with limited success during the twentieth century. But, there has never been enough money allocated either by the federal government or even by states to fund the program adequately. There has never been a local school district, even in the border counties where Raza board members control the curriculum, that has funded its program with local tax dollars. There have never been enough teachers produced by the nation's teaching colleges and universities to staff the bilingual classrooms.

We won the battle but lost the war because a huge debate ensued over instructional language policy that continues to this day. The fundamental question posed was whether the learning of Spanish would deter the learning of English, the ultimate goal. We let the opponents of Spanish define the issue. Consequently, some bilingual programs limit the teaching of and in Spanish to minutes of class periods and to elementary grades. Other programs use Spanish only to rescue non-English-speakers from drowning academically in an all-English speaking environment, particularly when taking tests for diagnostic or assessment purposes. There is no national standard for bilingual education. Therefore, there is no uniformity and no real bilingual education program across the board. The academic results have been mixed and subject to attack because of this lack of uniformity, funding, personnel, philosophy, and teaching methodologies.

What is saving bilingual education today are our numbers. Business wants to sell products to us, and they do it *en español*. Politicians want our votes, so they pitch us their messages *en español*. Labor needs our work ethic and youthfulness, so they will recruit, hire, train *en español* in order to keep us as employees, union members, part-time help, and at lower wage scales over white or black laborers. Churches conduct services *en español* because we are the emerging majority and they need members to replace their aging congregations. Middle-class and rich white people love us to attend to their service needs. They learn basic *español* in order to tell us how to cut the yard, clean the trash, feed the dog, care for the kids, wash their clothes, cook their food, and drive them to the malls. Educators must teach and graduate children in order to get promotions and higher salaries, and we are the majority of students in most school districts. Their success as educators is linked to our achievement.

They need us more now than we need them. Anglos have to learn *español*. There are more Spanish-speaking persons among us than there are English-speaking. We want bilingual education so our children can learn. These are some reasons why we will continue to have bilingual education.

2. Hell, Let's DO the Real Thing

There is no substitute for the real thing. Rather than read a book, look over a newspaper, watch a movie, or view a documentary to learn about Chicano life, it is better to go to a real event and get the Chicano life *en vivo!* The *Tejano Conjunto Festival* is one such event and is now going on twenty years of celebration at Rosedale Park in San Antonio, usually during the second week in May.

In Houston, Daniel Bustamante has been at it longer. His *Chicano Music Festival* is going on thirty years of continuous celebration. In Fort Worth, the *Tejanos* for *Onda Music* have been putting on their festival of Chicano music in August for decades. These celebrations are Chicano-produced and for the benefit of Chicano causes, organizations, or programs.

Recently, with the rise of corporate interest in our growing numbers as potential markets for their products, many corporations are "buying" events. This means they put up substantial amounts of money to underwrite the expense of the event in exchange for major publicity and name/logo prominence on banners, publicity flyers, etc.

It is not surprising to see Coca-Cola and Budweiser as the major sponsors of the Tejano Music Awards or Pennzoil-Quaker State as the major sponsors of a low-rider car show. It is not surprising to see non-Chicano, corporate-owned radio stations, such as KICK in Dallas (FM 99.1) or KQQK in Houston (FM 106.5) sponsoring "free" events with major Chicano, musical artists on various main stages in conjunction with the Cinco de Mayo activity or the Fiestas Patrias in September. On September 16, 2002, approximately 100,000 persons withstood rain and drizzle at Texas Stadium to be with the bands for the party.

Tejano music was called Chicano music before the major record labels depoliticized the music and established a rigid format on airplay at the radio stations. Before that, our music was simply called *Onda* music. See Ramiro Burr's *Tejano and Regional Mexican Music* (NY: Billboard Books, 1999) for reference on our music. See also the books by Manuel Peña and Guadalupe San Miguel on our music. My chapter on the evolution and politics of Chicano Music in *Roots of Texas Music* from Texas A&M University Press, 2003.)

3. Let's Try Letter Writing

As young students enrolled in those first classes on government and politics, our teachers implored those of us not satisfied with government programs or policies to write letters to a government official.

State Senator Frank Madla (D-San Antonio) never forgot that early lesson about letter writing, so he penned a request for information to University of Texas-Austin President Larry Faulkner. Senator Madla wanted to know why the university was not hiring more high-level Hispanic administrators and faculty. President Faulkner responded in writing, "There are not enough minority applicants who yet possess the education and experience necessary to compete for faculty or high-level academic appointments."

Senator Madla and the other minority senators claimed insult and denial of opportunity for Latinos in higher education as they waved the Faulkner letter on the floor of the senate chamber on April 25, 2001. The senators were debating the confirmation of appointees to the UT System Board of Regents, three white women. Also being confirmed were two white males and the Asian spouse of U.S. Senator Phil Gramm, Wendy, for the Texas A&M University Board of Regents. Of course, they were all confirmed.

President Faulkner clarified the matter to the offended senators. He apologized for creating the situation and explained that in 1999 only 4 percent of all PhDs granted in the country went to Hispanics and 6 percent to African Americans. That is why he and other previous presidents have found it hard to find qualified Mexicans, Latinos, and blacks.

At UT-Austin in 2001, the flagship school, among the 45 executive positions, there are only four Hispanics. Of the 15 college deans, only one is Hispanic. Among the 70 department chairs and program directors, three are Hispanic, and one of those is Dr. José Limón, director of the Mexican-American Studies Program.

As the saying goes, be careful what you ask for, you just might get it.

4. *Santa María, Madre de Dios, ruega por nosotros.*
Santa María, Madre de Dios, ruega por nosotros

These are the words that begin the "Hail Mary" prayer *en*

español. In Spanish, the praying people call it the *Ave María.* These are important words to Catholics and devotees of Mary, the mother of Jesus. María and the Virgen de Guadalupe are the two most important females to Spanish-speaking Catholics. San Antonio, according to the 2000 census, is 65 percent Hispanic. Catholic church attendance at Mass is overwhelmingly Mexican.

In San Antonio there are three Catholic universities. The University of the Incarnate Word is one of these, and Our Lady of the Lake and St. Mary's are the other two.

Incarnate Word recently settled a claim for money damages with eighteen *mexicana* housekeepers who worked at the college. The university had prohibited them from speaking Spanish and forced them into an English-only policy with much harassment. The U.S. Equal Employment Opportunity Commission sided with the *mexicana* housekeepers and helped them reach an out-of-court settlement in the amount of $2.44 million.

The university will have to call on area Catholics to say many more *Ave Marías* and drop more money in collection plates to pay for this wrong. The university, of course, denied any wrongdoing.

5. How Much Does Sainthood Cost?

We all have read of the tremendous life of sacrifice, deprivation, and risk that persons like Mother Teresa of Calcutta, founder of Missionaries of Charity, or San Martín de Porras, the black priest from Peru, undertook. We know there are orders of Catholic priests and nuns that take vows of poverty and live a life of extreme austerity. Some of these people become saints because of their intrinsic goodness. But first they must be nominated, and then canonized, if successful. To be successful, however, costs a lot of time, effort, and money. The process can take, on average, fifty years. The cost can be $10,000 at minimum.

First, a nominee must be identified and initial money raised. Paperwork supporting the nomination in the form of affidavits and testimony must be submitted, with copies to the Vatican. Printing can be expensive. The longer the nominee lived and traveled, the more expensive the documentation effort will be in preparing the case. The Congregation for Sainthood Causes of the Catholic Church has a "solidarity fund" to help with costs of cases coming from poor countries. The first major step is for the candidate to be declared "blessed." Then, the official sponsor of the nominee is declared the postulator. The postulator prepares the official position paper containing all the final documentation, *position*, which consists of a biography, written material from the nominee's hand, historical notes, affidavits, theological reflections, medical or scientific evidence on miraculous intercession, and reviews of material by third parties. These scientific consultants and reviewers are paid. Theologians that review writings or speeches or quotes of the nominee are also paid.

While the Catholic calendar that hangs in many of our homes has a saint's name *en español* for every day of the year and many of us carry first names associated with those saints because we were born on that day, no saints are Mexican or Chicano. Juan Diego of Virgen-de-Guadalupe fame had not even made the running. His supporters had not raised the necessary campaign money. How can we be *hijos de Dios* if we don't even have a saint? Then came the Polish Pope, John Paul II, and he decided to canonize Juan Diego and two other Spanish missionaries who worked in Mexico during the Conquest. We have our first *mestizo* saint!

Pope John Paul II canonized the first Central American saint also. The new saint is Pedro de San José Betancourt, a Spanish missionary in Guatemala during the seventeenth century. This pope has been busy. He has canonized more saints than any other pope. Juan Diego was number 464 for John Paul II. The pope also moved up the status on two more *mestizo* nominees known as the Cajonos martyrs: Juan Bautista and Jacinto de los Ángeles, two mixed-blood Zapotec Indians who were part of the staff of the Catholic colonial church. Their job was to inform on paganism and immorality among their own, and they did. Their villagers dragged them to their deaths after beating, hanging, decapitating them, and pulling out their hearts to feed to dogs. The case is controversial. The triumph of Catholicism over indigenous religions is wrought with violence and oppression.

Is it time to start a Chicano and Chicana for Saints Campaign Fund? Is it time to start a short list of nominees? I propose María

Hernández of Harlandale in South San Antonio and César Estrada Chávez as two nominees for the list. Anybody want to nominate Don Pedrito Jaramillo of Falfurrias, Texas? Anybody want to start the political action committee ("PAC") for El Niño Fidencio? (See www.houstonchronicle.com/pope for more information, and be sure to check out page 13A of the July 31, 2002 edition, for a view of the Spanish-language page in the front section of this daily. *The Houston Chronicle* is running full-length pages *en español* in the daily.)

6. Making History

Usually, the states are the entities that carry out the death penalty. The U.S. government has not executed a federal prisoner in almost four decades. On August 5, 2000, Juan Raúl Garza, an accused marijuana smuggler and convicted killer, was to be executed and would have become the first federal prisoner in this century to be executed. President Bill Clinton stayed the punishment, however, pending a review of death row inmates. Critics of capital punishment, among other arguments, claim that minorities are over-represented among the ranks of those to be executed. To be exact, there were seventeen minorities among the nineteen federal inmates pending execution when Juan Raúl Garza was finally put to death by lethal injection on June 19, 2001. He followed Timothy McVeigh by just a few days and was executed in the same chamber in Terra Haute, Indiana.

7. *El parqueadero o estacionamiento*[1]

One Sunday I went to brunch at the Fairmont Hotel in downtown Dallas, a rather prestigious hotel, for an event involving a famous personality. Hundreds of other interested persons were converging at

---

[1]The purpose of these next vignettes is not to encourage or incite anyone to commit a crime—rather, to alert persons to crimes committed in this way and to avoid becoming a victim. These are a few samples for illustration purposes, certainly not exhaustive. The Chicano criminal mind is most creative and enterprising; it does not need my help. Besides, the criminal element among our Raza does not enjoy a monopoly over scams.

the hotel entrance for parking services and were causing chaos because of their automobiles. I chose to park down the street at a parking lot along with thirty or so others. A shabby young man who appeared to be of Mexican ancestry was standing near the street entrance with a wad of dollar bills in both hands. Persons parking were walking up to him and handing him bills in $5, $10, and $20 denominations. He was busy making change.

I asked him *en español* why he was charging *por el parqueadero* on a Sunday, when the regular fee was supposed to be suspended. He looked at me worriedly and responded *en español, "No estoy cobrando. No más me están dando dinero. Te doy la mitad si no dices nada."* He wasn't charging. People going downtown to expensive hotels are so accustomed to paying for parking that without thinking, they handed him money. Of course, he took it. He offered to split the take with me for not ratting on him.

I laughed and walked away without paying. My thoughts raced instead to our instant communication, both *en español* and on the scam. I guess in his mind, technically he was not stealing, just taking the money being handed to him while standing in the *parqueadero* on a Sunday morning.

(As a kid and into young adulthood, I suffered with shallow high school and college teachers who believed Castilian Spanish to be the only acceptable Spanish. They drilled into my psyche that the proper word for parking lot was *estacionamiento.* They were forever correcting me. It was *estacionamiento* and not *parqueadero.* You can imagine my vindication when I emerged from the José Martí International Airport in Havana, Cuba, in 1975, and saw the sign indicating the parking lot, *El Parqueadero,* and later in Madrid, Spain's Barelas airport as *El Paradero.* In Mexico, the Castilian Spanish wanna-bes still use *estacionamiento.*)

8. The Sunday Newspaper

My favorite early Sunday-morning activity is to read the newspaper over cups of coffee. On several occasions while staying at not-so-fancy hotels that do not provide the ubiquitous complimentary *USA Today* or *The Wall Street Journal* at the front desk or room door, I've had to go to the outside newspaper vending machine to buy a copy. Loaded with a fistful of quarters on one occasion, I found the newspaper vending machines, but they were empty. It was either too early or they had sold out in record time. I got upset. It was not too late, and they couldn't have sold out. I just knew that somebody had stolen them.

Looking around for an alternative source, I noticed a Chicano kid at a distance selling Sunday papers from the median by the intersection with the freeway exit. I got in my car, maneuvered toward him, stuck out two bucks, and asked him for a paper. While he pretended to fumble for the change, I took the paper and told him to keep the change as a tip. Then, I asked him coldly, but smiling, "Did you steal all the papers from that hotel over there?" In two seconds, he went from smug at getting me to pass on my change, to panic and saying, "No way, man, not that one. I get them from the other machines."

Great way to make some pocket change for Sunday spending, just invest the initial $1.50, $1.75, or $2 bucks to get the vending machine open and take all the papers, including the one in the window, some 10 to 15. Sell them at the corner and make 1,000 to 2,000 percent profit in a few hours. And it is all tax-free.

9. Luby's Cafeteria: White-Hair Haven

When I was younger, I stayed away from restaurants that had an all-white clientele. Luby's, a Texas-based chain of cafeterias, was one of those. Now that I have gotten older and white-haired, I fit in with the regular, white, senior-citizen crowd at most food cafeterias. I guess I am looking more like an older white guy than a Chicano.

At Luby's you load up your tray with food items from the serving line and proceed to the cashier. She, usually a white female in the pre-1980s, rings up your food bill and hands you the itemized checklist and cost. It is not unusual for one person with a group, such as a family or office workers or just friends, to say, "I'll take the check." The cashier then rings all food items on all trays and hands you the global total. When you finish the meal, the group heads for the exit, and the person with the bill pays the full amount to another and different white female cashier. That is the way it is supposed to happen.

All types of customers rip off Luby's regularly, as they do a lot of restaurants and some bars because of individual billing.

The Luby's scam, or at any other such place, occurs when they serve a group but issue individual checks only. Then when the meal is over, someone offers to pay for the group; the others hide their checks and walk out together without paying. The designated payor then merely pays for his own meal and leaves. Members of the scam team take turns doing the same thing at other locations.

10. The Test Drive

Car theft is a major felony crime. An undercover Chicano cop working in New Mexico, Tim Chapa, once told me that he regularly stole cars from used-car lots while test-driving them. He would steal the car and deliver it to a surveillance target, usually a Chicano leader or higher-up in an organization the police wanted to bust. Another team of cops would then bust that person for possession of a stolen vehicle or even the car theft.

The scam worked this way: Any person or a police officer, in this case, presents a fake driver's license to a car dealer in order to take a car for a test drive. Then they just keep driving. Eventually, the car dealer will check on the license, learn it is invalid, and report the car stolen. If the car is not recovered, the car dealer can write off the loss on the business or personal income tax. If the car is recovered, the car dealer can still write off the loss on the business or personal income tax because the cops will not contact IRS and report they returned the car they stole in the first place.

Tim Chapa, an ex-state mounted police officer from New Mexico, admitted to stealing a Volkswagen from an Albuquerque dealer, driving it to El Paso with the hopes of enticing Cristóbal Tijerina, then residing in Ciudad Juárez, Chihuahua, Mexico, to come for the car. They had hoped to bust him on car-theft charges. Cristóbal, brother of Reies López Tijerina, leader of the Land Recovery Movement aka La Alianza de Pueblos Libres, already knew of this type of scam and never crossed the border for the "free car."

(See the video interview of Tim Chapa at the University of New Mexico's Center for Regional Studies, Zimmerman Library at Albuquerque.)

11. Free Food at Stores

Many grocery stores will often hire persons to provide food samples to their customers as a way to entice them to purchase the product. You can eat as much as you want, assuming you like the product and the hostess will let you. Sometimes the food sample is just sitting there for all to take. Take it all!

As Chicanos protesting one company or another over an issue, such as low wages, a labor strike, union contract violation, employment discrimination, an environmental concern, sexual harassment, English-only rule for employees, plant closing, and the like, we would personalize the protest by asking persons to boycott the product(s) of that company. Our most distinguished Chicano hero, César Chávez, used this weapon effectively and readily. He recognized that poor Raza only have consumer power and the power of numbers with which to fight in the public arena. In my day, the Raza stopped eating grapes and lettuce, drinking Gallo wine, buying Levi's, drinking Coors beer, and going to Disneyland, among many other boycotts over the years.

Chicanos would not only stand outside the store selling the product, urging customers not to buy this or that, but also enter the store and find the food samples. If there were none, they would help themselves to the cookies, the vegetables, the fruit, the soda pop, the juice, the cold cuts, the bread, and anything you could open and eat in the aisle. Poor Raza and recent arrivals *de México y Centro América* do this to this day. They look for surveillance cameras and those big oval mirrors in the store corner before they sample products.

When my first-born, Adrian, was due, my wife and I were in dire poverty. I was in graduate school and she was on maternity leave. I regularly would go to the local store and steal a potato, onion, chili, or tortillas and cans of sardines, tuna, or salmon. The canned goods would go in my back pocket to resemble a wallet bulge and the other products into my underwear front area.

(Disney Corporation heavily financed the campaign in support of California's infamous Proposition 187. Mickey and Minnie Mouse turned out to be real rats!)

12. Free Food at Bars

During "Happy Hour," bars regularly provide munchies or hors-d'oeuvres to their customers as a gesture of goodwill and also to limit legal liability stemming from drinkers ingesting too much alcohol without eating something. Happy Hours are usually held right after working hours, between five and nine, and the liquor is also discounted at these hours.

Honest persons are regular customers and will eat a little and drink a little before heading home. Dishonest persons are not regular customers and will eat a lot and drink little or nothing at all, especially if they employ the scam above.

13. Free Movies

Everyone, at one time or another, has paid to enter one of those cavernous, multiscreen theatres that are all the rage now, showing 15 movies in various salons at once. And many people have, at one time or another, paid for one show and stayed to see two or three more movies in other salons. The trick is to evade the attendants as you move into one salon from another. The other trick is to tell those who would evict you at a movie's end that you came in late and want to see the beginning of the next showing.

What Chicanos do for a group party is to have one person pay the full fare and take a seat before the movie begins. As the first screen announcements and previews begin, that person will race to the exit by the screen, not the entrance, and open the door to the group waiting outside to enter. Everybody gets in free and can stay for as long as they wish, provided they do not get caught without a ticket stub.

14. Free Food at Hotels

Major hotels always have giant meetings, conferences, and weddings going on. These gatherings attract hundreds of persons. They usually identify themselves as part of the group by wearing something around their neck, an identification card, or, in the case of a wedding, a suit or formal wear.

At every one of these events, there is lavish food and refreshment. In the mornings it is usual for coffee, tea, juice, and the like to be available along with pastries and fruit. Later in the morning, there is more coffee, juice, tea, and soft drinks, even water and more fruit and munchies. In mid-afternoon, again there is more of the same. At weddings and at the conclusion of some conferences, there may be an open bar with free alcoholic beverages for those invited.

The trick is to act as if you are invited and belong there. Talk intelligently when and if asked, "Who you are? What you are doing here? Where is your name tag? What room are you in?" The hotel directory will list all events occurring at the hotel that day, so getting a name of a group, organization, wedding party, or reception is not difficult. At these events no one knows who invited whom. And frequently, no one is policing the food to keep away freeloaders. Don't worry about the name tag; most persons I've observed just say they forgot it or left it in the room. These freeloaders are not homeless types and are dressed appropriately; maybe they are starving artists or graduate students.

15. *La Lotería, Tejano*-Style

The Texas lottery is big business. It generates many bucks from the millions of Texans that play twice weekly for the giant jackpot and the other games available. Many of our people play because they are addicted to gambling and also because poverty in our communities is at such epidemic proportions and the fantasy of winning millions is the best hope on the market, better than religion. Although Raza are the largest group among all that purchase tickets, not the same proportion of Raza win, but people do win regularly.

The state has a policy of not releasing the names of millionaire winners. The winners, however, usually go public themselves. They can't help but share the good news. Soon, long-lost relatives and friends find them and hit them up for one thing or another.

In a bizarre scam involving the Raza elderly, a Chicano couple approaches a senior citizen and shows him a lottery ticket, claiming to be the winners of millions. They ask, "Would you loan us $750 to rent a limo and drive down to Austin, the capital, to collect the winnings in exchange for $10,000?" There goes the $750 . . .

16. Another Lottery Scam

The poor *viejitos* among us can be duped as easily as any other one of us, because of greed and the hard life. The life of the poor is desperately bad. Grabbing for a sliver of hope is frequent. A guy with a lottery ticket, the winning ticket for $5,000 at that, approaches the *viejitos* above. He claims to have five of the six numbers correct. He explains that, as an undocumented person, he cannot identify himself to the state lottery officials to their satisfaction. Would the *viejitos* be willing to buy the ticket for $3,000? They do and the "undocumented" person with their $3,000 is nowhere to be found.

17. Obituaries and the Bible

Newspapers always report on some area deaths, particularly the passing of influential white males. Males do die at a faster rate than females, so the widow is left alone. The enterprising Chicano con man reads the newspaper regularly, jots down the names of those who died, and uses the telephone directory to find an address and phone number. He calls and asks for the deceased, to make sure it is the right household and to set up the widow.

He approaches the widow's home with a brand-new bible in his hand and knocks. He tells the widow that her late husband had ordered this new bible for them because it was a bargain at only $49.95. He says, "Do you still want the bible?"

Out comes the checkbook . . .

18. *El notario*

In Mexico and many other countries south of Toronto, Canada, the notary public, *el notario*, is a lawyer. In the good ol' U. S. of A., not so. Anyone over the age of 18 years and of reasonable character can become a notary public. In order to become a notary public in the USA, a person simply fills out a form, pays a licensing fee, and posts a surety bond. Then, he buys an official ink stamp with the notary logo and a record book. And he gets to work. Once approved, he is ready to acknowledge signatures and administer oaths.

The scam occurs when an unsuspecting client, thinking he or she is consulting a *notario* (a lawyer as in Mexico), is charged accordingly, but is not. The documents prepared, forms filled out and perhaps filed, and representations made are all illegal. It is practicing law without a license. Ask Jorge Rivera from Hondureños Unidos in Dallas, Texas. He was reprimanded in July 2002 for filling out applications for his countrymen and women for Temporary Protected Status.

19. The Tire Inflator Can

With regularity, K-Mart and Wal-Mart, and half a dozen other stores that carry auto parts, offer a sale on pressurized cans that will seal and inflate a flat tire long enough to get from the place of the flat to the auto-repair shop. Cunning Chicanos will buy several cans for under $10 and head for the nearest congested parking lot of a grocery store, mall, sporting event, church, and the like. The con artist will purposely deflate a tire on a given car and wait for the owner to show up and notice. After the typical cursing fit but before the car owner can whip out the cell phone or open the trunk, our scammer will approach and offer to fix it with his sealing can, but it will cost $10. He has to replace his can.

It is cheaper than calling a tire-repair truck.

20. The Guy without the Tire Inflator Can

Hermanas and other sisters, beware of the guy above that has the flat tire in a parking lot (which he did himself to someone else's car) and asks you for a ride to the truck-repair shop because he has no spare tire or inflator can. He may be a rapist, robber, lunatic, escaped convict, carjacker, or the like and not just some guy wanting to take you for a mere $10. Do not give anyone you do not know a ride anywhere! Instead, call the cops and report the guy.

(Thank you, Mónica González [now Hurtado], from Fort Worth, Texas, for this one.)

21. *Los papeles* aka Deed Records

Ask your grandparents about *los papeles,* and they will invariably go under their bed, pull out a *castaña* (small trunk), and show you deed records to real estate. And old folks' property is usually debt-free and paid for completely. Beware of the person who approaches your grandparents with a deed in hand about buying their house. Deed records are public information, and anyone can prepare a deed for a sale of real estate. The scammer will offer a nice sum, say $2,000 immediate down payment, for the property, who your grandparents are assured they can live there until they both die—rent-free! Meanwhile, the scammer promises to pay the grandparents a monthly mortgage payment of $600 on the balance, for example. They sign the new deed transferring ownership to the scammer, who tenders the $2,000 plus the first month's mortgage payment. Your grandfolks are ecstatic with the $2,600 in their hands and the promise of $600 every month thereafter until they die or the property is paid for.

Within a month, they get an eviction notice to vacate the premises. The scammer has recorded the new deed and is the owner. The note promising to pay the balance was an oral agreement and cannot be proven to exist. Fraud is very difficult and expensive to prove and usually takes place one-on-one, without witnesses.

22. The Case of Beer and Other Bottles

Hanging out by a liquor store or any store that sells liquor will reveal the party animals by the amount of beer, wine, ice, hard liquor, and wine coolers they buy. Any large purchase is a sure sign of a party somewhere! Rare are the big spenders who are going to replenish their home bar.

Our eagle-eyed thieves are on the lookout for people like me. And this did happen to me. I went to visit an uncle. Together, we went to buy booze to party all night. We had not seen each other in many years. The eagle-eyed thieves followed us home. And party all night we did until about two. By three, the eagle-eyed thieves were hotwiring my van and taking off with it. They knew, once the lights went out, that we too were out from too much booze. Fortunately, the neighbors and the family dog raised a fuss and alerted us in time to see the van being driven off. The police did recover the van several miles away. Of course, the thieves took off with part of our belongings left in the van, including our dirty clothes, photos, video camera, and spare tire.

23. Free Computers and Palm Pilots

Given the panic and scare most Americans have felt since the attack on U.S. soil (New York's World Trade Center, aka the Twin Towers, and the Pentagon) September 11, 2001, security measures have increased by quantum leaps. One such security measure previously in place for some years and now made more rigorous is airport security. All persons, baggage, and hand-carried articles must go through x-ray and other metal-sensitive machines. The security guards are taking extra precautions; consequently, passenger lines quickly form and time spent at these entrances is prolonged. All persons entering the main airport area where the boarding gates are located must surrender all articles to these machines and then stand in line to go through the personal metal detector.

I have already seen thieves in pairs work the security line to their advantage. Two crooks will spot a traveler with what seems to be a laptop computer in a bag headed for the line. The crooks will get in front of the traveler, with one maneuvering immediately in front of the unsuspecting traveler. As soon as the traveler places the laptop on the conveyor belt of the x-ray machine, after the security person has asked to turn it on, one crook will go past the metal detector and to the other end of the x-ray machine to wait for the laptop to emerge. The other crook directly in front of the traveler will cause the alarm to go off requiring the security guard to admonish him to return to the line and step through the machine again but not before placing all articles in the plastic receptacles: coins, watch, pen, gum package, etc. While this is being done, the first crook is already with the laptop and headed out the exit door, usually located near the same security entry area. Finally, the second crook clears the x-ray machine, and the traveler behind him also clears the x-ray machine, but soon is shocked to find the laptop missing. All the protests to the security guards will not find the laptop. By now, it is out the main airport doors, probably in the trunk of the getaway car in the parking lot.

24. U.S.-Mexico Border: Supply and Demand

The U.S. is a nation of addicts. Some 4 million Americans are chronic drug addicts, and 20 million more are casual, recreational addicts of hard drugs and marijuana. If we factor in the use of legal drugs such as tobacco and alcohol, we are a nation of addicts. This is big business for federal cops involved in policing this criminal behavior.

U.S. policy toward Mexico and other neighbors to the south is to police the supply, not the demand. In so doing, the federal cops in various agencies use computers, vehicles, airplanes, and weapons, to apprehend the suppliers.

Over the last three years, according to an internal audit done by the Justice Department on five of its premier agencies, they found at least 775 weapons and 400 laptop computers "reported" lost or stolen! The five agencies were the Bureau of Prisons, the Drug Enforcement Agency, the Federal Bureau of Investigation, the U.S. Marshall Service, and *la migra*. The FBI lost or had stolen the most laptops at 317, and *la migra* had the most weapons lost or stolen at 539.

Has anybody been charged or arrested for these losses or thefts? No!

25. La Llorona in 2002

The legend of La Llorona is about a woman who killed her children by the river and then spent the rest of her life wailing over their loss. Most of us heard the story during childhood and were fearful of that woman monster, but we grew out of it. During the Chicano Movement, many of us enjoyed witnessing the one-woman play *La Llorona*, put on by Dorinda Moreno of the Bay Area in California.

Today, women and men still kill children. According to the Texas Department of Criminal Justice, there are 70 women in Texas prisons as of June, 2002, who killed 83 children. Only two Texas women have been sentenced to die for killing their children, neither one of whom was Hispanic. But there are Latinas in jail for killing their children, make no mistake about this. In fact, most of them are mothers, and they constitute 32.9 percent of all killers.

As we grow in numbers of the population, will these grim statistics increase for Latinas and Latinos?

26. Compensation for Victims: Twice a Victim

Most states have a Victims of Crime Compensation Act that provides for the victim of a crime to receive some compensation for the injury or death, usually for medical treatments, funeral expenses, and lost wages. This is not to be confused with the compensation for workers injured in work-related accidents that most states also have. Would you believe that female victims are compensated at a lower rate than male victims? In Texas this is true! And Texas has had this fund for victims of crime for the past 22 years.

According to the analysis of the Texas fund from 1980 to 2001, there were 36,119 claims in which women were compensated. The average compensation was $3,681. On the other hand, some 49,070 men filed claims and were compensated. The average compensation was $6,434. The disparity is almost twice the amount. Even in cases involving sexual assault and criminally negligent homicide in which women more often are victims, the men received higher compensation than women: $4,191 to $2,635, respectively, in sexual-assault cases. The figures were $9,450 and $7,116, respectively, for men and women in homicide cases.

Women are twice the victims, and for our Latinas, particularly those without documents who do NOT report any crime to the police for fear of deportation, much less file a claim, the victimization is triple.

27. Double Whammy!

Rich kids don't need government-sponsored financial aid, grants, or scholarships, much less Affirmative Action, to attend and complete college. Their parents probably dine regularly with the area college president, know a regent on a first-name basis or at least play golf with him or her from time to time. Their kid is not going to flunk or be denied admission. Rich kids have had Affirmative Action forever. There is such a thing as white privilege.

Poor kids get a double whammy. Their parents are too poor to help them with college tuition, fees, and books. At best, they can afford to house and feed them a few more years past the age of 18. Poor kids have to rely on financial aid, mainly loans. And, as a consequence, they graduate heavily in debt. "An estimated 39 percent of student borrowers are graduating with unmanageable levels of student loan debt," according to "The Burden of Borrowing," a report by the State PRIG's Higher Education Project. The average debt among student borrowers has doubled to $16,928 in the last decade, according to the Department of Education's National Postsecondary Student Aid Study.

Of students who graduate from college and come from families with incomes of less than $22,000 (read migrant families, read undocumented families), approximately 71 percent walk away with diploma in hand and heavy debt. Compare this statistic with the 44 percent of students with debt that come from families with incomes of more than $100,000.

The problem of debt for higher education does not stop at graduation. In fact, the real problem begins: paying it back. The rich kid will pay less monthly on the debt for a shorter period and have more disposable income than the poor kid with a higher payment due to the greater debt and pay for a longer term, which results in less disposable income.

How about starting a debt-retirement scholarship for Raza graduates or a non-interest revolving loan fund to retire college debt of graduating seniors? How about both?

(See www.prig.org highered for more information on the Higher Education Project. PRIG organizations are nonprofit, nonpartisan public interest advocacy groups.)

28. Making Money Off Mexicans

The age-old custom and practice among those entrepreneurs addicted to cheap labor and cheap goods has been perfected off Mexicans. We perform the cheap labor and have for centuries. We have to! There are no enforced minimum wage standards, accident insurance coverage, health benefits, or closed union shops for Mexicans to join. We buy the cheap products and have for centuries. We have to! We are poor, and we don't have credit cards or ATM machine accounts or money to spare.

When a pope comes to visit or a Mexican president comes to visit, the entrepreneurs get busy making cheap souvenir products with their images to sell by the hundreds of thousands. We have to buy one! Be it a photo, a coffee cup, a T-shirt, a bandanna, or a cap.

When Mexican President Vicente Fox announced his trip to Texas for August 26, 2002, the entrepreneurs got busy ordering products galore. The products were ordered with George Dubya and Fox's images, with the date of the visit to the Crawford, Texas ranch, with flags of both countries and the dates, with you-name-it products.

Then, Fox cancelled his trip because the state of Texas was to execute a Mexican national without first advising him of his right to assistance from the Mexican government in defending himself against the crime alleged. This right is protected by international law, a treaty signed by both Mexico and the United States and scores of other countries. It is the law of our land also. We insist that our citizens abroad have the fundamental right to contact their government for assistance when they are charged with a crime in another country. We demand that right be respected or we'll send in the Marines! But in this case, the state of Texas ignored that fundamental right. President Fox had called Texas Governor Rick Perry to ask for a reprieve of the death penalty. No dice.

President Fox also called George Dubya for a reprieve. No deal.

President Fox couldn't come and be seen toasting, hugging, laughing, and otherwise being entertained while his countryman was being killed in violation of international law. So he didn't come. There was no money to be made off this Mexican at this time.

What do you do with a product commemorating a non-event? What do you do with a dated product after the event did not occur?

Business venture is a risk. Never count your chickens before they hatch. *El que mucho abarca poco aprieta.* On the other hand, loss is a tax write-off in business. Fox never came to Crawford,

Texas, before 2002 was over, as some had hoped and prayed for. To come at a subsequent time but still in 2002 would have helped vendors of these products, but then the partisan general election of November 5, 2002, got in the way. Fox could not come and be seen as favoring one candidate for governor over another, much less be seen with Governor Rick Perry, who told him, "No dice," on sparing the other Mexican's life (his name was Javier Suárez Medina). He couldn't do that and expect to be welcomed back in Mexico.

29. *El* Lease *del Pueblo*

All states have a fee for all kinds of licenses, from driver's license to fishing to hunting dove, deer, hog, and in Texas, even alligators. Texas has a list of Big Time Texas Hunts. You can hunt alligators, ducks, deer, doves, and wild hogs, even exotic game. The license to hunt gators costs $10, and you are entered into a lottery.

As a kid growing up in South Texas, I saw hunting as a fact of life. But it wasn't for sport; it was for food supplement. Invariably, around wintertime someone would ask you to go hunting for deer *en el* lease *del pueblo,* meaning the open highway, for extra meat to make *tamales y guiso.* Leasing private land for hunting is cost-prohibitive for most Raza, still to this day. Plus, the guns used in hunting larger animals are expensive. The bullets for such guns are also expensive. Usually, when we went hunting, we borrowed a gun or two, bought some bullets from the rifle owner, and shared both the guns and bullets, taking turns shooting and driving the car or pickup. Hunting was not a poor man's sport, unless you hunted on the open road illegally and without a license, as we did. It still isn't. We just risked getting caught. Sometimes we did. Some of us still do. A last factor: we were also ignorant of the process to enter the state lottery for hunting on public land. That also kept us away, not to mention the cost of buying the license to hunt.

But we also bagged deer and wild hogs more often than we got caught while hunting *en el* lease *del pueblo.*

(Call 800-895-4248 for information on these hunts.)

30. Greatest Inventions?

Is it the air conditioner? Is it the automobile? Is it the gasoline engine? Is it the computer? Which is it?

I vote for the flush toilet. Without the indoor, flush toilet, we would still be going to *el cuartito* and saying, *"voy pa' fuera,"* because it was outside. That is because it was called the outhouse in English. Do you recall "holding it" because it was too cold to go *pa' fuera* during winter nights. Do you recall and miss the adventure of knocking over outhouses, especially during trick-or-treat on Halloween? Do you recall holding your breath inside the *cuartito* because it was smelly? Did you smoke to kill the odor? Do you recall the choice of wipe you had? Was it pages from the Sears catalog or plain old newspaper or grocery bags? Did you munch on grapes or read the print on the newspaper wipe while you did number two? Did you always go inside or just stand behind *el cuartito* for number one? Did you miss the cutout hole often? Those were the days, eh? You didn't have any lid to up or down, you just sat in the cutout hole and hoped that no spiders or snakes would bite your cheeks.

Some interesting toilet facts:

- Flush toilets were also found in Persia and Crete from 1700 to 1000 B.C.
- Roman Emperor Vespasian levied the first tax on toilets in 69 A.D.
- The Chinese invented toilet paper on a roll in 1391.
- The French loved the toilet so much they made it illegal NOT to have one beginning in 1668. They also added features to the toilet and invented the bidet.
- Alexander Cummings in 1775 invented the S-curved pipe at the bottom of the toilet to trap the fumes. Thank you, Alex.
- In 1778, Joseph Bramah invented the floatie valve thingamajig that goes in the tank to get the right amount of water to flush.
- In 1859, Queen Victoria had a gold toilet made in the form of a throne.
- Thomas Thyford made the first porcelain toilet in 1885; others were of wood or metal.

- In 1980, the first automatic flush toilet went into use in public restrooms across the U.S.A. These are the ones without handles or buttons to push. You just walk away from them, and they will flush automatically.
- In 1992, the U.S. government mandated new standards for toilets. They must be low-flush ones using a maximum of 1.6 gallons of water to flush.

I won't go into toilet lids and designs . . .

I'm glad the meshicas invented the flush toilet while setting up Tenochtitlán near the floating gardens of Xochimilco. Professor Bindeswar Pathak of India claims the Indians invented the flush toilet in 2500 B.C. You believe whom you wish. I choose the Meshicas; perhaps they got the idea from their predecessors: Toltecs, Mayas, Olmecs. Who knows, but they had it. Hernán Cortez and his band of killers reported noticing indoor, flush toilets in the Aztec temples and dormitories during the conquest of the empire.

(For more toilet fun, go to www.jamminjohns.com, www. extremeglow.com, www.toilet-humour.co/uk, and if you are in San Antonio's northern neighborhood of Alamo Heights, visit Barney Smith's Toilet Seat Art Museum for a view of more than 600 seats and toilet covers.)

31. Don't brag!

The *Pendejo* Prize for 2001 goes to Humberto Pérez of St. Hedwig, Texas. He and a buddy cooked up a scheme to defraud his auto insurance and auto alarm companies, State Farm and Safe Touch of Texas, respectively. The *movida* was to file a claim for his stolen pickup that had an anti-theft alarm. He did and he received $7,000 from the alarm company and a new truck from State Farm. What the companies did not know and never found out was that his buddy "stole" the truck after Humberto had made him a spare key.

Everything went according to plan until December 11, 2001. On that date, Humberto, unable to contain himself, called into a talk radio show, and gave a detailed description of how they committed insurance fraud. He said his name was John. Listening to the radio talk show was FBI agent Steven C. McGraw, who took it upon himself to find John and bust him. First, he got the tape recording of the show for the confession to the crime. Next, he got caller identification on the number of John's call. Then, he got a warrant for his arrest, and it turned out to be Humberto, not John. Humberto was charged with two counts of mail fraud in federal court.

Don't brag.

32. Yesenia Hernández, the Lifer, and Libby García, *la tía hoochi-mama*

Yesenia Hernández got a life sentence from State District Judge Manny Alvarez in Dallas, Texas, for killing her eighteen-month-old son, Roy Aguilera, the summer of 2001. She bit him. She burned him with an iron. She hit him repeatedly with a broomstick. Little Roy had four broken bones when medical examiners did his autopsy, in addition to multiple burns, bruises, and bites. Some people commented that she should have received the death penalty, but prosecutors didn't seek that punishment. There are 59 Mexicans across the country on death row.

Then, there is Libby García, who took in her 15-year-old niece. The niece was from Amarillo, Texas. Aunt Libby brought her to Dallas and put her to work as a prostitute. After two months of turning tricks for *la tía hoochi-mama*, the young girl caught the attention of Sergeant Byron Fasset and Detective Vidal Olivárez. They busted her when caught in engaging situations near the Shady Oaks Motel on Fort Worth Avenue.

Compelling prostitution in Texas is only a second-degree felony, with penalties of up to twenty years in prison and a $10,000 fine.

33. Sometimes Nothing Is Better Than Something

Several years back I was so embarrassed and humiliated by the antics of Dr. Juan Flores, who works for the Dallas Independent School District. He was asked to deliver *El grito* during the *fiestas patrias* celebration (September 15 and 16) held by the city and school district in Dallas, Texas. Rather than give the speech that *el cura Hidalgo* gave on the eve of the Call for Revolution, *el grito de la Independencia,* as is the tradition, he gave a shout, *"Viva México"* and gave a scream, truly a *grito,* like we do after several *tequilas* and a good *canción.* The man did not know what the tradition was and assumed *el grito* was a *grito!*

The administration at the University of Texas-Arlington during the *fiestas patrias* of 2002 has taken this ignorance to a lower level. In support of Hispanic Heritage Month, the Center for Multicultural Cooperation and the Center for Mexican American Studies, under the direction of Georgina Vázquez, coordinator of the event, and with the Multicultural Services Office, are holding an *el grito* contest. Ms. Vázquez is quoted as explaining, "It's a scream for independence. Participants have to do a traditional Mexican scream." She added that screamers do not have to be Hispanic to join in the fun. "An Indian guy won third place last year."

Sometimes it is best to do nothing at all to celebrate the *fiestas patrias*, if you don't know what you are doing. Screamers . . . Where did this come from? How did *¡Viva México!* become a traditional Mexican scream? Father Hidalgo must be thrashing in his grave!

When *el cura* Hidalgo made the call for *revolución*, he gave a speech and closed by crying out three times, *"¡Que viva México!"* Since then, the president of Mexico and the one called upon to make the call at a local event, to give *El grito,* usually exhorts those in attendance at solemn ceremonies with these words:

"¡Mexicanos! ¡Que vivan los héroes que nos dieron patria y libertad! ¡Viva Miguel Hidalgo! ¡Viva Guadalupe Victoria! ¡Viva Ignacio Allende! ¡Viva José María Morelos y Pavón! ¡Viva Doña Josefa Ortíz de Domínguez! ¡Que viva México! ¡Que viva México! ¡Que viva México!"

(See *The Arlington Morning News,* August 31, 2002, p. 2Y.)

34. Cyberathletes at the Olympics?

Yes, there is such a sport as cyberathletes, and you have seen them in action. Next time you pass an arcade or on your own TV, if you have little brothers and sisters, watch them playing video games. These are cyberathletes in training. They are called cybergamers. They are everywhere.

Angel Muñoz is the prophet for the cult of cybergamers. Muñoz has organized the Cyberathlete Professional League (CPL) and hosted the fourth summer championship in July 2002, at the Hyatt Regency Hotel in Dallas. A Swedish team, Shroet Kommando, won first prize, $25,000.

Angel Muñoz began this business in 1995 and went full-time into the venture in 1997. Previously, he was an investment banker with New World. Forty-two years old and the father of two kids, he loved to play video games. He still does. But, now he is organizing his fun sport into a major business venture. CNN televised the championship this summer. Intel became *the* corporate sponsor for the event. Two thousand players came from around the world to the championship games that lasted five days.

This is serious stuff and big money! The video game industry topped $31 million in sales this year. This is an increase of 12 percent from 2001.

(Check him out at his website: www.avault.com.)

35. Phone Book or Voter Guide?

You have seen a big city phone book. They are fat and weigh several pounds each, one for business listings and the other for residences. A voter guide to most of us is usually a two-page insert in the daily newspaper a few days before the major election. You have not seen a voter guide unless you have lived in Oregon, California, and other locations where the League of Women Voters is active. The League publishes a voter guide in many jurisdictions.

The San Francisco voter guide has more than 300 pages and will cost in excess of $2.8 million to print. Delivery to the 440,000 registered voters in San Francisco will also be a problem because the guide is too big to fit in mailboxes, especially the slotted ones. The mail carriers are protesting the weight of the books. Plus, the mail carriers also have to deliver the California voter guide, and that one has 112 pages.

Oregon has a vote-by-mail system so every registered voter in the state gets a voter guide. In 2001, the Oregon guide was split in two volumes that totaled more than 400 pages and cost $2 million to mail.

The average length of voter information guides is 100-150 pages, according to the Initiative and Referendum Institute in Washington, D.C.

And guess what? The League of Women Voters of Texas will also print a guide *en español* for 2002. (See Lwvtexas@lwvtexas.org.)

36. Nick Zúñiga Has Diabetes

Diabetes is a major killer of Raza. Those with diabetes take it a day at a time, with some good days and lots of bad days. Nick not only has diabetes, he has a two-year-old daughter, Natalie, and a seven-month-old son, Jacob, and is carrying a full-load at North Texas State University in Denton, Texas. Nick also is on the varsity football squad and plays guard. Nick is a big man at 295 pounds but small compared to other guys playing football and that position. Last year, he weighed 315 pounds, but the diet he is on because of the diabetes has cost him some weight. Because of diabetes, he has to check his blood sugar four to six times a day. Ouch!

He changes that many diapers a day to help his wife, Sonya, with the baby. And after football practice and games, he finds time to read, study, and do homework for his courses leading to a degree in applied arts and sciences.

Nick is from Grand Prairie, Texas, where they eat lots of *tortillas de harina, frijoles refritos, tripitas, barbacoa de cachete, chorizo, mollejas, menudo*, in other words, great Mexican food . . . *pero ¡te mata!* Diabetes comes from eating too much of that food. Diabetes is also genetic. We get it from our relatives. So, get on a diet, a push-away diet. Push away the second plate of *barbacoa* and *chorizo*. Push away the fourth *tortilla de harina*. Push away the third *taco de frijoles refritos*. Push away all that *manteca* . . .

Live longer. Keep all your limbs and eyesight. Control diabetes. Don't let it control you. See your grandchildren marry and make you a great grandparent. *¿Qué no?*

37. Little League World Series

You already know about this "world" title stuff. It basically is the United States playing by itself and on occasion with others, as in Little League. The 2002 Little League World Series was between Sendai, Japan, and Louisville, Kentucky. Japan won. Louisville had beaten Worchester, Massachusetts, in the final U.S. championship game and Fort Worth's *chicanitos* (most of the team) from the West Side in the semifinal playoffs. Maybe next time, *razita*. You did well, anyway! Hundreds of cheering fans greeted them at the Dallas/Fort Worth International airport, August 23, 2002.

38. Selena

Oh, she was a beautiful Chicana, *morena*, leggy, powerful voice, luscious bottom, creative, full lips, multi-talented, wealthy, and *simplemente toda una mujersota.* She was on her way to becoming our best ambassador to the world. And then Yolanda Saldívar murdered Selena on March 31, 1995. Yet, her music and image live on. Millions of dollars continue to be made off her legacy by many, including her family. *People* magazine sold out the special issue on Selena. The movie *Selena* has grossed millions and made the director, Gregory Nava, and the actress, Jennifer López, famous and wealthier. Dolls in her image were an instant hit. Books on her life sold thousands of copies, regrettably even the worst of them.

María Celeste Arrarás cashed in on the Selena legacy with such a cheap book, *Selena's Secret: The Revealing Story Behind Her Tragic Death* (New York: Fireside, 1997). Arrarás was the host of Primer Impacto, a newsmagazine show on Univisión at the time of the tragedy. She reported on the murder and televised an interview with the killer that became the highest-rated show in the history of Spanish-language television. From that vantage point, Arrarás obtained her information about Selena's life. She took the information, added the drama of the trial and Yolanda's ravings, to write a book full of malicious innuendo about Selena's secret.

What is the secret?

Arrarás writes on page 251 almost at the end of her book, "If you should see me on the street, ask me whatever you wish, but do not ask me about the secret. It's not only that I can't discuss it; it's also because it's time to give it a rest. Selena deserves it."

The secret is you can make money if you call it Selena's secret. (For the Spanish version, see *El Secreto de Selena*.)

39. *Elote* with *Crema y Chile*

Many years ago, the corner *raspa* stand was about the only Mexican delicacy doing business in the street. Then came the *barbacoa* outlets and door-to-door *tamale* vendors. Now it is the *paleterías* doing street sales from carts and the selling of *elotes*. In each of these cases, permits from the city of various sorts had to be obtained. But in the case of the *paleterías* and *paleteros*, a city ordinance had to be passed permitting such street vendor sales, just like the ice-cream truck.

The *elotes* are sold in two ways: straight on the cob with garnish of *chile, limón, mantequilla* or *mayonesa* or *crema, sal y pimienta,* usually sold in front of a grocery store or as Ninfa Juárez does. She sells *elotes* in a cup *con todo,* for two bucks. Ninfa cuts the corn kernels off the cob, boils them, and adds *limón, chile, mayonesa, crema,* and parmesan cheese. It's less messy than corn on the cob. The *chile* sauce is hot, three-alarm.

Before you know it, Raza vendors and concessionaires will be bidding on city, county, and state contracts for selling such items and more, maybe even in the District of Columbia with all its federal buildings. This activity will require hardball politics and business acumen. But, we are the future concessionaire contractors, as well as in other sectors. Jesus Chavarría reports in his magazine *Hispanic Business*, June 2002, p. 8, that "Between 1987 and 1997, the number of U.S. minority-owned firms grew 107 percent, or four times the rate for non-minority firms . . ." I know you, the readers, are already thinking, "Yeah, some white female or African American or Asian is the 'minority.'" NOT! According to Jesus, "The rate of increase for Hispanic firms was even greater, 129 percent." ¡*Órale*, Raza! And, keep preaching, Chuy! (www.hispanicbusiness.com)

Meanwhile, go see Ninfa in action by Shed 1 (look for the yellow roof and her multicolored umbrella) from 9 a.m. to 6 p.m. daily in the Farmer's Market at 1010 S. Pearl Street, Dallas, Texas.

40. Latino Per-Capita Income

The Census Bureau reported in 2001 that the median per-capita income of Latinos is lower than that of all other groups. Whites, of course, earn an estimated $29,606. Blacks are close behind with $21,662 in annual earnings per person. Latinos, however, are way down at only $19,833, and we have larger families! Some among us do make tons of money, but they are the exception.

Take Alex Rodríguez, the athlete, for example; he makes a ton of money for playing baseball. On December 11, 2000, at the winter baseball meetings held in Dallas, he signed a contract to play ball worth $252 million with the Texas Rangers, the former Washington senator's baseball team, not the governor's private army, police thugs in Texas with the same name.

He is worth every penny.

On his twenty-seventh birthday, on July 27, he worked a game. He hit a grand-slam home run in an extra-inning game against the Oakland Athletics that won the game. The final score was Rangers 10, Athletics 6.

Alex Rodríguez, "A-Rod," is the highest-paid player in team sports in the United States of America. His progeny will inherit a bulk of this money and more, particularly the royalties from endorsements, products, investments, and the like. We can't all be paid as much as A-Rod, but we all can begin to accumulate wealth and pass it on.

(The Census Bureau has many publications and products. The Census Bureau is always coming out with new material daily, weekly, monthly, annually, and decennially. Check the latest products out at www.census.gov.us.)

41. "Let's Get Ready to Wrestle and Clinch . . ." The Heavyweight Championship of the World

John Ruiz is the heavyweight boxing champion of the world. Whites love to claim world championships when only their teams play: basketball, football, baseball, etc. Soccer, for example, is the only truly worldwide competitive sport, the World Cup. The Tour de France draws cyclists the world over to compete, but the title makes it clear that it is a French thing, not a world championship. Wimbledon is the same thing in tennis, as is the British Open in golf.

Ruiz is the undisputed heavyweight boxing champion, holding the World Federation of Boxing's (WBA) title for a little while longer. He defeated Kirk Johnson in a nationally televised match aired on HBO on July 27, 2002. But the defeat came by way of Johnson's disqualification in the tenth round for continued low blows. Ouch! With all the low blows, clinches, head butts, rough-and-tumble wrestling, missed knockdowns by the referee Joe Cortez, and Ruiz's failure to finish off Johnson when he had him in deep trouble in the ninth, this was not a boxing fan's match.

Ruiz, in years past, battled the mightiest boxers, including Evander Holyfield. In fact, Ruiz and Holyfield fought three times! Ruiz beat him once, and the last match was declared a draw. Ruiz took the title from Holyfield in March 2001, and that victory made him the first U.S. Latino heavyweight champion of the world.

42. Criminal Social Capital

Robert Putnam made a splash with his article and subsequent book on the concept of social capital. He entitled both *Bowling Alone,* to explain that volunteerism and joining organizations was on the decline to the point of threatening the underpinnings of American democracy. He recommended we practice the accumulation of social capital—joining with others, volunteering, making contacts, maintaining networks, getting involved. I am sure he did not include criminal gangs and networks.

A federal grand jury in Laredo, Texas, has convicted five Webb County men accused of conspiring to fix dozens of criminal cases for bribes amounting to $200,000. They were two investigators associated with the state district attorney's office, Alfonso Rodríguez and Agustín Mendoza, Jr., a bail bondsman Jesse Castañeda, and two relatives of the D.A., José Rubio, Sr., his father, and Carlos Rubio, the brother of Webb and Zapata counties' top prosecutor Joe Rubio. He has been D.A. since 1988. He was reelected to a fourth term in November 2002. He apparently had nothing to do with his relatives working dirty deals with information and cases coming out of his office.

(See *The Dallas Morning News*, August 29, 2000, p. 23A and September 2, 2000, p. 50A.)

43. Republican Snake-Oil Formula

Edward Rincón of Dallas, Texas, does polling. He conducts survey research on consumer trends among Hispanics and polling on issues and candidate preference in elections, among other topics. He analyzed the 2000 general election for impact of the Raza vote in California and Texas.

Republican presidential candidate George "Dubya" Bush spent millions on getting out the Raza vote messages and appeals. Heavy hitter in advertising, Lionel Sosa of San Antonio, was directing the effort. Exit polls from the 2000 general election indicated that 81 percent of Raza in California voted for Democrat Al Gore and only 19 percent of Raza voted Republican. In Texas, Raza voted 68 percent for Gore and only 32 for Dubya, according to Edward Rincón. Most Latinos didn't buy the GOP message. The Republican snake-oil formula of photo opportunities with Vicente Fox, the Mexican president, and Dubya's Spanish-speaking nephew, George P. Bush, did not work as well as expected. Dubya spoke in Spanish in some of his political commercials. Dubya publicly stated his opposition to English-only legislation. Dubya had a photo-a-week with some Mexican border governors. Dubya called the Mexican governors by their first name on television. The Republican National Convention was a lavish pro-Raza event. There were more Raza on stage during the week-long media event than as Republican voting delegates, however.

Sorry, Lionel, all of this was not enough to make Raza voters fall in love with Mr. Bush and forget that he was a compassionate, conservative Republican.

44. Call Them on It! Call Them on It!

Bidal Agüero is the founder of a Chicano newspaper in West Texas, *El Editor*. He and his wife, Olga, have run this paper for decades, and they have sponsored and organized umpteen other related Chicano activities in the region, from baseball tournaments to folklore dancing contests and Chicano musical concerts. Bidal's appearance is not that of a typical Chicano from the 1960s. Bidal wore a baseball cap before it was fashionable. Bidal has a full, full beard, now graying. Bidal does not tuck his shirt in nor does he button the top button ala *cholo*-style. And, he wears thick glasses.

Victor Hernández, on the other hand, dresses very much like the lawyer and city councilman that he is. His wife is also a lawyer and judge. The Hernández couple is very fashionable. So when Victor, the councilman, invited Bidal, the newspaperman, for early lunch over at the Lubbock Club, located on the fourteenth floor of the Norwest Bank building in downtown Lubbock, Texas, all hell broke loose. Historically, the only Chicanos and blacks allowed in the club were those who work there.

Bidal arrived first and on time at 11:45 a.m. Victor arrived later at 11:55 am, but Bidal was gone. Victor inquired where Bidal was and was informed by Mary, the hostess, that Stewart, the general manager of the club, had refused to seat Bidal because he was not properly dressed. Victor then located Bidal and picked him up. They discussed the incident, but Bidal said, "Let's just go to Lala's Restaurant." Instead, Victor drove Bidal over to the bank building and called Mary on the mobile phone, asking for Stewart. "Honey, he's, he's real busy, and where are you anyway?" Mary asked Victor. "I am outside of the bank building. I will be right up." Mary greeted them and offered to seat them both upstairs. The upstairs area is away from the general seating and is reserved for special functions. Victor insisted on talking to Stewart and found him walking toward his office. Victor introduced Bidal to Stewart as the editor of the local Chicano newspaper. And Stewart started talking a mile a minute, excusing himself for his decision to oust Bidal. ". . . It was a business sort of environment," that they, "dah, dah, dah, dah. . . . And I'm talking to you as a friend . . ." So Victor finally asked Stewart, "If Bidal tucks his shirt and takes off his cap, we can be seated? In the main dining room?" "Oh, yes sir, yes sir," said Stewart and took off toward the main dining area to seat them, but Victor and Bidal talked it over and decided the point had been made, and they went off to Bryan's Steakhouse for a better meal.

Victor states it succinctly, "I needed to call him on it, not only for

Bidal's sake, and not only for the Hispanic community's sake, but for their own sake. I mean you know, the majority community, especially in relation to the Hispanic populace, has been able to get away with a lot of things, in my opinion, because people don't call them on it." (See Interview with Victor Hernández, General Libraries, Special Collections, University of Texas at Arlington, p. 37.)

45. Take This Job and Keep It!

Carlos Truán got a job early in life as an insurance salesman with New York Life. He sold a lot of policies, and the company liked him. The company was also based outside of Texas. Carlos got bit by the political bug during the Chicano Movement, and he ran for state representative from the Kingsville-Corpus Christi area. He won and won and won until he moved up to be state senator. He won there also, and won and won. He lasted so long, he was referred to as the dean of the Texas Senate. He served until 2002.

But all was not milk and honey during his career. Some jealous and envious Anglo colleagues, he surmises, snitched on him to the national headquarters about his partisan political involvement. Insurance salespersons are unlike regular contract labor; they work odd hours and earn commissions on sales. In other words, if Senator Truán had had to work an eight-to-five shift in order to earn an hourly wage, he would not have succeeded in politics as he did. Fortunately, Mr. Truán had the foresight to request and obtain written permission from the company to run and hold public office. He also was able to sell many more life insurance policies by his involvement in politics. (See Interview with Carlos Truán, General Libraries, Special Collections, University of Texas at Arlington, Arlington, Texas, pp. 13–15.)

46. *Corre la palabra*

When I was elected county judge for Zavala County, Texas, in November 1974, the road administrator for the county was a fellow by the name of Jackie Hooks. Before I took office on the first of the year, between Christmas and New Year's, I drafted a letter asking all county employees to resign and reapply for their jobs, as I was going to restructure county operations, particularly the Road and Bridge Department. I personally delivered the letter to all employees and inadvertently crashed a beer party and cookout that Jackie Hooks was having on county property and county time. He didn't resign nor wait for me to fire him; Hooks moved out of town to Uvalde, Texas, and eventually was hired as the road administrator for that county.

Years later, Gilbert Torres was elected the first Chicano commissioner for Uvalde County. Torres had heard from me about Jackie Hooks. *Corre la palabra.* And Torres, as county commissioner, got after Hooks every chance he got for not hiring Mexicans to work for the county road department. Commissioner Torres took his complaints against Hooks to the county judge. "And Judge White said, 'Gilbert, I am in favor. All I want is just something to say why he got fired.'"

"For drinking on the job," Torres told him.

So, a new road administrator, Wayne Grant, was hired, who hired Mexicans for about half the Road Department positions.

(See Interview with Gilbert Torres, General Libraries, Special Collections, and University of Texas at Arlington, Arlington, Texas.)

47. Havens for Criminals

In many U.S. cities it is a crime to walk around as Raza. In Dallas, Texas, scores of Raza were busted, convicted, and deported for drug use by Dallas police officers, county prosecutors, and uncurious juries during the latter part of 2000 and early 2001. After some investigation by inquiring minds and sharp lawyers, the drugs turned out to be fake, the informers compromised, and the police less than clean in the matter. In Houston, Texas, police routinely in years past used to throw down guns to make arrests stick and to enhance misdemeanors to felonies. They, too, were exposed.

In the media, we have read and seen on video police beatings of innocent suspects or even unsuspected persons.

Well, this is good news for criminals. *The San Francisco Chronicle* reports that the San Francisco, California, Police Department (SFPD) solved only 28 percent of violent crimes during the years 1996 and 2000. According to this source, the SFPD routinely does not investigate the vast majority of serious assaults and robberies. Is San Francisco the only place where crime does pay? No! Detroit has a 29 percent rate of crime solving. Phoenix has a 31 percent rate. Baltimore has a 32 percent rate.

But criminals stay away from San Diego. There you have a better than 50-50 chance of getting busted; they have a 64-percent rate of solving violent crimes. For the 50-50 chance cities, try Jacksonville, Florida, with a rate of 54 percent and Indianapolis, with a 52-percent rate.

(See Otis White, "Urban Notebook," in *Governing,* July 2002, p.14 or www.Governing.org.)

48. *El Boogeyman*

As a child, I always heard about *el cucui, la llorona, el viejo,* and *la* miss, all euphemisms for the evil thing, the wailing woman, the boss, and the teacher, respectively. I heard of El Boogeyman *y* Jumping Jess as an adult by listening to KQQK radio, a former Chicano music station in Houston, Texas. El Boogeyman is Alberto Rodríguez and Jumping Jess is Jesús Rodríguez, but they are not related to each other. They are disc jockeys (DJs). I should say, were disc jockeys. The Chicano music format or Tejano music, as those who would divide us further apart and regionalize us into petite, ethnic enclaves call it, has been shut down in most cities across the country. Chicano music is being replaced by *norteño* and *regional* or in some cases, *internacional,* the newest Mexican and Latino formats on radio. A McAllen, Texas, station has been reprogrammed away from Chicano music. KQQK has been reprogrammed away also. Dallas's KICK-FM is on the way to reprogramming. The collateral damage of this reprogramming away from Chicano music is the loss of employment for the DJs, such as Alberto and Jesús Rodríguez. But not to worry!

El Boogeyman *y* Jumping Jess are on the air again, on www.bandidoradio.com. Check it out! *La onda chicana* has gone global over the Internet, Raza! Let's hope they stay on the air in cyberspace and do not forget to pay their music royalties.

49. OPCs

While growing up and even while in college, I learned what "OPCs" meant. I didn't have much money then (and still not enough now), and I had a habit, a nicotine habit. I smoked cigarettes sporadically beginning at age 11 and habitually by age 17. When I could not afford to buy my own cigarettes, I smoked "OPCs," other people's cigarettes; they were cheaper. Then came the realization of the evils of smoking in January 1964, with U.S. Surgeon General Luther L. Terry's warning that linked tobacco use with cancer and other serious diseases. Smoking is not only bad for your health and costly, but also smoking makes for real bad breath. Add coffee and drinking alcohol to smoking, and you have really, really bad breath, which makes you very unkissable. I like to kiss and be kissed.

My eldest daughter, Tozi, asked me to quit smoking as a gift for her *quinceañera*, and I did for many years. Later, in 1994, while writing a book, I took up cigar smoking, drinking red wine (Concha y Toro, a Chilean blend of cabernet sauvignon and merlot) and black coffee. That was worse. This time, my youngest daughters, Andrea Lucía and Clavel Amariz, stopped kissing me. I like to kiss and be kissed, especially by my children. Again, I quit and still abstain.

Did you know that the more education you have, the easier it is for you to quit smoking? Did you know that the less education you have, the harder it is for you to quit smoking? Did you know that whites are able to quit smoking more easily than Raza?

Did you know that only 43 percent of Raza are able to quit smoking?

Did you know that 7 in 10 adults want to quit, but their success is related to educational attainment level and race/ethnicity?

(Find out more by clicking onto www.cdc.gov/tobacco.)

50. *"Abriendo Caminos"*

The term above is the Spanish-language name for the National Republican Party's campaign initiative targeting Raza. The Republicans are spending a million dollars on this campaign aimed at us in electoral battleground states. The National Democrats are busy also.

The Democrats have weekly Spanish-language radio addresses, are promoting and organizing voter registration drives in major cities and the entire Southwest, and propose legislation to legalize all undocumented workers in the United States.

Presidents Carter, Reagan, and Bush, Sr. all signed immigration legislation into law that provided legalization for some undocumented workers. And just like blacks more than a century ago who became Republican when President Abraham Lincoln issued the Emancipation Proclamation that "freed" the slaves, some Mexican immigrants are becoming Republican stalwarts. Take, for example, the cases of Jorge and Carlos Olamendi in California and Luis de la Garza in Texas. They are but three of the new former undocumented immigrants, now U.S. naturalized citizen recruits into the Republican column.

When Nixon was in the presidency, he ate the Veracruz-style chicken plate at a California restaurant where Jorge Olamendi washed dishes. He was fired for greeting Nixon. But the next time Nixon came to the restaurant, Jorge owned it. He has Nixon photos plastered all over the walls. Carlos Olamendi came across illegally and worked at his brother's restaurant as a busboy, dishwasher, and waiter. When Reagan was president, the Olamendis sought legalization in 1986, along with 2.6 million others. Then, the brothers became U.S. citizens and loyal Republicans to the political party that provided them U.S. citizenship.

Luis de la Garza, another illegal entrant from Mexico, also got his start as a lawful resident under President Carter's legalization programs and became a U.S. citizen under Bush, Sr. In the case of de la Garza, he became a Republican when George, Jr. ran for governor in Texas. De la Garza is a premier political opportunist. He and I go back a long time in Dallas-area politics and U.S.-Mexico relations.

If the Olamendis and Luis de la Garza have their way, the Republicans will come around to supporting more legalization programs. And if the Republican members of Congress cannot or will not support Minority Leader Dick Gephardt's (D-Missouri) legalization bill or any other such legislation, then maybe George, Jr., the anointed president, will issue an executive order to invoke national security and grant amnesty to all illegal persons in the United States as he closes the U.S.-Mexico border tighter.

Raza voters still prefer candidates of the Democratic Party running for congressional seats, by a 53 to 23 percent split, according to Sergio Bendixen of Bendixen & Associates, a political polling outfit based in Miami.

51. Here Comes the Judge

Bush appointee Priscilla Owens as judge for the 5th Circuit Court of Appeals was severely criticized and scrutinized by the media and members of the Senate Judiciary Committee, because of her extremist conservative views. When Owens served on the Texas Supreme Court, she was among the most strident conservatives. Former State Supreme Court Justice Al González, now President Bush's White House counsel, also served with her. He was critical of her judicial activism. González now has been called upon to support the nominee publicly. And he did. But the Judiciary Committee did not recommend Owens for approval. Her nomination went down in flames, for now. Along with that, the nomination of Miguel Estrada, a Honduran refugee and federal judge, to the U.S. Court of Appeals (D.C.), also went down. Estrada is extremely conservative in his views, and is a member of the Federalist Society.

52. What Is the First Union Classic?

No, it is not a golf tournament. It is a four-race cycling series and one of ten official events on the U.S. 2002 Pro Cycling Tour. And you thought the Tour de France was the only big bicycle event? Big, yes. Only, no. In one of the races of the four held in Trenton, New Jersey, the course consists of a 13-lap, 7-mile route through the city.

And, there is one rider who has won all three men's races in the First Union Cycling Series: a Latino named Fred Rodríguez. He won in 1995, 2000, and 2001.

53. ¡No Valió Valiente pero Accent Sí!

Valiente magazine, a slick Hispanic magazine venture out of Dallas, Texas, did not make it. That happens in both the restaurant and magazine businesses. The National Council of La Raza (NCLR) has a publication called *Accent.* It is produced for NCLR by Valiente Ltd. Q*ué padre, ¿no?,* to land on your feet again and again. Valiente Ltd. also produces the program book for the Alma Awards, another NCLR project. The folks at Valiente are very well connected to NCLR. *¡Adelante!*

54. *La Tía Betes*

La Tía Betes actually is a character in a children's health book about diabetes. This affliction attacks Latinos with a vengeance. It is our dietary consumption of the good stuff: *chorizo, tripitas, barbacoa, frijoles refritos, tortillas de harina,* and *gorditas enmantecadas, pan dulce, azúcar con café,* and little exercise. I know we work hard, but that is not exercise.

Whites have only a 12-percent rate of diabetes. Within the Raza community, Cubans have a relatively low, white-like-rate at 15.8 percent, but Mexicanos and Boricuas—forget it, my friends. We are at 23.9 percent and 26.1 percent, respectively. We are seriously working on diabetes symptoms: frequent urination, excessive thirst and hunger, numbness in feet and hands, fatigue, irritability, blurry vision, and unusual weight loss. Sometimes there are no symptoms. "If you are older than forty-five, you don't exercise, and you're overweight, you're at risk! Call 1-800-DIABETES or visit www.diabetes.org.

If we are the future, shouldn't we count on you to be there?

55. *¡Paletas! ¡Paletas! ¡Paletas!*

It used to be that the ice-cream truck would cruise the neighborhoods at the right time of the day, playing catchy tunes and sounding bells to attract the kiddos. Sometime in the 1980s, Africans, particularly Nigerians, took over the trade, selling the ice-cream treats. Nowadays, Raza is moving in on the market with pushcarts. Raza vendors peddling from a cart are out in the streets of major cities across the nation, selling *paletas.* The *paleteros* are at the bottom of the entrepreneurial ladder. They are subcontractors to the *paleta*-makers. These poor guys walk the streets, pushing their carts all day without much of a break. They cannot leave the cart unattended for a second. And many of them are victims of crime because young thugs beat and assault them not for the *paletas*, but for their money. *Paleteros* are also uninsured for health or accidents.

The *paleterías* are a different story. The makers of *paletas* are doing well. Take Irma and Norma Paz in Nashville, Tennessee. The Paz sisters own and operate *Las Paletas* Gourmet Popsicles, located at 2907 12th Avenue South, in a trendy neighborhood. They sell about twenty kinds of flavored *paletas*. Call them to see if they have your favorite taste at 615-386-5501.

Latina entrepreneurs are the fastest-growing segment within the Raza business start-up explosion happening across the U.S.A.

(See Mabel Tinjaca's book on the subject, *Vision! Hispanic Entrepreneurs in the United States* [Heritage Publishing, 2001] and the *Hispanic Business* magazine issue on 50 top Latina business-women, April 2001.)

56. Chicano, Hispanic, Latina, Mexican American, What's Next? *¡Musulmán!*

Yep, there are 40,000 Latino Muslims in the United States and counting. Hispanic reverts to Islam are running 6 percent a year. And why not? It is about the same god, just different prophets.

Besides, somewhere in our history around 711, the Islamic conquest of the Iberian Peninsula took place and continued until 1491. That's about 800 years! Islamic soldiers from northern Africa did not bring women with them during the early period of conquest.

Our Islamic roots are everywhere: music (guitar), food (rice), architecture (arches), livestock (horses), and language (almost every Spanish word that begins with "Al," as in *alfombra, algodón, almuerzo*, and *alambre*, to name a few).

The Nation of Islam (Farrakhan's group) is actively recruiting and converting Latinos, particularly on the East Coast and in the Bay Area, claiming that Latino ancestors, the Olmecs, were Africans. The orthodox Islamic groups are also recruiting us. They call us reverts because they claim we come from people who once were Islamic.

And, today, many of us exchange greetings and farewells in traditional Islamic-Christian ways of yesteryear when we say *adiós,*

"To God," and *ojalá*, or "Allah Willing." Bet you didn't know that! (Subscribe for more general information to *Islamic Horizons* magazine or visit www.isna.net, and for the Raza Islamic connection, try www.LatinoDawah.org; LuzDeIIslamPub@yahoo.com; or www.HispanicMuslims.com.)

57. *Dime con quién andas y te dire quién eres*

My grandma, María del Refugio Casas Fuentes, used to quote me *dichos mexicanos* regularly. The one above comes to mind in the recent U.S. Customs bust of Tish Hinojosa, a well-known regional singer out of Austin, Texas. She sings well in both English and *español* and has a large following. *The Dallas Morning News* (August 9, 2002, p. 41A) and assorted national media (CNN, Fox News) reported that last August 5, 2002, Tish Hinojosa, 52, and her companion and friend 25-year-old Jason Miles Phillips were caught crossing the border in Laredo, Texas, with 30 pills of Rohypnol, the date-rape drug. The pills were found in her buddy's boot. The feds claim in the indictment that she asked him to smuggle the drug ecstacy. How the date-rape drug got in there will be explained in court. It is still illegal to possess controlled substances, regardless of kind.

Meanwhile, Tish's publicists at Milam & Co. of Austin declined comment other than to say that Tish is known for her community involvement, public service, and political activism. That is very true, but she was not doing any of that when crossing the border. "Just tell me who you be hanging out with, and I'll tell you what kind of dawg you are," *dicen los brodas en el barrio*.

58. *Católicos por la raza*

In the late 1970s, the Catholic Church and Raza got it on. The issue was the lack of concern by the church personnel for Raza issues. Raza are the main constituency of the Catholic Church in the Americas, both of them. During the Chicano Movement, the Raza priests and nuns formed organizations within the umbrella of the church to press for increased responsiveness to Chicano issues. The Chicano priests went by the acronym PADRES. The nuns used the moniker HERMANAS for their organization. With the demise of the *movimiento* also went these organizations; besides, the priest leaders were co-opted as they became bishops and archbishops, such as Patricio Flores in San Antonio.

During the late 1990s and early in this century, the Catholic Church has been rocked with major scandals involving pervert priests and some nuns. The Catholic followers are in disbelief at the extent of the scandal, both in the number and character of the incidents. The Catholic followers have had to pony up more donations to shore up the church's liability to pedophile victims. The settlements for these transgressions run into the billions of dollars.

In the midst of all of this and during the pope's last visit to North America, St. Rita's Catholic School in Dallas imposed a new requirement for parents of students. The school is demanding a background check on parents as a pre-condition of enrollment of students. While the parents will not be fingerprinted, the school will run criminal background checks on all parents and require them to attend a three-hour training session on appropriate behavior with children.

You read this correctly: parents are to be screened and trained, not priests.

And over in Los Angeles, Cardinal Roger Mahony has built a new cathedral for more than $190 million! Parking will cost $2.50 for twenty minutes, but you can get the ticket validated if you attend Mass. If you want to be buried in the mausoleum of the cathedral, in the basement, sign up now while you can; spots are available at a high of $3 million to a bargain low of $500,000. Hurry . . .

¡Por Dios santo!

59. Working it!

Anita Pérez Ferguson was chair of the National Women's Political Caucus (NWPC) from 1995 to 1999. She was the first Chicana to hold that position. She has been "the first" in other situations. She always worked it. In her book *A Passion for Politics: Encouraging Women in Leadership* (Santa Barbara, CA: Luz Publications, 1999), Anita lists the positions she held, beginning with being the fundraiser for Gordon College near Boston. At a training seminar while she had that job, she realized she had to get involved in electoral politics. And she did with a passion. She became a volunteer in the Mondale-Ferraro presidential campaign. She worked for a congressional candidate in Santa Barbara, California, in 1986. She was a paid staffer for State Senator Gary K. Hart. In 1990, she took the big leap and filed for the Democratic Primary as a candidate for the U.S. House of Representatives (23rd district, Ventura and Santa Barbara counties). She won the Democratic nomination, but lost in November. She tried again in 1992 and lost again. She then ran for the Vice Presidency of the National Women's Political Caucus (NWPC) and won. In 1995, four years later, she ran for president of the NWPC and won.

In that capacity, she promoted the training of women for leadership positions. In earlier years, she obtained a B.A. in communications and two master's degrees, one in management and the other in counseling psychology. Several hundreds of speeches, thousands of comments, and scores of media interviews later, she returned to higher education. Princeton University invited her to be a Woodrow Wilson Visiting Fellow for the 1999-2000 academic year. And she compiled her book.

Anita works it and works at it. Good lessons.

60. The Porvenir Massacre

Violent conflict between Mexicans and Anglo Texans occurred frequently along the U.S. border with Mexico in West Texas, particularly in the early 1900s. Noted *revoltosos* in the area of Pilares and Porvenir on the border were the Cano brothers, Chico, Manuel, and José. The U.S. authorities accused them of every crime committed in the area and called them the usual gringo epitaphs, *bandidos, sotoleros, Villistas, terroristas, Carranzistas,* and outlaws. To area defenseless Mexican farmers, Chico and his brothers were protectors.

It is alleged in *gringo* books that Chico stole cattle and horses from big ranches in the Big Bend area and drove them into Mexico for resale. It is also alleged that he stole cattle and horses from big ranches in Mexico and drove them into the U.S. for resale. Who knows for sure? The fact is Chico Cano and his brothers were hunted by Texas Rangers, local police, and the U.S. Army for various alleged murders: John S. Howard, a river guard (1913); Joe Sitters, a U.S. Customs inspector; Texas Ranger Eugene Hulen (1915); and four others at the Luke Brite Ranch (December 1917). Chico Cano never was tried for any crime and died in 1942 in Juarez, Chihuahua, two years after a serious fall from a horse.

Even before his death, when Chico Cano was blamed for a crime, the local Mexicans paid the price, such as those in Porvenir, Texas, in January 1918, right after the Brite Ranch raid. Texas Rangers under the command of Captain J. M. Fox, and with assistance of forty troopers from the U.S. Army under the command of Captain Anderson, broke down doors of shacks in Porvenir in the middle of the night. The Texas Rangers dragged out sleepy Mexican farmers. The wives and children of these innocent and unarmed men were prevented by the soldiers from giving chase as their husbands and fathers were marched out of town by the *rinches* for questioning. The soldiers surrounded the village. All total, sixteen men, one a boy of sixteen, were murdered in cold blood by the *rinches* using dum-dum (hollow-point) bullets that tore holes as big as a man's fist on exit. The women and children could hear the shots and the screams for mercy *en español*. When the soldiers and *rinches* rode out in full gallop, the villagers raced to the scene to find the bodies piled in a bloody and unrecognizable heap.

A victim was Juan Flores. His son, Juan, Jr., age nine then, saw the *rinches* drag his father out of their home. He was helpless before the armed and mounted soldiers standing guard at the door of his *jacal*. He heard the screams and the shots. Together with his mother and other siblings, they found the bodies. With all the villagers, Juan Flores and his family loaded the bodies into a cart and raced for Mexico to bury their dead in a common grave. Immediately after the burial, the Flores family left their belongings in the *jacal,* their harvest in the fields, their livestock in the brush, and left Porvenir forever. On August 4, 2002, I interviewed Juan Flores in Odessa, Texas, at age 93. The next day, a film crew led by Gode Davis, making a documentary on the lynching and murder of Mexicans in the United States, captured his story on tape, as I have.

This current-day episode came about because María Flores, daughter of Juan Flores, is married to Evaristo Alvarado. The couple has been researching and documenting the massacre. The Alvarados live in Uvalde, Texas, and they contacted the local Chicano newspaper publisher in the community, Alfredo Santos of *La Voz de Uvalde*. Santos put them in touch with me as someone who could help research the incident a bit further and bring public notice to the atrocity. I interested Gode Davis in the story and also pointed him to the photograph postcard collection held at the university museum at Kingsville, Texas, depicting lynched Mexicans and other scenes of violence against Mexicans by *gringos*.

Perhaps tomorrow you'll see a PBS special on *gringo* violence against Mexicans in Texas.

(*Sotol* is a Mexican liquor similar to *mezcal* and *tequila*. During Prohibition, *sotol* was smuggled into the United States in large quantities, but it never caught on as well as *tequila* has. See Robert Keil, *Bosque Bonito* [Alpine, Texas: Center for Big Bend Studies, Sul Ross State University, 2002] for an edited version by Elizabeth McBride of a U.S. trooper's diary of events along the border; Elton Miles, *More Tales of the Big Bend* [College Station: Texas A&M University Press, 1988]; and Ron C. Tyler, *The Big Bend: A History of the Last Texas Frontier* [College Station: Texas A&M University Press, 1996] for accounts both on Chico Cano and the Porvenir massacre.)

61. Ted Williams Was Part Chicano?

During the heyday of activity in the Chicano Movement, I started a volunteer group named the Voluntarios de Aztlán. The volunteers renamed themselves as the Chingaremos Brigade. Mario Longoria was one of those volunteers. He had been a student of our great historian Rodolfo Acuña.

As time went on, Longoria developed an academic interest in Latinos in sports and has published in that field. He is the author of *Athletes Remembered: Mexican Professional Football Players, 1929-1970*. During the recent scandal over the freezing of Ted Williams's body, the noted all-time baseball great, widely reported in the press, Longoria penned a piece in the *Express-News* of San Antonio, Texas, and Web-posted on August 11, 2002, in which he reported that the mother of Ted Williams, María Venzer, was a Mexican. And her mother, Ted Williams's grandmother, was from El Paso. But Ted Williams did not live his life out as a Mexican; in fact, he avoided the reference. Longoria, however, claimed Williams as a Mexican.

Forever the professor and mentor, Rodolfo Acuña Web-posted an open reply to Mario Longoria and all of us with: "A legitimate question is if he did not claim to be Mexican, why should that community claim him?" See www.tedwilliamsmuseum.com or call 352-527-6566 and ask if Ted Williams was part Mexican.

62. Texas Ranger Rubén Rivera at Bat: Second Chance

We are writing here about a baseball player with the Texas Ranger team, not some new Chicano recruit into the evil police force that once upon a time victimized Mexicans at will in Texas. Rubén Rivera was signed by the New York Yankees to play baseball for $1 million a year. The kid was hot! During spring training with the Yankees in 2002, Rivera stole a bat and glove from teammate Derek Jeter's locker. He sold it to a memorabilia dealer for $2,500 and got caught. The Yankees released him for $200,000 and cancelled what remained of his million-dollar contract. Fortunately, the Texas Rangers picked him up and signed him to a minor league contract. At the All-Star break he moved up from the farm club once again to the majors. He has started in every game since then.

Rubén Rivera got a second chance.

Rubén Rivera risked $1,000,000 for $2,500. What was he thinking? What math did he NOT learn in grammar school?

63. Questionable Doctors?

You have read the newspaper accounts of medical providers accused by patients of sexual misconduct and malpractice and other criminal, and, for sure, unethical practices. What is this world coming to? You can't go to the priest for confession. Now you can't trust your doctor?

You can read all about allegations made against Fred Armendáriz, M.D., of El Paso, Texas, and learn of what he did to get on the list of those disciplined by the Texas Board of Medical Examiners, but you have to pay $10 for the report. Is your medical care worth $10 to find out if your doctor appears on the list? How many Latino doctors are on the list? Who are they? Where are they practicing? Is the Fred Armendáriz listed the one I know? (See www.questionabledoctors.org and let me know what you find out.)

64. Questionable Records

In my years of practice as an attorney and experience with family law matters, I have seen it all. But the biggest headache is the birth certificate with wrong information. The usual problem is the name of Raza. The spelling and order of names confuse white hospital administrators and clerks, not to mention the doctors and nurses. The racial category is the second source of grief for both them and us.

During my investigation of this matter, I met a parent, Rebecca Baeza, who had just given birth to María del Jesús at the local hospital. Becky told me she filled out the birth certificate information and entered "Chicana" for race of her baby girl. The hospital clerk called on her to ask which country she was from. When she replied "U.S.A." The hospital clerk promptly changed the race category to "Hispanic."

I guess in Weatherford, Texas, we still are another race. Becky did try to maintain her Chicanismo, but not hard enough.

65. Memorable Quotes

"Extremism in the defense of liberty is no vice," said Barry Goldwater in 1964. "Communication of the truth is not a universal right," said Bishop John Yanta of Amarillo, Texas.

Goldwater, a U.S. Senator from Arizona, was the Republican nominee for president in 1964. He lost by a landslide to Lyndon Baines Johnson, the Democrat. For Yanta, a Catholic bishop in the Texas Panhandle area for the past 14 years, the future does not look rosy. He hid from his parishioners information about men under his direction who had been "program priests." The term "program priests" refers to those who were accused child molesters and sent by their superiors to a church-run treatment center for that perversion. In other words, the church officials, when faced with such an accusation, rather than investigate and prosecute, sent the accused for in-house treatment, covering up the whole affair. After release from treatment, the priests were put back on the job, usually in another parish, and no one was told about their background or sexual interests.

Yanta, formerly the executive director of the San Antonio Neighborhood Youth Organization (SANYO), a War on Poverty Program during the late 1960s, is still adamant about disobeying his superiors on this matter. The U.S. bishops in early 2002 admitted to having a serious problem with pedophile priests and changed the rules to basically a zero-tolerance on sexual abuse by their men. Yanta lost priests in 16 of 35 parishes in his diocese; at least eight of them had been "program priests." For example, former Bishop Leroy Matthiesen, Yanta's predecessor, forced Rosendo Herrera out of the seminary in Mexico for sexual misconduct but brought him to the Amarillo diocese in the United States. Herrera failed to win ordination in Lubbock and was accused of misconduct in 2000 in Amarillo. He is on lay status at his request. A more egregious example is John Salazar-Jiménez. This priest went to prison in California for sexually molesting two teenage boys attending Catholic school in Los Angeles. Matthiesen brought him into the Amarillo diocese in 1991 while the man was on parole. He made him pastor of Church of the Holy Spirit in Tulia, Texas. Monthly, Salazar-Jiménez traveled to meet with his parole officer in Albuquerque. He spent nine months in Jemez Springs, New Mexico, while on leave from the Holy Spirit in Tulia to complete his parole conditions. The parishioners never knew any of this. Salazar-Jiménez is now in Ontario, Canada, in another treatment program for priests with a secret, dark past.

When Yanta took over as bishop from Matthiesen in 1997 and for the past 14 years, the records of past misconduct and the "program priests" were there at his elbow.

Yanta also kept quiet.

Now, with the rule of zero tolerance for sexual abuse, Yanta says about the secret, dark past of his "program priests" that "communication of the truth is not a universal right."

I wonder if he would say that about the holy sacrament of confession?

Will you ever believe a priest? Whom can you trust with your kids?

66. Catholic Review Boards

The demand of the 1960s was for a civilian review board of police. The cops were out of control in many cities across the country. Police brutality was an epidemic. Most cops and their leaders and employers opposed the civilian review boards. A few cities organized such oversight committees.

In the late 1990s, a new epidemic made headlines: sexual misconduct of Catholic priests with boys, some girls, not many. By the beginning of the 21st century, the money judgments awarded victims of sexual abuse by priests drained financial reserves. The extent of sexual misconduct prompted the church to admit wrongdoing and set new policy. The church also began forming sexual misconduct review boards.

Regrettably, these review boards from the national level to the local level, mirror juries in criminal and civilian cases. While some reform has been made in the make-up of juries from basically all-white, retired professionals or moneyed persons to some minorities and working people, juries are still composed of mostly whites in urban areas. There will be a dark-skinned face here and there among the jurors, but not many. For sure, few Latinos or Chicanas are to be found in the jury box.

The Fort Worth diocese sexual misconduct review board has 18 members, three of whom have Spanish surnames and these are all professional Hispanics. Bettie Reyes, a school principal, is the chair. A third of the group, six of the members, are of church employees. This packing device is called a safe harbor. There is no victim represented. There is no blue-collar, working-class representative. There is no *Hijas de María* representative, *cursillista,* or *Guadalupana* representative, and those are the vast majority of *católicos* in this area.

The National Board of Review has no Latino or Latina, unless a surname has fooled me. We are the majority of *católicos* in the United States, at least the ones who go to Mass and have images of the Virgen de Guadalupe in our homes.

67. Oops, I Goofed!

It is not always the bad guys who are the real bad guys; sometimes the good guys are also the real bad guys. Let me introduce you to Mark Aguirre, captain of police in Houston, Texas. At this writing, he is enjoying job suspension with pay for wrongdoing, along with twelve other police officers with the Houston PD. What happened?

On August 18, 2002, a police raid of a Houston K-Mart parking lot took place. The objective was to curb drag racing. The police arrested 273 people that night at the parking lot on orders from Capt. Aguirre. What's wrong with that?

Nobody was drag racing.

68. I Can Do Both!

There are professional athletes that double-dip in sports. That is to say, they play two sports professionally and do it well. How they manage their schedules and negotiate their money are other issues.

Tony González plays tight end for the Kansas City Chiefs. He is a Pro Bowl player. For two months he held out for more money to play football and to start an NBA career. He missed training and the preseason games. He rejected an $8 million signing bonus and a long-term deal that would have reached $28 million. Instead, he signed for a one-year deal worth $3.05 million and is still pursuing the NBA career. González is not happy, and neither is his agent, Tom Condon, who now will take home less of a cut.

The main difference between Condon and González is that Condon takes a cut from each player he represents, and that adds up to big, big bucks for a long, long time, while González gets only what's left for as long as there is to have. And, doing two sports at once is risking injury, harm, and danger, suffering pain, soreness, stress, and time away from home, family, and friends at twice the rate. And Tony is really, really good. In the season opener, the Chiefs beat the Browns 40 to 39 largely because of his efforts. Tony had five catches for 87 yards and a touchdown that night.

If there are Latino players and actors and entertainers in all fields now, are there Latino agents?

69. Let's Go to the Bathroom and Talk

It used to be that when a group of members of an official governing body wanted to sidestep the law on open meetings, they would go hunting together, go drinking together, go play golf together, or go to the toilet together, if there was a female office-holder they really wanted to exclude. The Texas Open Meetings Law, like those of most states, prohibits the discussion of official business by a majority of members of a governing body in private meetings. The discussion of public business must be in an open meeting in full view of the public.

The school superintendent of Somerset Independent School District near southern San Antonio, Texas, filed a complaint in the mid-1990s charging some Chicano school board members with violating the Open Meetings Law. She not only got them indicted but convicted with her testimony that a secret meeting was held by the Chicano members who constituted a majority, and they also excluded Anglo members from the secret meeting. The president of the Somerset board, José Luis Tovar, Jr., was convicted and sentenced but got probation. He cannot run for public office again. He insisted it was a setup by the angry, white female superintendent.

In 2000, three members of the fifteen-member State Board of Education of Texas (SBOE) met at a restaurant for lunch. Two members sat at one table and another at another table with a trust fund consultant. The State Board manages $17.5 billion in teacher retirement funds. The fee to manage these funds is considerable, and many consultants want the work. They will do just about anything to get the management contract. Three of fifteen is not a majority of the SBOE, but three of five is a majority of the SBOE's finance committee, and Joe Bernal of San Antonio was one of those charged with the crime. Joe Bernal is a former state senator from San Antonio. He was instrumental in passage of bilingual legislation while in the Texas Senate and of confronting the brutality of the Texas Rangers in the Rio Grande Valley during the melon strikes at La Casita Farms in the late 1960s.

If you are in public office, be careful where you go, whom you sit with, and who is watching, especially if you have recently made someone angry with you or your decisions.

70. *Los galleros*

Cockfighting is an old Mexican tradition. The cockfights are also gaming events. People bet on their favorite cock. Cockfights are almost as big an event as bullfighting in Spanish-speaking countries. The game of cockfighting and the raising of cocks for fighting is big business. When I drive the countryside in rural Texas, New Mexico, Oklahoma, Arizona, and Louisiana, I still see rows of the little cages behind rural homes; they are miniature chicken coops, evidence that someone there is raising fighting cocks.

When Laura Miller, now mayor of Dallas, was a city council member, she managed to pass an ordinance banning the keeping of roosters in residential areas of the city. She argued that they crowed too early in the morning and were a nuisance to day sleepers. She also argued that they were being raised for an illegal activity, cockfighting. Texas has outlawed cockfighting for years, since 1907, as have most states. Arizona and Missouri banned it in 1998. There are three that do not: Louisiana, New Mexico, and Oklahoma. New Mexico allows it in only nine counties.

On the Oklahoma November 2002 ballot, Measure 52 seeks to outlaw cockfighting in that state. Proponents of the ban argue it is cruelty to animals. Opponents of the measure say it is a sport with a long history and profitable to the forty-plus cockfighting pits in operation across the state. Cockfighters say they will sue the state for lost property in the amount of $75 to $100 million if the measure is passed. This is a big business involving some 7,000 members of 42 game clubs, with 12,000 plus families involved in the breeding side, *los galleros*. The annual revenue projected by the Oklahoma Gamefowl Breeders Association from cockfighting and related support interests is approximately $100 million. This is not pocket change.

The battle over cockfighting is the battle of suburban voters versus the rural ethos. The winners, if the banning measure is passed, will be Indian reservations and Louisiana, where gaming over cocks is allowed. The losers will only go underground, as in Texas. *Los galleros siguen.*

71. Divorce: American Polygamy

The Church of the Latter Day Saints (Mormons) no longer holds polygamy as a fundamental tenet of their religious dogma. Muslims in some sects still do. In the United States, we are beginning to permit polygamy via divorce and remarriage. We can have as many wives, one at a time, and make as many kids as we can afford or not afford by hiding from collection of child support. There are many, many deadbeat dads out there. Child-support collection, lack of it, is a big issue in most states, and it is growing as an international issue because collection, when possible, is limited to in-country boundaries.

Divorce causes the impoverishment of Latinas, all women for that matter. Usually, the woman will obtain primary responsibility for the welfare of the child(ren). And usually the father will pay child support and get specific rights of access and visitation with the kids. In most cases, the divorce process is acrimonious. The couple will fight viciously and tenaciously for months over issues that in retrospect will be seen as minor, but not in the heat of battle. Lawyers are hired to fight over these issues. Many divorces, rather than be settled without trial, proceed to litigation because the parties cannot come to an agreement and prefer that a judge settle the issues for them.

Acrimonious divorce proceedings are harmful to children. The kids are made pawns. The rate of divorce among Raza is going higher by the year.

(See www.collabgroup.com for information on dispute resolution in family law and www.dallascollaborativelaw.com for a site of lawyers in family law practice.)

72. ¡El rocanrol, raza!

Our Spanglish or Tex-Mex always amuses me as some folks refer to our use of mixed English and Spanish in sentences and conversation. Examples are *la troca* (truck), *el rayte* (ride), *ay te wacho* (see you later), and *rocanrol* for rock-and-roll.

Communication is the key, so Tex-Mex is okay to use. *¡Dale gas!*

Music is also communication. And all the great Chicano bands of yesteryear began their careers playing *rocanrol*. Ask Little Joe, Sunny Osuna, Latin Breed, Rubén Ramos and his brothers, Laura Canales, to name a few. Recall Richie Valens, Question Mark and the Mysterions, Doug Sohm, Tortilla Factory? How about the origin and dream of Selena Quintanilla's father, Abraham, in music: to be a *rocanrol* band. The lead singers in these bands were all doing *rocanrol* at first chance.

In a big way the influence of U.S.A. rock-and-roll is felt by the entire world. This influence is cultural imperialism. We live in the United States and adapt and cope with what is. That is the Chicano life. But what about Mexico and the rest of Central and South America? Why do they go for *rocanrol*? I told you, cultural imperialism.

Some folks grow out of it with age. Little Joe, Rubén Ramos, Laura Canales, for example, became hot property in the music of *la Onda Chicana* for decades. Others never grow out of it because they rock and make money. El Tri is one of the hottest Mexican bands, *rocanroleros,* and has been for 35 years! The lead man is Alex Mora, now 49 years old, and still ranting and raving, shrieking, stroking his guitar neck until it squirts (his gag), and strumming the steel guitar until your ears hurt. Catch their latest tune, *"Todo sea por el rocanrol"* in their 35th album, *No Te Olivides de la Banda.*

73. Échale más agua al caldo, llegó la visita

This is a famous saying in Spanish, to put more water in the soup because company has arrived. In other words, you must make do with what you have, and you share what you have by spreading it around. This *refrán* or *dicho* was the favorite of Don Vero Garza from Mission, Texas.

When I review the past antics of U.S. Commerce Secretaries for the past two decades, I think of this *dicho* because I feel like the guests were served watered-down *caldo*, as in the saying above.

At issue is the decennial count of population in the United States. In both the 1990 and 2000 census enumerations, the Secretary of Commerce has rejected demands to adjust the total numbers in favor of minorities who were undercounted by the process, some 3 million in 2000. Raza population is the most undercounted. NALEO estimates that 1,000,000 Latinos were not counted in the 2000 census. We lose millions of federal dollars in services because of the undercount, and we lose out on political representation during redistricting that follows the census release of numbers.

Although we are more, we get less. *Échale más agua al caldo . . .*

74. Pipeline Politics

Graduate study in the United States is the study of pipeline politics. Who gets into the pipeline for a terminal degree? How large is the pipeline? How fast can you go inside the pipeline? Who opens and shuts the pipeline valve?

The numbers of Latinos who graduate from high school are not impressive, and the numbers of Latinos who enter college are less so. The number of Latinos in graduate programs is dismal. There is a very thin pipeline for Latinos entering graduate programs in search of terminal degrees. We do not control access, speed, selection, or success in the pipeline.

There were approximately 1.77 million U.S. graduate students in 1998. Latinos comprised only 5 percent of these, 83,000. In the professional schools, there were approximately 303,000 students. Latinos were only 5 percent there, also with 14,000. Locally, at Southern Methodist University Law School, a private school, 17 Latinos were enrolled, 7 percent. There is no public law school north of Austin and east of Lubbock.

The good news is that the pipeline is full of whites and some blacks, but those are all that are left. Whites are declining in number and blacks are not growing. The only other group gaining is Asian.

(See www.pewhispanic.org for their latest report on Latinos in higher education.)

75. Electoral Politics

Henry Cisneros was the great hope of U.S. Latino politics, beginning in 1972 and into the early 1990s. He had been the first Hispanic mayor of a major city, San Antonio, since the Anglo conquest of the Southwest and Texas in the early to mid-1800s. Toward the end of the Carter administration, Vice President Walter Mondale considered him for his running mate. There was talk of Henry C. running for governor or U.S. senator in Texas.

During the first Clinton administration, Cisneros was appointed Secretary of Housing and Urban Development. Then, he admitted to lying to his wife, the FBI, and congressional committee members overseeing his confirmation about an extra-marital affair involving an Anglo political fundraiser named Linda Medlar while being considered for the HUD position. He left HUD and eventually pleaded guilty to one federal misdemeanor charge, paid a token fine, and was placed on probation.

Henry rehabilitated himself before the public and reconciled with his wife. Univision, the Los Angeles-based Spanish language television network, picked him to head the company, and he made good money there. He quit the network in 2000 and formed a housing development corporation with headquarters in San Antonio.

In a gesture of goodwill, President Clinton, in the final hours of his presidency, granted Henry Cisneros a pardon for his federal crime. The Cisneros pardon is significant in the fact that the former San Antonio mayor and U.S. cabinet official is one of the first Chicanos ever to obtain one. Ben Reyes, Betti Maldonado, Ramsey Muñiz, Reies López Tijerina, Albert Bustamante, and Kathy Villapando never have been able to do so. Perhaps Henry's recent treatment under the law suggests that we are finally gaining something approximating a more equal status in American justice, at least when we have sufficient money and power on our side.

[By the way, Raymond Telles was the first Raza elected mayor of a major city, El Paso, in 1959. This historical oversight by the pundits and Cisneros's biographers is part of the enduring mythology surrounding Henry C.]

PART II

MID-RANGE POWER STRUCTURE AND LEVEL OF POWER

1. Justice from Justice Justice

In the lore of judicial figures, there is a Texan by the name of William Wayne Justice. He was called Justice Justice for decades while on the federal bench in the Eastern District of Texas. Justice from Justice Justice came to many quarters, including prison reform, school desegregation, voting rights, and open housing.

One of the cases he heard involved the battle between school districts in Del Rio, Texas, home to Laughlin Air Force base, a former strategic air command center, and home to thousands of Mexicans. In fact, in Del Rio there were two segregated school districts, one for Anglo students and one for Mexican students. The problem was that the air base was adjacent to the San Felipe Del Rio School District, the Chicano school, yet the soldiers' kids were bused through the Mexican barrio over to the white school. By this maneuver, the whites not only perpetuated segregation but also financial inequality because the federal government paid the white school district good money to bus and teach the military kids. The white school also hired military personnel as teachers and support staff, but not Mexicans.

Mike González, winner of the South Texas Iron Man competition while in high school in Uvalde, Texas, joined other lawyers to sue the white Del Rio Independent School District. Venue was proper in Justice Justice's court because he has assumed statewide jurisdiction of all school cases. Justice Justice had gone to law school and was a former drinking buddy with one of the lawyers representing the Mexican kids and parents, Warren Burnet from Odessa.

Mike, Warren, Abel Ochoa from El Paso, Texas, and Richard Clarkson with the Burnet law firm won the case. The districts were consolidated into one and renamed San Felipe Del Rio Consolidated School District, the true name of the city. And the court ordered a comprehensive educational program to benefit Chicano kids, including remediation for past discrimination, plus attorney fees.

The judge set a Monday-morning, nine o'clock hearing on the matter of attorney fees. The opposing attorneys, mostly from Houston law firms with hundreds of attorneys, chose to fly into Tyler, Texas, for the hearing. Tyler is but a hundred miles from Houston.

Mike González chose to drive the entire distance from Del Rio to Tyler. The Houston lawyers were delayed. Mike was there on time. Finally after a two-hour delay, Federal Judge William Wayne Justice gavels the court to order and inquires of the Houston lawyers, "How come you were late?" "Our plane had problems with fog." Justice Justice then queries Mike González, lone attorney for the plaintiffs, "Mike, how far did you have to travel?" "Four hundred some odd miles." "Did you fly up here then?" Mike answered, "I drove." "And you were here on time this morning?"

The judge looked sternly at the Houston lawyers and said, "From now on, if you are not here on time, I am going to hold you in contempt and put you all in jail."

The plaintiffs and lawyers got their entire attorney fees awarded.

Justice William Wayne Justice is now a retired judge on senior status. That means he hears only the cases he wants to when he wants to. Justice Justice rules.

(See Interview with Mike González, General Libraries, Special Collections, University of Texas at Arlington, Arlington, Texas, pp. 86–87.)

2. Hall of Fame Without a Hall?

Hall of Fame, Wall of Fame, Hall of Heroes and Heroines, Museum of Icons—whatever you want to call it, there must be a physical location. Or should we give life to the idea first and then raise the money to build, rent, or lease it?

There is a National Hispanic Music Hall of Fame. The inaugural inductees were Flaco Jiménez, Little Joe [Hernández], Johnny Gonzales, Rubén Vela, Johnny Canales, Los Aguilares, Los Pavos Reales, and six others. The ceremony was held in historic La Villita by the river in San Antonio, Texas, in June 2002. But there is no actual building to memorialize the inductees, yet.

If you want to help, call Sam Zúñiga or Marcelo Tafoya (512-928-1797). Zúñiga started the idea of a hall of fame for the Texas Talent Musicians Association, aka Tejano Music Awards. Tafoya at one time owned five Chicano radio format stations in Texas. "If you build it, they will come," someone said in a movie, but this saying should be Chicano-improved-upon with "If you think it, create it, and award it, then you can build it and they will surely come."

The same idea is being implemented in Alice, Texas. In Alice on June 9, 1999, Tejano ROOTS Inc. (Remembering Our Own Tejano Stars) was chartered. The group sought out State Representative Ignacio Salinas, Jr. (D-San Diego) and State Senator Carlos Truán (D-Corpus Christi) to establish a Tejano Music Hall of Fame and designate Alice, Texas, as the official birthplace of Tejano music. So that, Armando Marroquín, Sr. and his company could focus on Chicano music exclusively. Marroquín also was the first man to place Chicano music in the jukeboxes in South Texas.

In Edinburg, Texas, the county government subsidizes the local Hispanic Chamber of Commerce's attempt to keep open a museum with its budding Music Hall of Fame. Roberto Pulido y los Clásicos are from that part of the Rio Grande Valley. More important, Roberto Pulido's brother, Eloy, was the county judge for Hidalgo County from 1998 to 2002.

Better to have three Halls of Fame than none at all.

3. Ever Heard of MASA?

No, not the corn or wheat dough to make *tortillas* and *tamales* and *buñuelos*, rather the Mexican-American Student Alliance of New York. MASA is a student group at the City University of New York (CUNY). This is an organization that was formed post-September 11, 2001, because of Mohammed Atta. Atta was one of the perpetrators of the September 11 attack on the Twin Towers of the World Trade Center. Atta had an expired student visa. Another perpetrator of an earlier attack was Timothy McVeigh. Remember him? The Oklahoma City bomber?

What do McVeigh and Atta have to do with MASA?

In 1989, undocumented New York students could attend college and pay in-state tuition, $1,600, at a four-year college/university or $1,200 in a two-year college if they proved that they had lived in the state for more than a year. The undocumented students additionally had to have a GED or high school diploma.

In 1996, after McVeigh's evil deed in Oklahoma, the federal

government passed legislation that denies undocumented students in-state tuition. CUNY, however, refused to increase the tuition. After September 11 and Atta's evil deed in New York, State Senator Frank Padavan (R-Queens) railed against undocumented students attending New York colleges and universities. He called the undocumented students a national security threat. The CUNY trustees read these allegations in *The New York Times* (October 31, 2001) and changed their minds. Trustees upped the tuition for undocumented students to $3,400 per semester.

MASA got organized in response. MASA members and some professors went on a hunger strike. MASA members scripted and performed street theatre to let people know about the issue. MASA members lobbied for new legislation. Assemblymen Peter Rivera (D-Bronx) and Adriano Espaillat (D-Manhattan) introduced legislation to provide in-state tuition rates for high school graduates of a New York school, as is done in California and Texas.

(See www.masany@att.net or call them at 212-860-6705, 145 East 116th Street, New York, New York, 10005. See also *In Motion Magazine,* April 30, 2002.)

4. Spanish, English, Spanglish, Tex-Mex, *¿qué onda?*

Older Hispanics, by and large, speak, read, and write *español.* Younger generations of Latinos communicate in both languages, Spanish and English. Some critics of our way of communicating call it Spanglish and Tex-Mex. And the number of Spanglish-speakers is growing.

To be sure, not enough research has been done on the subject, but there are some dozen recent surveys done with small samples. The surveys show that up to 70 percent of all Latinos choose Spanish as the language of choice. But two recent surveys conducted in Los Angeles revealed that young Latinos, ages 14 to 24, prefer English over Spanish when talking among themselves or while channel surfing and reading magazines. A large segment of these young Latinos, three fourths or 74 percent, claim they speak Spanglish. These are very significant findings because:

- Raza buying power is growing at a rate nearly three times that of non-Hispanic whites.
- Half of the U.S. Latino population is younger than 26 years of age.

(See "The Story of Two Cultures: Hispanic Youth of Los Angeles," Cultural Access and Sapo Communication, Los Angeles, California, June 2002.)

5. Hall of Heroes

The Pentagon has a Hall of Heroes and the U.S. Army has portraits of the past Secretaries of the Army. The 17th Secretary of the Army was Luis Caldera, the son of Mexican immigrants to California. Prior to the army stint as secretary, Caldera served as a legislator in California for five years. And prior to that, he attended various schools to complete degrees: Harvard Business School (MBA), West Point (BA), and Harvard Law School.

Caldera was the first Hispanic Secretary of the Army. The man had connections.

6. Buy a House

Buy a house! Interest rates are at an all-time low at present. Builders are promoting home sales with fantastic gimmicks and come-ons, such as vacation trips to Hawaii, added appliances, upgrades on carpeting and landscaping, large discounts, and almost everyone qualifies. They will qualify you to sell the house, regardless of how bad your credit history was or is. If you default, they do get the house back. The most important thing about buying a home is that it is the only real wealth accumulation a person does in a lifetime. All you have to figure is: Can you make the payments?

According to the 2001 Census data, home ownership among Latinos is on the rise. It grew from 42 percent in 1990 to 46 percent in 2000. There is a problem in some areas where minorities pay higher interest rates on their mortgages than non-minorities in similar financial circumstances. This is called red-lining in the industry, where a lender draws a red line on a map and instructs the staff to not lend in that area or to charge higher rates.

7. Marín on the Money

Rosario Marín is the 41st Treasurer of the United States for the Bush administration. Rosario's signature is on every paper money bill printed during her term. Find a two-dollar bill with her moniker and frame it as a historical conversation piece.

Born in Mexico, Rosario was brought from Mexico City to the U.S. at age 14. She attended a community college at night and later obtained a bachelor's degree. When she became a U.S. citizen and filled out a voter registration card, she asked her boss what to mark in the box asking for political affiliation. He said, "Republican, register Republican." She did. It did not matter to her at the time because she didn't know the difference between one political party or another. When she did realize the difference, she stuck with the Republican Party and became an activist party loyalist and candidate for public office. She is the former city council member from Huntington Park, California, and served as mayor for a term. She worked at the California Department of Social Service under Governor Pete Wilson of Proposition 187 fame. He recruited her to work for him. President Bush looked for Republican Latinas to appoint in administration slots and tapped Marín. She was, and still is, an active Republican Party member.

It sure helps to be a Republican Latina at the right time and in the right place, *¿qué no?*

8. "Doesn't Go Away," Diana Flores

"Doesn't Go Away" is the establishment's nickname for Diana Flores, trustee of the Dallas County Community College District, first elected and sworn in June 11,1996. They tried to keep her off the board through legal maneuvers, but Diana fought back and didn't go away. Their trick on her did not work. Diana holds the token Chicano district, and there is a token black one as well; all the others are for "Whites Only." While the "Whites Only" signs are no longer visible in public places and businesses, the reality is not so clear, particularly in setting single-member districts for electing representatives to governing bodies. The Dallas County district has seven seats while most community college districts in Texas, especially the urban districts, have nine. The more seats on a governing board, the greater the chances for Raza-elected representation.

All new members of any governing body MUST go through a learning curve. Diana was no exception. She was told early on at the first board retreat, held three weeks after she was seated, that the Dallas trustees speak with one voice or not at all. In other words, she had to vote with the majority and not be a dissenter. But, the token minority representative MUST be a dissenter on almost all agenda items beginning with contracts, personnel, and most policy initiatives. Maintaining the status quo and voting with the majority spells doom and gloom to minority constituents because it means no change from the same-old-same-old *modus operandi* that only benefits the insider majority, or should I say monopoly group? She was also told that a board member could only get an item on the agenda if the member had four votes—a majority of the board, in other words. But Diana and the black trustee were only two votes! Soon she found out that individual trustees could, if they talked to the chancellor, place items on the agenda at will, and she did with frequency. When Diana asked for information about personnel hiring, expenditures, and the like, she was told that information requests had to be approved by the board—in other words, four votes again.

As for trustees speaking with one voice or not at all, Diana wrapped herself in the American flag. She announced for the record that in America a person has freedom of speech and the right to vote as their conscience and principle dictate, and she was not going to give those freedoms up for anyone. She was going to exercise her democratic freedoms to speak and vote how she felt, and if the board did not let her place items on the agenda or get information, she would file Open Records Requests through the state attorney general. It made the other board members appear to be hiding information, from the public. Diana got what she wanted and still does. Diana was reelected to the board in 2002. Under her tenure on the board, to date there has been a steady increase in Chicano enrollment (66%) and graduation rates of Chicanos

(62%), plus a steady increase in Chicano and Chicana faculty.

If you follow the Diana lesson, you can be a majority of one.

9. Missing in Action: National Hispanic Hall of Fame

In 1988 the Central California Hispanic Chamber of Commerce, together with the Fresno Unified School District and Chihuahua, Inc., founded the National Hispanic Hall of Fame. The first inductees included some very prominent and deserving national figures: César Chávez, Polly Baca, Mario Obledo, Danny Villanueva, Ricardo Montalbán, Rita Moreno, Tom Flores, Carmen Zapata, and me, of course. I was deserving and prominent. Okay, maybe only in 1988. There were posthumous inductees also: Dennis Chávez, Rubén Salazar, and William C. Velásquez, as well as an international inaugural inductee, Vicente Fernández.

It was a gala affair. I still remember the event to this day and glow with warmth when I do.

In 2000, I had occasion to travel via Fresno. I called the originator of the Hispanic National Hall of Fame idea, Gloria Palacios Morales, and her cohort, Helen Rael Giddens. At the time of the event, she was the president of the sponsoring board and of the regional Hispanic Chamber of Commerce; now she was not. I wanted to see the building housing the Hall of Fame and see the other inductees since 1988. Regrettably, she informed me, her successors-in-office did not continue support for the project, and it died without further inductions. It was a flash in the sky.

Charismatic leadership is like that: a flash, intense, attention-grabbing, beautiful at the time, but expiring as quickly as it comes. Leadership must be sustained over time. The lesson here is not so much excellence in a leadership role, but consistency. Would you not rather have someone in charge who continues the project, year after year, than someone who moves on to another project? Stay the course, Raza, and finish what you start.

10. Evaluation of Judges

It used to be that the American Bar Association, the premier gatekeepers of the lawyers' profession, was called upon by presidents to evaluate potential nominees to the U.S. Supreme Court and other high-level judicial posts. Then came George Dubya, the anointed president, and he, on advice from his White House counsel Al González, dropped the protocol. Bush's potential nominees now go to other Republican politicians and a somewhat nebulous ad hoc committee of Republican stalwarts for a nay or yea vote of confidence. The Bush ad hoc committee has cleared a few qualified Latinos, or is this a contradiction in terms, given the heavy hand of Republican partisan politics?

At the local level, the scenario is similar. Usually, municipal judges are appointed by city council members. Sitting judges are evaluated from time to time by the prosecutors, and potential appointees are evaluated and screened by some citizen panel, also appointed. The prosecutors' poll, in my opinion, is suspect.

In Dallas, the city council received the survey of prosecutors' ratings of municipal judges the first week in August 2002. On a 30-point scale, the three Chicanos out of nine full-time and eighteen part-time municipal judges received poor to fair ratings. The ratings were: Victor Ortiz-18, Gustavo E. González-21.9, and Daniel F. Solís-22.5. These ratings were accompanied by anonymous remarks on specific judges. One such remark about Judge González said he was too proactive in aiding *pro se* defendants (those who represent themselves) by giving them instructions on how to play the system in order to beat a probation violation.

Can you imagine a Chicano judge actually helping a *pro se* defendant? That strikes me as a clear oxymoron. Why else would you be in court, if you weren't guilty to begin with? What is this world coming to?

11. *O'Reilly Factor* Has Become the Oh Really Factor on *The Pulse*

William "Bill" O'Reilly got his start in broadcast journalism on WFAA in Dallas, Texas, back in the 1970s. He has a degree from the Kennedy School of Government at Harvard University, but he is no flaming liberal. Today, he is the hottest TV news personality on the air with two shows, *O'Reilly Factor* and *The Pulse*. He is extremely right of center in his views, vocally aggressive, physically imposing at six-foot-seven, of Irish ancestry, and very much in your face while "debating" a topic on his programs. He rarely lets a guest finish a sentence and always edits the final cut that airs to make himself look good and the guest terrible.

Why would anyone want to be on his show?

It is a rare opportunity for Raza to be seen and heard by a national audience. You get your message across. I should say, you hope to survive the final edit and hope to get at least part of your message across. O'Reilly's notion of balance, fairness, and truth is to let the guest get in one or two good points.

Last March 2002, Ron Gochez, MEChA chairman at San Diego State University, squared off on the O'Reilly Factor with two opponents. Not only did he face Bill O'Reilly, but he also faced a member and officer of the California Patriot and Berkeley College Republicans, Bret Manley. The actual pretaped debate went somewhat well for Gochez, but in the final aired show, he did not fare well. Gochez was made to appear nervous, dry-mouthed, circular in his argument, defensive, and otherwise outnumbered and out-talked. He was made to look like a lunatic demanding the return of lost Mexican territory.

Over KUCI Radio in Irvine, California, last July 15, 2002, Armando Cervantes, a local MEChA leader got it on with Hal Netkins, city council candidate in the possible new Valley City (if the vote to secede passes). The topic was also the *reconquista de Aztlán*.

I got my chance to pretape a show for *The Pulse* in August 2002, that aired nationally on the Fox channel on August 15. The topic was immigration. And we went at it for 30 minutes in the pre-tape version of the debate. It was one-on-one, O'Reilly and me. I gigged O'Reilly repeatedly and got the best of him well over two dozen times. I have the transcription of the pretaped show to prove it. I audiotaped the entire debate.

The show that aired was entirely another scenario. He was presented as the rational, normal, patriotic American. He called me a lunatic for my views. I was made to appear as the crazed, aging Chicano militant on the subject of Mexican immigration. I was allowed a couple of gigs on national television.

La Raza will love the face-off. La Raza will applaud that I got in some gigs. La Raza will appreciate that we are still in the fight. *No dejamos caer la bandera.* La Raza has to take the offensive on issues, frame the policy questions, define the debate parameter, seek the public forum, and prepare with talking points.

(Send $10 for a copy of the transcription or $17 for video and transcripts to Box 19539, Arlington, TX 76019.)

12. The Diamonds?

What do these names have in common: Dallas Diamonds, Austin Rage, New England Storm, Missouri Prowlers, Arizona Knighthawks, and Houston Energy? They are teams in the U.S. Women's Football League. Yes, women play professional football and every other sport you can imagine, particularly after 1950 with the founding of the Ladies Professional Golf Association. Remember our golf champion Nancy López? In 1970 the Women's Tennis Association was founded. In 1976 the Women's Professional Billiards Association was started. In 1981 the Professional Women's Bowling Association got chartered. In 1997 the National Women's Basketball Association was formed. The Women's Professional Softball League was started in 1997 but suspended in 2001 with plans to relaunch in 2003. Lisa Fernández was an Olympic champion of the fast-pitch. Women have been in boxing since the first bout was sanctioned in 1997. There are several associations for women's boxing, just like those for men, an alphabet soup of acronyms: WISBF, IFBA, WIBA, IBA, and WBF. The greatest female bodybuilder of all times *es la Rachel de Harlingen.* Her professional name is Rachel Elizondo McLish. In handball, the champion during the 1980s at the Pan American Games, the U.S. Cup, and the 1984 and 1988 Olympics, was Sandra Lynn de la Riva-Baza from Los Angeles.

In 1999, the Women's Baseball League was organized. In 2000, the Women's Professional Football League took off. In 2001, the Women's United Soccer Association began play. In 2002, the latest association formed is the United States Professional Volleyball league.

In 1972, the national act that prohibits sex discrimination in federally funded education programs, Title IX, was passed. The year prior, 1971, one female in 27 participated in high school sports. Those numbers are now one girl in 2.5. During the past academic year, 2000–2001, approximately 2,784,154 girls in U.S. high schools participated in athletics, with some 500,000 playing basketball. Good progress has been made.

Will these women's sports survive by drawing spectator attention? Probably. The men in basketball, for example, started as the Basketball Association of America in 1946, renamed the National Basketball Association (NBA) in 1949. They drew few crowds. The focus was and remains on football. Men's basketball broke the 10,000 average attendance mark in the 1975–76 season. That was the 29th season for the league.

Will women in sports be paid as well as men? Probably not. The average NBA salary in the 2001–2002 season was $4.5 million. The average for the woman basketball player in 2002–2003 is $46,000; that is two cents to the dollar. Women in bowling made 70 cents to the male dollar. In golf it is 36 cents to the dollar, while in tennis it is 67 cents to the dollar. These statistics are from a study of professional athletes' salaries in 1999–2000 conducted by the Women's Sports Foundation. Overall sponsorship revenue in women's sports has reached the $1 billion mark. The sponsorship revenue for men in 2001 was $25 billion. Coverage by television of women's sports is also growing from 5 percent in 1989 to 8.7 percent in 1999. More importantly, within Fortune 500 companies, 80 percent of the women identified as leaders played sports as children.

Is there a future for women in sports? You bet! There are more women in the U.S. population than men. Increasingly, more women are spectators at sporting events than men. And, more of the younger generation in the United States, under 18 years of age, is female, overwhelmingly Latina.

Check out Jessica López, an outfielder with the U.S. softball team. She traveled to Yokohoma, Japan, during the last days of August 2002, to compete in the Japan Cup Tournament in softball. Jessica drove in both runs to defeat Japan, 2-1, for the gold medal! Japan got the silver and China the bronze.

Latinas, hit the field! You are the future.

13. Fight Fire with Fire Equipment

In the 1980s, some Hispanic firefighters from across the country got together to discuss the formation of a national Hispanic firefighters' association. They eventually did get organized. The Texas bunch lobbied their legislature to amend the state constitution to allow the donation of used firefighting equipment to *compadre* firefighters in Mexico. First, the enabling legislation to amend was passed because the Chicano legislative caucus in both houses worked for passage. Second, the Raza firefighters and others interested in the issue campaigned for passage by the voters. Third, the amendment passed in the general election of 2000. Fourth, President Fox and his wife hosted the Hispanic firefighters at Los Pinos to honor them for this work. Fox named his wife to head the commission to receive such donations. The collaboration through donations has led to an obvious need to train Mexican firefighters on the use of U.S.-made equipment. Now, border firefighting units, such as the ones in McAllen, Texas, and Reynosa, Mexico, are not only donating and receiving equipment but also training on the equipment.

Are we on the way to One Mexico or are we still on the notion of Aztlán?

(Note: Mexicans have a different view of ethics and nepotism. In the United States, it would be illegal and unethical to have your wife get the donations. In Mexico, if you don't take care of your *familia, no eres buen hombre o mujer*. You are without ethics and illegal for not doing it.)

14. What Is Your FICO?

I never heard of FICO until I tried to buy a car for one of my sons, Olin. I was rejected for credit because of a low FICO. Huh?

FICO is a numeric score now assigned to you based on your credit report. Having good credit is not enough to get a loan. It is the absence of bad credit that will help you get a loan. How many of us don't have bad-credit skeletons in our closet?

FICO is a formula developed by Fair, Issac & Co. (get it, F, I, Co?). Your credit report is analyzed utilizing a FICO model, and numerical scores are assigned to various parts of your credit history.

Payment history is 35 percent of your score. A 30-day late payment can hurt you by 50 points, but a 60- or 90-day late payment can kill you and does. So does a recent late payment because the analyst views this as the beginning of a serious late payment problem. If an account of yours has gone into collection, you are dead in the water. Don't fight over that magazine subscription bill you received and you know you did not order. Pay it before you get the nasty collection letter.

The amount owed is another 30 percent of your total FICO score. Watch the debt limits on your credit cards. If you owe near as much as the limit on a card, the analyst thinks you are living on credit, from card to card. Too many credit cards with debt, even little debt, are bad indicators to analysts. But don't pay off all the cards; use one or two and keep the balances about half the limit (but watch the interest rates!), and pay regularly. Not using your credit cards is as bad as not having charge accounts. The analyst will knock off all points on this part of the score for not having a credit card or account history (remember this is 30 points!).

The length of credit history is worth 15 percent of your score. The older you are, the more favorable the potential rating. Young borrowers need to get into manageable and affordable debt as soon as possible to max their score.

New credit and the mix of accounts add the final 20 percent of the score with ten points each. New credit can be bad if you open too many accounts. Inquiries of your credit can hurt you also; so watch the number of applications you submit. Account mix means the types of credit, such as mortgage, car payment, credit card, tuition loans, and medical payments, for example. A debt to a finance company is real bad news; it implies no one else will loan you money. Defaults, bankruptcies, like collections, are deadly to your score.

As we increase our wealth with the purchase of a home, major appliances, vehicles, and education loans, we will need enhanced FICO scores. For tips on how to increase and improve your scores and for answers to your specific questions, try www.lone-wolf.com or read the book, "How to Save Thousands of Dollars on Your Home Mortgage" by Randy Johnson.

15. *Revista Chicano-Riqueña (RCR)*

A collaborative project between a Chicano, Luis Dávila, and a Boricua, Nicolás Kanellos, both at Indiana University in the early 1970s, produced a literary magazine, *Revista Chicano-Riqueña*. Both of them had their own incipient publications, Kanellos had *La Cadena de la Herencia* and Dávila had CACA. With a little seed grant of $500 from the Latin American Studies Department, actually carry-over money, they printed the first issues of RCR. The rest is history.

Kanellos went on to establish himself as a major force in American letters.

Everybody has great ideas from time to time, but you need money. Carry-over money is a good source. Carry-over money is that leftover money from a grant. You would be surprised at how much carry-over money is laying around. Find it and ask for it.

16. Carry-Over Money

Back when Ronald Reagan became governor of California, he immediately set out to eliminate legal aid for the poor in the state. But he couldn't because it was a federally funded program. When Reagan became president of the United States, he cut legal aid out of the budget, but Congress restored the funding. As Reagan moved from governor to President, many legal aid programs didn't wait for the axe to fall; they shifted carry-over money from a prior fiscal year to newly and expressly formed, independent, tax-exempt, legal-aid organizations. These entities did not have the rules and restrictions that Reagan was able to place on legal-aid programs, e.g., no class actions, no voting rights litigation, etc.

So, legal aid for the poor continued as long as the carry-over money lasted. In the case of the Texas Rural Legal Aid Foundation, it is still funding lawyers in 2002 to do battle on behalf of the poor. Don't wait for the axe to fall; have a contingency plan.

17. The Blame Game, Part I

The public schools in France are designed to produce loyal,

skilled, literate, and productive French citizens. That is the job of public schools the world over, to produce the next generation of loyal, skilled, literate, and productive citizens. The U.S. public schools are like the schools the world over; they are designed to make Anglos out of all of us. The curriculum is Anglo-centered; the teachers and administrators are predominantly Anglo; the governing boards are predominantly Anglo; the school sports, festivities, and extra-mural activities are Anglo-centered; the cafeteria food caters to the Anglo taste; the language of instruction is English; the textbooks prominently feature and exalt Anglo heritage and accomplishment; the tests favor middle-class Anglo students. Anglos attend the better equipped, staffed, designed, and modern schools; segregation of non-Anglos is maintained within schools by programs and between schools by geography; and those tracked for college are predominantly Anglo students.

But we are not all Anglos.

Children in the United States come in black, brown, yellow, in between, and white. Not all children are citizens. Not all parents of children residing in the United States intend to stay. Some persons come escaping tyranny, hunger, ravaging floods and hurricanes, brutal police, political and religious persecution, sexual abuse, and some come looking for relatives who migrated to the U.S.

The U.S. public schools make little allowance for these different and diverse children's needs; they are all taught the same material. Some exception is made with language instruction, but the goal remains the same: get them into English as soon as possible so we can make Anglos out of them. English as a medium of instruction should be an exit criterion for graduation from high school, not an entrance criterion in the primary grades to enter the world of learning!

It is not surprising to see that non-Anglo children are pushed out of the public schools at alarming rates. I use the term "push-out" over "drop-out" because kids do not choose to leave schooling; they are pushed out of schools by adults involved with the educational system.

The "drop-out" problem is not news. This has been the case since the educational system in the United States was forced to admit non-Anglo students, usually by federal court order, beginning in the late 1940s to early 1950s. Today, however, non-Anglo children are the majority minority if not the majority in the Southwestern and Southeastern states, most urban school districts, and the border region with Mexico. But the schools have not changed to meet the needs of these different and diverse students. The "drop-out rates" are criminal.

The blame game continues: "It's the parents' fault, they don't care." "It's the students' fault, they don't want to learn." "It's the language spoken at home, they just don't speak English." "These kids just don't have the I.Q. other students (read Anglo) have." "This is how we have done it in the past, no need to change." "Give them the standardized test and if they flunk, it's the teacher who is not teaching." "We'll not bring in a multicultural curriculum, this is America." "If we fix the problem and the kids drop back into school, who is going to pay for the new buildings and more teachers?" Yada, yada, yada, yada . . .

Today, for the first time in history, we have non-Anglo administrators in charge of education in some states: Oregon, New Mexico, and Texas. Felipe T. Alanís, a native of San Juan, Texas, for example, is the new Commissioner of Education for Texas appointed by Governor Rick Perry (Republican). He is the first Chicano in history in this position. He has publicly promised to develop a more accurate formula on computing "drop-outs" by 2003. The school districts bordering Mexico have for some years in recent decades had *mexicano*-led school boards and central administration officials of Mexican ancestry, often products of those very schools they now administer. Large urban school districts, such as Los Angeles, New York, Chicago, and Dallas, for example, have had non-Anglo school superintendents. The current U.S. Secretary of Education, Rod Paige, is non-Anglo. There has been a *mexicano* U.S. Secretary of Education in years past, Lauro Cavazos.

The "drop-out" or, more accurately, the push-out problem is severe. Dr. María Robledo Montecal, executive director of Intercultural Development Research Associates, based in San Antonio, Texas, has estimated the number of push-outs from Texas schools since 1986 to the present at almost 2 million students. That is about the entire population of San Antonio and Austin or Dallas or half of Houston.

Will all these brown faces rather than white faces in charge make a difference in the drop-out rate? I hope so. These brown faces should not continue the blame game.

18. Box-Office Hits

Revenue generated by movies is measured by tickets sold at the box office. Can you guess which was the biggest box-office hit in Mexico up to mid-year 2002? Another drug-related escapade? Another singing mariachi movie? A border-crossing saga? A Cantinflas-type comedy?

Not! You never heard of Cantinflas?

The box-office record-buster in Mexico was *The Crime of Father Amaro*. This movie has outperformed the next bestseller in Mexico, *Y tu mamá también*. The latter has been shown in U.S. theaters and in other international venues to rave reviews. *Y tu mamá también* was about the explicit sexual activity of a middle-class, middle-aged Mexican woman with grown children. This subject-matter has been taboo for centuries in Mexico. The prevailing notion has been that NO Mexican woman should enjoy sex, much less one with children. *The Crime of Father Amaro* is about a decadent priest who drinks, has mistresses, fathers children, sells dope and guns, and otherwise is a sinner of some magnitude. This subject matter has been taboo for centuries in Mexico also. The prevailing notion has been that NO Mexican priest ever transgresses a parishioner member of his flock.

I guess many people have not heard of Father Ernesto Villaroya, a Catholic priest in Ennis, Texas. Sylvia Abano Martínez Arámbulo alleges he raped her in 1982 in the parish office while both served in the Philippines. Sylvia was a nun then. She got pregnant from the rape and had a son. She left the order and was told to drop the case against the priest, she claims in court documents filed in Los Angeles, California, where she now resides.

The *Father Amaro* movie may not fare so well in the United States, where the priests making the news are not decadent. They don't make babies or love to women. Those in our headlines have boy toys and are otherwise perverted, except those like Father Ernesto, who says sex with Sylvia was consensual.

19. Lesson for Chicano Mayoral Candidates

Chicanas and Chicanos are now running for mayors of large cities. We've had mayors in decades past but usually of small to medium cities, and usually along the border with Mexico. In Texas, we have had several Chicanas win as mayors in medium to large cities, such as Laredo and Brownsville. Chicanas in Texas have also won in small cities since the advent of the Chicano Movement. Chicanas and Chicanos have run and lost in big-city races, such as Houston and San Antonio and Dallas. And Chicanos have won some mayoral races— for example, Raymond Telles in El Paso in the 1950s and Henry Cisneros in San Antonio in the 1980s. Denver has had its Federico Peña and Los Angeles almost had Antonio Villaraigosa.

Chicano Domingo García has run for mayor of Dallas twice and lost. In those elections he did little campaigning among *mexicanos* because he was quoted as saying, "They are only 8 percent of the vote." He also shaved off his mustache to appeal to non-Mexican voters. *No aprende.*

The last time he ran for mayor was in a special election in 2000. The sitting mayor, Ron Kirk, resigned to seek the Democratic nomination for U.S. Senator.

García ran and lost badly again, coming in last in a three-person race. He did not make the run-off contest to decide the winner. García thought he had a chance because the other two candidates were whites, a male and a female, and they would divide the declining white vote in Dallas. But it did not happen, and he had a large campaign debt as a result. One of his campaign zealots, Adelfa Callejo, an old-time Hispanic lawyer, announced in a press interview with a Spanish-language television station reporter that Domingo García would endorse whichever one of the white candidates would help pay off his campaign debt. García also told the media he was endorsing the white guy, Tom Dunning. The media had a field day with this announcement. How much was the payoff for the endorsement, they all wanted to know. Soon thereafter, the criminal prosecutors got into the investigation picture because they smelled a crime in the making. Allegations flew from one white candidate's camp to the other about what Domingo had said to each of them in exchange for his endorsement. Both camps said Domingo had called them to concede defeat and congratulate them on making the run-off, then that he got into the endorsement discussion.

Another Hispanic, Roland Castañeda, the general counsel for the Dallas Area Rapid Transit (DART), was dragged into the investigation fray because Domingo told the media he had called on behalf of Tom Dunning asking for García's endorsement. The media had another field day because Domingo proclaimed his innocence and offered as proof the taped conversation with Roland Castañeda. Now the question became what was said to Domingo about his endorsement, when and by whom. Matters got more complicated when the media alleged that the woman candidate, Laura Miller, had called García asking for his endorsement and offering money.

The Dallas County district attorney (D.A.), himself running for reelection in another race, announced he was withdrawing himself and his staff from the investigation. He sent the matter to the district attorney in a neighboring county, Tarrant. That D.A. announced that he would investigate promptly before the final run-off election was to be held, so the voters would know who did what when. He did not keep his promise. The run-off election was held, and still the public had not heard of the results of the investigation. The ultimate winner was Laura Miller, second woman mayor in Dallas history.

Months went by and no indictments were had in this case. Finally, on August 19, 2002, Tarrant County Assistant D.A. Joe Shannon informed the Dallas County grand jury, "We did not see any money moving from one party to another."

Meanwhile, back at election headquarters, García also lost his race for reelection as state representative. He blamed his loss on the endorsement controversy.

Never ever trade endorsements for money. If you do, never ever have your campaign confidants, financial supporters, and advisors speak for you. Cut your own deal without a taped conversation as record. Reread above or the citation below for what the actual finding was: No money moved from one party to another. In other words, the deal may have been cut, but money did not flow. The public announcement made of retiring García's campaign debt to the highest bidder in exchange for his endorsement followed by García's actual endorsement provided no time for the money to flow from one account to another. *No aprenden.*

(See *The Dallas Morning News,* August 20, 2002, p. 18A.)

20. Taped Conversations, Part I

It is illegal in most jurisdictions, unless you are the government, to tape a conversation without permission of another. There are ways, however. I was invited to appear and debate right-wing Bill O'Reilly on his program, *The Pulse* on Fox News, during the summer of 2002. I told the show producers in advance and prior to arriving in New York for the taping that I wanted a copy of the entire debate, unedited. I was told that for sure I would get a copy of the entire program (read edited, aired copy). When I was done with make-up and ushered into the recording studio, I asked about my audio recording the debate and was told it was not possible because they had the exclusive rights to the show. I said, "I am also the exclusive owner of my part of this show. If I can't audiotape the entire debate to see what you edit, I'm walking. Thank you for the flight and hotel room."

Immediately, the in-studio crew leader and producer, David Lewis, said, "Just put the recorders (I had two, just in case) where they cannot be seen." I placed them, one each, near O'Reilly and me, under the chairs.

The transcript of the debate is in sharp contrast with the transcript of what was aired on prime-time national television, August 15, 2002. I have both copies.

You see, in shows like this one, the star is made to look good and the guest is not. Be sure you tape the entire conversation. Force the right to tape to the wire. They have no choice at the last minute but to let you. With an unedited transcript of the entire debate, a record exists of who won the debate.

(If this anecdote is in this book, who do you think won the debate? Send $17 to Box 19539, Arlington, Tx., and I'll send you copies of both for an educational experience.)

21. Taped Conversations, Part II

Angel Noé González was the first Chicano school superintendent in Cristal City, Texas, my hometown. Early in the first months on the job, agents from the San Antonio field office of the Federal Bureau of Investigation called him about wanting to come visit to discuss allegations of wrongdoing in his administration. Angel panicked. He had never been investigated by the FBI. He knew of no wrongdoing. What do you do in a situation like this? I was the school board president and told him to ask them for identification, nature of the complaints, and to be sure to tape the entire conversation from the beginning. Smart and resourceful Chicano that he is, Angel called Zeke Rodríguez, a federal official in Washington, D.C., for a second opinion. Zeke (Ezequiel, formerly from Rio Grande, Texas) also told him the same thing, with an additional caveat: check the batteries, tape, and recorder before they arrive to make sure you get a good copy.

Superintendent González greeted the FBI agents and quickly informed them he was taping the conversation, and proceeded with the script: Would they present their identification badges, names, and numbers? Who complained? What did they complain about? Would they give him copies of the written complaint? And would two weeks to respond be sufficient time for Angel to investigate the matter and report to the FBI?

The FBI agents were intimidated by the tape recording. They could not begin to process the questions. They did flash their black-vinyl-cased badges and excused themselves with, "We'll get back to you on that," and left as quickly as they arrived.

22. Her Story or His Story, Still Not Our Story

"Herstory" is a term used to denote a woman's rightful history and not just a mention made in white male-written history. Regrettably, "herstory" is a white woman's perspective and does not include other women's perspectives, especially those of Chicanas. Ana Louise Keating, as editor, aided Gloria E. Anzaldúa in the writing of *Interviews/Entrevistas* (New York: Routledge, 2000). This book, a compilation of interviews that Anzaldúa did with others, is about her growing up Chicana in South Texas, her turning points in writing, spirituality, feminism, and life in general.

It is her story.

23. An American Story

Ramón "Tianguis" Pérez was born in a Zapotec village, Macuitlianguis, deep in the recesses of the Mexican state of Oaxaca in the late 1950s and decided as a young twenty-something-year-old to migrate to the U.S. in search of work in the early 1980s. Jorge Agustín Bustamante was also born in Mexico, but he was a lawyer. Bustamante, in the 1970s, was in pursuit of another degree, a Ph.D. at Notre Dame University in Indiana. Both Pérez and Bustamante have a lot in common. Both wrote a book about their experiences in crossing into the U.S. without legal documents, e.g. passport, visa, or other work permits. Their stories are replete with the horrors of victimization, abuse, exploitation, and chronic poverty. Bustamante did it for his dissertation to earn his doctoral degree, and Pérez, because he wanted to share the experience with others. Bustamante's book never made it into print, but he became the first *Chicanólogo*-in-residence to Mexican President Luis Echevarría Álvarez and expert on Mexican migration to the United States. Pérez's book, *Diary of an Undocumented Immigrant,* was written *en español*, translated by Dick Reavis and published by Arte Público Press in 1991, made possible by a grant from the National Endowment for the Arts.

The Pérez book is a true American story.

24. Babies, Ballots, Not Bullets

In the 1970s, the Brown Berets of California announced the launching of *La Marcha de la Reconquista.* The march, starting in

Los Angeles and traversing the Southwest, was to ignite the passions and capture the imagination of Chicanos in order to spur them on to insurrection and to reclaim the lost homeland of Aztlán. The Brown Berets trekked across each state in their yellow bus, doing early-morning physical training and marching to cadence in formation, usually in town squares. Locals in these cities and towns took their picture as souvenirs of the Chicano Movement come to town. The marchers made it across the Southwest and back and culminated with the physical occupation of Catalina Island off the coast of Los Angeles. According to the Brown Berets, that island was not adjudicated as gringo land; it was still Mexican. They reconquered it.

After the food ran out and the FBI tired of feeding them pizza, hamburgers, and Pepsi, they brought them back by boat to Los Angeles. No insurrection followed. No bullets were fired. Some babies were made. The Brown Berets faded into Chicano Movement obscurity. A book was written about the *marcha*.

In fact, many babies have been made over the years. And in a few years, these babies will cast ballots for candidates of Mexican ancestry running in U.S. elections. The reconquest of Aztlán, for re-establishing political sovereignty by Mexicans over Aztlán, is under way with every election.

In Texas, for example, Mexicans were run out of the state after the gringos took over in 1835. By 1850, shortly after Texas became a state of the United States, black slaves accounted for 28 percent of the total population. Whites were 72 percent of the Texas population. Mexicans weren't even counted as part of the census enumeration in Texas in 1850!

But, we made babies. And we came back to Texas, particularly after 1910 and the outbreak of the Mexican Revolution.

By 1950, blacks had dropped to 13 percent of the population. By 1990, whites were 60.6 percent of the Texas population. By 2000, blacks were a mere 11 percent of the population, and whites continued to drop to only 56 percent. We have now reached 47 percent of the Texas population, and climbed to 13 percent in the nation, surpassing blacks in number and percentage of the whole.

We are making more babies. And we continue to come back to Texas and all other parts of occupied Mexico and the rest of *gringolandia.*

(See John Sharp, *The Changing Face of Texas* [Austin: Comptroller of Public Accounts, 1992]; Steve H. Murdock et al. *The Texas Challenge: Population Change and the Future of Texas* [College Station: Texas A&M University Press, 1997]; and www.census.gov for the 2000 statistical data on population.)

25. SummerFest in Milwaukee, Wisconsin: A Chicano Gathering

Almost every community in the U.S. with some Mexican population has some sort of Chicano fiesta or gathering. The celebration of cultural tradition dates back to the days of the *mutualistas* that held patriotic ceremonies every *Diez y seis, 20 de noviembre, Día de las madres, Día de la Raza, Pascua, Día de los Reyes Magos, Día de la Virgen de Guadalupe*, and other such fiestas, despite the *gringo* harassment and ridicule, not to mention the denial of parade and dance permits, use of public facilities, funding for the arts and culture, and police protection for crowd control.

During the Chicano Movement, our activists revived the fiesta celebrations by adding more components to the existing schedules, with such events as *conjunto* and other music festivals (Tejanos for Onda Music in Fort Worth), film festival (Guadalupe Cultural Arts Center in San Antonio), Raza on the Rocks (NEWSED in Denver), and SummerFest in Milwaukee, Wisconsin. The Hispanic generation has added scores of golf tournaments, after-hours networking socials (usually business-card exchanges), and sit-down dinner banquets to honor somebody.

But SummerFest has typical Chicano origins. It started as a protest, "Struggle for Education," at the University of Wisconsin-Milwaukee in 1970 because only about a dozen Latinos were enrolled out of 25,000 students. Negotiations with UWM officials reached no settlement. On August 27, 1970, just weeks before the fall semester, about 150 Chicanos and some Boricua activists stormed the chancellor's office and staged a sit-in. Days passed and the Raza would not leave. Finally, some were arrested, and the university chancellor, J. Martin Klotsche, agreed to the founding of the Spanish-Speaking Outreach Institute, specifically designed to increase Latino enrollment.

Next, the issue of money became a concern to the Raza in Milwaukee. What good is an open door toward enrollment if you can't afford the education? So the activists initiated a Mexican fiesta on the corner of 4th Street and National Avenue to raise dollars for scholarships. In 1977, the fiesta moved from the barrio to the edge of Lake Michigan on the grounds of SummerFest, the traditional white celebration. Thousands of dollars have been raised in the past decades benefiting hundreds of Latino students. In 1996, the Institute was renamed after Roberto Hernández, one of the takeover Chicano activists. He died of heart failure at age 50.

In 2002, Wisconsin Governor Scott McCallum, Milwaukee Mayor John Q. Norquist, State Representative Pedro Colón, Alderman Angel Sánchez, County Supervisor Anthony Zielinski, and County Executive Scott Walker honored the Chicano and other activists of the takeover with a ceremony of recognition. The honorees were Ernesto Chacón, Dante Navarro, María Anderson, José Luis Huerta-Sánchez, Jesús Salas, Gregorio J. Rivera, Tony Baez, Luis López, Juanita Rentería, Delfina Guzmán, Ricardo Fernández, and Jaime Dávila.

The last academic year at UNM, there were only 938 Latino students enrolled; and only 19 Latino faculty members, both tenured and nontenured, were among the 786 total faculty. It still is not so good, but a measure of progress has taken hold.

Education is not a right in the United States; neither is health. You have to pay handsomely for both. Sometimes you have to go to jail to get access to health and education so others will not be denied. Hopefully, others will follow in the activists' footsteps and continue the struggle.

(See *Milwaukee Journal Sentinel*, August 21, 2002.)

26. The Crawford Retreat

Crawford, Texas, is the location of the current President's ranch. He plays at being a real cowboy. And he also plays at being a real

President. Like his predecessor, Bill Clinton, not his daddy, George "Dubya" convened a summit at the ranch to discuss national economic recovery. The list of participants included many Latinos and Latinas. *The New York Times* of August 13, 2002, published the list of participants. I found Carmen Aguilar from Bellevue, WA; Ana Cabral of HACR in D.C.; Delia García from Arizona's Hispanic Chamber of Commerce; Rosario Marín, the Treasurer of the United States, formerly from California; Mario Rodríguez from San Clemente, CA; Héctor Barreto, head of SBA; José Cuevas, Jr., from Midland, TX; Lupe García from Santa Cruz, NM; George Herrera from the U.S. Chamber of Commerce and formerly from Chicago; Arturo Juardo from Las Cruces, NM; José López from El Paso, TX; Alex Soto from Miami, FL; Patricia Pliego Stout from San Antonio, TX; Milagros Colón from Camp Springs, MD; Jerry Contreras from Laredo, TX; Dianna Hernández from El Paso, TX; Mike Jaramillo from Arlington, TX; Eduardo Padrón from Miami, FL; Rudy Galvín from Lubbock, TX; María de Lourdes Sobrino from Vernon, CA; Héctor de Jesús Ruiz, the CEO of Advanced Micro Devices; Ariel and Jessica Rodríguez from Fontana, CA; and Fred and Berta Salazar from San Antonio, TX.

These folks are important to know. Somebody up in the White House knows them, and you should also. Look them up. Hopefully, they realized how much of an elite they are to have had an opportunity to rub elbows and share ideas and exchange numbers with others attending the President's Economic Forum. The President's list also included some real heavyweights, such as the CEOs of Albertson's, the grocery chain; American Express; Harley-Davidson, the motorcycle manufacturer; Chick-Fil-A; New York Stock Exchange; Pfizer; Fannie Mae; Charles Schwab Corporation; Cisco Systems; The Home Depot; Yahoo!; and AARP.

If I had been there, I would have come away with a personal computer from Cisco Systems, personal commitments for a discounted Harley-Davidson road-hog cycle, a Chick-Fil-A franchise, sample pills of Viagra, insider info on stock gainers, a preapproved platinum credit card from American Express and one from The Home Depot with discount coupons, and membership in AARP. If you are not going to contribute something to the meeting and bring home some goodies, why go? Don't tell me it was to get a photo with George Dubya to frame and put up in the office.

(HACR is the brainchild of Rick Bela, the lawyer who helped me outline the legal strategy for the Raza Unida Party in Texas. He also founded the Hispanic Association on Corporate Responsibility.)

27. *Gotitas: Primero Fue Tomás Rivera,* Then Came France A. Córdova

Tomás Rivera is known for many reasons: for example, being from Cristal City, Texas, my hometown, being jovial, being the author of several award-winning works, such as ...*y no se lo tragó la tierra*, but his crowning achievement was to become the first Chicano chancellor of the University of California at Riverside. After his untimely death, we had no other Chicano chancellor in the UC system for many, many years.

In April 2002, the UC Board of Regents named France A. Córdova the seventh chancellor at UC Riverside.

We advance a drop at a time, *gotitas . . . gotitas . . . gotitas.*

28. ¿*La Christina Aguilera o la Britney Spears o la Shakira?*

I admit that I cannot tell the difference between them. To me, they all look too skinny, too fake blonde, too overgrown to act like teenagers, and too untalented to be vocalist stars. Aguilera does have a voice. I like her voice.

I do not like Spears or Shakira. And now, along with millions of Mexican and Latino fans in the Americas, I am not buying or letting my children or anyone I know buy any product Britney has to offer, or Pepsi, her sponsor, until she apologizes and asks forgiveness.

You do know how to atone as Raza for a transgression? It is not a simple white-like, rote-memory utterance: "I'm sorry." That does not cut it. As Raza, we must first apologize and then ask forgiveness. You must transfer the power of absolution to the victim of your transgression. Let them decide if they can forgive you.

In Britney Spears's case, she went to Mexico on tour. She land-ed at the airport on July 23, 2002, and disembarked. She proceeded to flash her middle finger to the adoring crowd of fans. She said her "bird-shot" finger was not aimed at the fans but at *paparazzi* that had been dogging her. The Mexican newspaper, *Milenio,* ran the photo.

Then, while in concert on July 28 at the Foro Sol stadium, which was jam-packed, she sang four songs. In the middle of the fifth song, she said, "I'm sorry, Mexico. I love you. Bye," and walked off the stage. The fans were furious and demanded their money back. *Y nada.*

Ándeles, pendejos, sigan con la güera flaca . . .

Now thousands of Mexicans are doing what I am doing: not buying her product or that of Pepsi until she apologizes and asks forgiveness. I have a lot of time and lots of other uses for my money.

29. Jimmy Santiago Baca

No, that is not a character in one of Rudolfo Anaya's novels. This is a real live action *vato* from Santa Fe who has become famous for his own writings. *Este pinto* has written screenplays and books and poems. He wrote parts of "American Me" and "Blood In Blood Out." *El carnal* has taught courses at Yale and other campuses. He travels the country doing readings at major bookstores and promotes his books and himself.

He also was a druggie in his youth and paid a heavy, heavy price. He went to prison in Arizona. But that was 27 years ago, and he is 50 at this writing. The *gringo* world, however, does not let him forget it. He will always be a *pinto*. They sometimes, like *People* magazine, seek to make him a celebrity for going from *pinto* to poet. He is not buying into that.

El Jimmy says, *chale con ese jale,* "I am not adhering to their stereotypical model."

The person that defines wins.

30. Victor Morales, the Guy in the Pick-Up

Victor Morales is remembered fondly by Texas voters as the guy in the pick-up because during the 1996 U.S. Senate campaign, Victor stole the show. As part of a class discussion, Victor, the teacher, took the challenge that someone like him could win the Democratic Party nomination. He bet he could prevail over money and television in a statewide race in a huge state.

Of course, he didn't call me. I could have told him differently, given my experience as a candidate for the U.S. Senate in a special election in 1993. But I called him and offered my assistance with a list of donors, contacts, unsolicited advice, campaign debate tips, and I also gave him some money. I know how extremely difficult it is to raise money, even after you get past the ugly feeling of having to ask for it.

In 1996, Victor Morales, an unknown classroom teacher traveling the state on weekends in his white, Nissan pick-up, beat all the professional politicians, some of whom were sitting members of Congress. In the run-off election between him and John Bryant, a member of Congress, he whipped him again and became the Democratic Party nominee. He was given a cameo spot on national television at the National Democratic Convention. The media went crazy over Victor. The Democratic Party didn't. Victor posed a major problem; he would not accept any donation from a political action committee (PAC). The Demos tried and tried to get him off that position with no success, so they denied him any help. It is the Demos' way or the highway, and Victor took the highway and lost, narrowly, but lost, anyway. If you lose by one vote, it does not matter if it is one or one thousand or more. You lose.

In 1998 he ran for the House of Representatives and still held to his pledge of no PAC money. He lost again.

In 2002, he ran again for the U.S. Senate and whipped everyone in the primary election held by Democrats. But on the eve of the run-off election, literally the day before, the other Chicano running a statewide race, Tony Sánchez, candidate for governor, endorsed Victor's opponent, Ron Kirk, the black mayor from Dallas. Victor lost narrowly but lost.

The Democratic Party did not want two Mexicans at the top of the ticket. The Democratic Party wanted a white, a Mexican, and a black at the top of the ticket. It matters not that down below the ballot you have many, many white male candidates and only a handful of Raza, women, and black candidates. At the top of the Demo ticket is a one-Mexican rule. At the top of the Republican ticket it is a no-Mexican rule.

We gotta keep trying and someday we will prevail.

31. *Hispanic* magazine

Efforts were made in decades past to found a national magazine of general interest to our community. I recall the first issues of *La Luz*, published in Denver during the early 1970s. It did not survive. I recall the first issues of *Hispanic Link* published in Washington, D.C. It has survived. I recall the first issues of *La Raza*, published in Los Angeles. It did not survive. And, I recall the first issues of *Hispanic* magazine, originally published out of New York. It has survived and relocated to Austin, Texas. I recall the first issues of *Nuestras Vidas,* published out of Houston. It did not survive.

Why some survive and some fail is linked to our growing numbers and national advertising dollars aimed at our consumer interests. As we have grown demographically, so have the advertising dollars allocated to media products directly targeting our community. The amount of advertising dollars is not adequate by any means, but it is growing.

Today we have specialty magazines: *Latina* and *Latina Style* are but two such publications vying for readership among our women. In Dallas there was a startup, *Valiente,* a slick and classy monthly for the upscale Latino/a. It folded in months. Out of California come *Low Rider* and *Q Vo,* for the custom-car, *bajito* enthusiasts. *Low Rider* has been sold to a non-Chicano syndicate.

It is only a matter of time before we get magazines that tap into our sports, entertainment, and political activity—that is, if other competitive journals do not preempt the field; *Reader's Digest en español, People en español, Playboy en español,* etc., have already done so. These are nothing more than Anglo-market material packaged in Spanish.

Visit *Hispanic* magazine at http://www.hisp.com or call 800-251-2688 for subscription information.

32. Chicano Press Association

In the mid-1960s, a flood of Chicano newspapers was evident. Almost every city in the U.S. with a Chicano community had at least one such newspaper. I am not referring to the old-time newspapers *en español*, such as *La Opinión* in Los Angeles or *La Prensa* in San Antonio that date to the early 1900s. I am writing about the newspapers that grew out of *el movimiento*. There were so many that they organized themselves into the Chicano Press Association. They were the precursors to the current National Association of Hispanic Journalists. Some newspapers from that era are still around. *El Editor* in Lubbock, Texas, dates to that era and is still published by Bidal and Olga Agüero. *El Sol de Texas* in Dallas is still around, although Jesús Gutiérrez and Sara Suárez have sold it to Anglo owners. *La Gente* in Los Angeles continues to be published. *El Malcriado*, the publication of the national farm workers, lasted a long time. The National Council of La Raza, formerly known as the Southwest Council of La Raza when it was based in Phoenix, sporadically came out with *Agenda*, a hybrid publication in English that seemed like a newspaper, newsletter, and magazine, all in one. It has been published quarterly for the past sixteen years, along with another piece called *Boletín*.

A resurgence of Spanish-language newspapers in our communities has occurred. There is not a major city in the U.S. without at least one such publication, and in some cities there are over a dozen Spanish-language newspapers. In Dallas, there are nineteen such publications. In Chicago, there are seven. In Los Angeles, there are twenty-two. And, if I add the publications that are in English with some Spanish but aimed at the Chicano reading market, such as *Tejano USA* in Dallas and *La Voz de Uvalde County* in Uvalde, Texas, there are more than ever. These are subsidized by local advertising dollars, not national, which indicates that our local communities can support various communication tools, such as newspapers. The trend across the nation among English-language newspapers is to have only one in every town. In our bilingual communities there is room for the one newspaper in English and the more than one *en español*. But we have to relearn to write, read, and practice our Spanish. The people with these skills will be more employable in the near future.

The National Association of Hispanic Journalists, the current point organization for Raza in this field, argues that there has been a reduction in Latinos working in English-language newspapers during 2000. While there was a rise in Latino employment in such newspapers from 1982 to 2000, there was a decline during the last year. Latinos in English print media only comprise 3.66 percent of all newsroom employees, according to the American Society of Newspaper Editors' annual newsroom survey.

33. The Newsletters

Printing a newspaper, even in these days of desktop publishing, is exhausting, and the pounding of the pavement trying to get advertisements to fund the endeavor is never-ending. Some persons, particularly organizations and programs, turn to a simple newsletter to communicate, educate, organize, and inform.

As is the case with newspapers and magazines *en español* or in both languages, the newsletters across the country that inform our community are varied. Generally, there are two types: those specific to an organization or program and those aimed at capturing a niche in a specific market. For example, *El Noticiario* is the newsletter of the Texas Association of Chicanos in Higher Education (TACHE), and *CHCI News* is the quarterly newsletter of the Congressional Hispanic Caucus Institute, Inc. These are both organizations seeking to inform and communicate with their membership or interested public. An example of the niche-market newsletter is *Amigos,* a product of Semos Unlimited, Inc. from Santa Fe, and *El Mesteño,* published in Premont in South Texas. The latter is a newsletter "about Mexican-American culture and heritage in South Texas and Mexico."

34. Publish Your Own Book

I told you earlier that I had to self-publish my book on power relations, *A Gringo Manual on How to Handle Mexicans.* In the 1980s, Bettina (Elizabeth) R. Flores at age 50 wrote her book *Chiquita's Cocoon,* and for a decade was not able to find a publisher. She published it herself in 1990. By 1994 her book had been picked up by Villard Books, a division of Random House in New York. A few years back, in 1998 to be exact, Juan Haro had to self-publish his autobiography, *The Ultimate Betrayal*. The book is a very severe and critical narrative of his disillusionment with and betrayal by Rodolfo "Corky" Gonzales of the Crusade for Justice in Denver.

In earlier years, few if any publishers were interested in Chicano material. There were no Chicano publishing houses, either. You had to do it yourself. Today there are publishers very interested in our writings and our market. We buy books more often than writing them.

Under these new circumstances and in the field of creative writing, Anna Orozco Flores has made inroads into self-publishing her novels loaded with Chicano characters and settings. This Chicana from Denver, early on, made her decision to write, publish, and market her own books. Her first book was *Deadly Union*. Her second book is *Without a Trace*, about a Chicano activist attorney, John Romero, involved in a local election. But someone is "determined to be rid of him . . . and this sets into motion a disappearance . . ."

Clearly, building a loyal group of readers takes time, and sales will depend directly on her marketing ability. She will, as all successful marketers, make more money without a publisher and all the middle people.

35. Have Someone Else Publish Your Book

Victor Villaseñor is the author of *Rain of Gold*, which some have acclaimed as the Chicano *Roots*. (Ever wonder why we have to compare ourselves with black accomplishment? Isn't our accomplishment worthy in and of itself?)

Villaseñor tells the story of how he sold his manuscript for a handsome price to a major book publisher in New York. He quickly grew to be very upset with them as the editing process unfolded. Villaseñor wanted the story to remain as he had written it. Having spent most of the advance money, he had to scrounge around for enough new money to buy the rights to his book back from the publisher and he did. Victor then sought out Nicolás Kanellos at Arte Público Press (University of Houston). Arte Público (AP) is one of two Chicano/Latino publishing houses in the country. The other is Bilingual

Review Press in Arizona. Nick took a chance with *Rain of Gold* by printing a hardback edition in 1991, which is always a more expensive product for the customer and publisher. The hardback, cloth-bound edition at $23.95 usually sells fewer units than a trade paperback at a cheaper price. Nevertheless, Arte Público and Victor soon had a bestseller on their hands and were able to auction the paperback rights to Bantam-Doubleday-Dell for big bucks. In 1992, Dell came out with a paperback edition and in 1996 with a version *en español,* both priced at $14.95.

36. César Estrada Chávez

The big push in recent years since the death of César Chávez in 1993 has been to celebrate his accomplishments and contributions by obtaining a holiday in his honor. At the federal level, the efforts have been minimal. At the state level, some states have come forth with holidays. In Texas, the law that was passed makes César Chávez Day an optional state holiday. In some cities, streets, parks, and schools have been named in his honor. Houston and Dallas Independent School Districts, for example, have schools named after him. In the Fort Worth Independent School District, there are schools being built with his name and that of Dolores Huerta on them. In Lubbock, Texas, there is a community celebration with awards, rally, symbolic march, and food at Aztlán Park on 1st and Buddy Holly Avenue. In California, the legislature passed a law creating a new state holiday: César Chávez Day of Service and Learning on March 31.

María Lucía Gómez, a fourth-grade teacher at Whitehead Elementary in Woodland, California, learned late in 2000 that funding was available to celebrate the new holiday. She organized students and parents and asked her school principal for the afternoon off from work so she could meet the due date and time for proposal submission (January 19, 2001, at 5 p.m.). She began to prepare a funding request for $7,940 with which to buy books, conduct a food drive for local striking cannery workers, paint a mural on the outside wall of the school cafeteria, and celebrate other heroes and heroines, such as Gandhi, M.L. King, Jr., and Rachel Carson.

Opposition to teacher Gómez's plan soon mounted from expected and unexpected sectors of her community. The area growers were opposed. The PTA warned her not to teach about the conflicts César had with growers. Some local Mexicans raised questions about her motives in celebrating a Chicano when she was a Colombian native. Others accused her of dividing the community with this controversial proposal. The principal canceled his permission for the afternoon off, ordered her to remain on the campus and not submit the proposal. She did, anyway, and got funded.

During the school assembly called the week of March 31, the principal allowed student awards for perfect attendance to be issued, along with information about upcoming summer camps, everything except homage to César Chávez. At the conclusion, the principal asked if anyone had anything to say about Chávez. María Lucía Gómez stood up and said a few words in his praise. She had been beaten but not defeated. *¡Sí se puede!*

37. Target a Market

If you have something to sell, someone will buy it. The trick is to find that someone. Salesmen operate on the theory of 1-in-10. They can handle rejection better than anyone I know because of this theory. The concept is simple: Ask ten people to buy something and nine will say, "No!" But, one will say, "Yes!" and buy. So, ask at least 10 people to buy and you hit a 10 percent rate of sales.

But what if you have a product that people will buy if you take it to them, like ice cream.

The era of the dairy truck bringing fresh milk to the home is gone, along with the ice-cream truck. Now, *los paleteros* have taken over these routes in the neighborhoods of most Southwestern cities. The jingle of their bells signals their presence. Most people, especially kids, will not drive to the store to buy a Popsicle, but they will walk outside the house to buy the refreshing treat. *Los paleteros*, while they sell a lot of Popsicles, unfortunately, do not earn a great deal. The profit margin on a dollar ice-cream bar is too low. The *paleta*-maker is the one who earns the money. And to make matters worse for the *paleteros,* often they are the victims of crime. Local gangsters beat up on them and steal their money and ice cream.

Many of these street vendors are Mexican immigrants without the required U.S. documents, so they can't complain to police for fear of apprehension and deportation. The local gangsters know this and pick on them for this very reason. Other, more astute criminals beat up on the *paleteros* to steal their money, ice cream, and dry ice. Dry ice mixed with a carbonated drink can make an explosive. (Don't try this! You run the risk of blowing off your hand, eyes, face, fingers, or hurting someone else.)

38. Make It a Fiesta and They Will Come

For decades in the United States, if not centuries now, Raza has celebrated the *diez y seis de septiembre* with *gusto* and great aplomb in many cities and all barrios. Of more recent vintage is the celebration of the Cinco de Mayo. *El cinco* is probably celebrated more in the United States than in Mexico itself. The reasons are twofold: (1) it is another fiesta we can have, and (2) it is a business opportunity for those who would use our culture to make money.

Now, the trick is to come up with yet another fiesta. There is not a city that does not have Chicano and Latino cultural entrepreneurs at work organizing fiestas, signing up corporate sponsors to underwrite the event, subcontracting food-and-drink vendors, imprinting T-shirts and other paraphernalia, and getting bands to play. Look at *Calle Ocho* in Miami, Fiesta in Fort Worth, Texas, LatinoFest in Houston, SummerFest in Milwaukee, and the Mexican 4th of July celebration in Las Vegas, New Mexico, for variations on the same strategy.

39. Make It a Targeted Audience Fiesta and They Too Will Come

I bet you no one would have believed, much less placed a bet that Raza could build a fiesta in Freer, Texas, around catching rattlesnakes. How about a fiesta around garlic in Gilroy and Watsonville, California. They celebrate picking cucumbers in Wautoma, Wisconsin, and the Spinach Festival is held in my hometown of Crystal City, Texas, every November. Popeye has a statue in front of City Hall. But that is exactly what has happened. Raza have taken a product they pick as workers, or an aspect of their labor (killing snakes while clearing land), and made it into a fiesta. Perhaps in Robstown, Texas, they will start a fiesta on the picking of cotton. The high school football team name and mascot is already the "Cottonpickers."

40. Make It a Food Fiesta and They Will Certainly Come

First, it was the chili cook-off fever that hit as the rave fiesta for an organization to have as a fundraiser. Then, came the *menudo* cook-off marathons, followed by *fajita* cook-offs, and in Fort Worth, Texas, the making of the largest *enchilada* in the world. It is the making of *pan de campo* in San Diego, Texas, that is the big fiesta, while *chorizo* and *tortilla*-making wait for sponsors. It won't be long because the trend is to share our special and unique food with the world. Food is culture. Already at all fiestas, Chicano-sponsored or not, some of the food booths are from local Mexican restauranteurs. Check out SummerFest in Milwaukee, Wisconsin, the state fairs in New Mexico and Texas, the Ice Festival in St. Paul/Minneapolis, Minnesota, and, of course, the mother of all fiestas, Fiesta Days in San Antonio, Texas. This latter fiesta celebrates the defeat of the Texas Mexicans by whites in 1835, but nobody remembers that anymore. All they know is that it's party time.

41. Make It a Music Fiesta and They Will All Watch and Buy

More than two decades ago, a high school teacher named Rudy Treviño teamed up with Gilbert Escobedo, a Chicano musician and promoter in San Antonio, for a project. They began the Tejano Music Awards. Previously, no one had acknowledged, much less celebrated our Chicano music. Some of us called it *Onda* music, certainly not *Tejano*, because our music is made, played, and heard all over the Southwest, Midwest, West, and in northern Mexico. Our music is our culture.

The Tejano Music Awards grew in attendance each year by the thousands. The organizers had to keep changing venues to accommodate the crowds. They made videos of the annual event for resale. They put it on television. They put it on the radio. They organized pre-award events and post-award events, even in Las Vegas, Nevada, all to standing-room-only crowds. The Grammy Awards have had to incorporate a category for our music. *Billboard* magazine, the music industry journal, reports on our music as a regular feature now.

Many cities, such as El Paso, Tucson, Chicago, and Los Angeles, hold mariachi festivals. In San Antonio and San Benito, Texas, they hold *conjunto* festivals. The Tex-Mex Fest at the Arena Theatre in Houston was held on September 27, 2002, featuring some *veteranos* of *la Onda Chicana* music, Little Joe *y la familia*, Sunny Osuna, Alfonso Ramos, Latin Express, and others. The *veteranos* are still moving the agenda forward. Little Joe has produced the first Chicano DVD entitled "Celebration of Life."

Now that there are so many of us, annually the National Council of La Raza puts on the ALMA awards on national television during prime time. Local Chicano organizations in San Antonio, Dallas, and the Rio Grande Valley, for example, sponsor film festivals around Chicano and Latino movie productions and documentaries.

(San Antonio's Richard Dávila, radio KEDA personality, *el Güero Polkas*, has consistently played Chicano music from up-and-coming talent on his early-morning show for decades, is Mr. Onda Music in my book. See Boogieman@Bandidoradio.com for the information on Tex-Mex Fest.)

42. LatinoFest in Houston

Vehicle owners who lower their cars closer to the ground with hydraulic systems that make the cars bounce and sway (*bajitos*) and spend thousands on chrome accessories, powerful sound systems, and rich paint jobs, are low-riders. There are now van, truck, and bicycle low-riders, as well. Most of them are Chicanos, although there are also whites and blacks in the car-club culture. There are low-rider magazines, low-rider movies, low-rider car clubs, low-rider car specialty shops, and low-rider car accessories galore on the Internet.

In El Paso they have had low-rider parades. In Dallas they have had low-rider car shows. In California they have developed and successfully marketed a national magazine, *Low Rider*. But in Houston they have put it all together and combined the attraction of other fiestas into one giant party they call LatinoFest. Eastpark Productions organizes the annual event. They are not a Chicano enterprise. They are whites making money on a Chicano enterprise. LatinoFest attracts tens of thousands of people to the Pasadena Fairgrounds in early November, each paying $15 to $20, with children under 12 admitted free. The list of national and local corporate sponsors is impressive. LatinoFest has, of course, hundreds of low-rider cars, trucks, bicycles, motorcycles, and vans from all over Texas on display. The low-rider owners compete for cash prizes and trophies. The ubiquitous voluptuous Chicana models sporting thong bikinis with high heels are also on hand. Big-name Chicano music performers, usually the winners from the last Tejano Music Awards, are on two main stages located at opposite ends of the site. Area Mexican restaurants staff food courts. There is an arts-and-crafts bazaar for people to sell their wares. There even is a supervised children's play area for spectators to leave their children while they enjoy the fiesta.

This fiesta, like many others, makes a ton of money. The major reasons are threefold: it is a gated event with paid admission; corporate sponsors and other vendors pay for it all with their donations; and the promoters target both an audience and monopolize a niche, the Raza, low-rider, car-club culture. Wanna see homies? Wanna see *vatos* in wife-beater T-shirts? Wanna see *las* home girls, *las* cuties? Go to LatinoFest!

43. Speaking Spanish Is Child Abuse?

Texas State District Judge Lisa Millard (Harris County, Texas) issued an order in a lawsuit affecting a parent-child relationship (SAPCR) in April 1999. Judge Millard prohibited a mother, Natalia González, of a six-year-old girl, Carolina, from speaking Spanish at home "because Natalia's English skills were said to be weak." The order was extended to cover more family members, including the father, Ramón. Natalia's lawyers alleged Judge Millard was biased and urged her removal from the ongoing custody battle. Then, after word got out in the press and people began objecting to this horrible decision, Judge Millard changed her mind. To her credit, she rescinded the ban.

Natalia's lawyers then formally filed a motion to recuse (Millard) with visiting judge Fred Edwards. He promptly ordered Judge Millard recused from the case.

Sometimes there is justice for some.

(See *The Dallas Morning News*, August 25, 2000, p. 32A or visit www.courts.state.tx.us to find either Judge Millard or Edwards.)

44. The Bingo King

Eddie García of San Antonio was known as the Bingo King for his many connections with bingo parlors across the city and state. With bingo money, Eddie built many more business ventures; Home Health Care Solutions was one of the many ventures. His executives in Home Health were Helen and Frank Madla. The problem was that Frank Madla was also a Texas state senator and has been since 1992, and prior to that he was a state representative for nineteen years. The man is deep in politics and experience. Senator Madla was the chair of the legislative oversight committee on bingo.

In 1998, Eddie García was murdered in his office, shot at point-blank range by an unknown assailant. The case remains unsolved. But a multiagency comprised of the attorney general, the Ethics Commission, and the Legislative Council, in 2000 began looking into the records of the oversight committee and Home Health Care Solutions.

It is not that Senator Madla did anything wrong. It just looks bad, and that sometimes is more damaging than wrongdoing.

45. Internal Colonialism or Affirmative Action (AA) for White Cops?

Back when I was in graduate school, I ran across the work of Robert Blauner on internal colonialism. I loved his conceptualization of ethnic and racial minority plight in the industrialized nations, particularly the United States. You know what colonialism is, the setting up of a colony of soldiers, administrators, and managers in a foreign land and making the natives supply you with raw material and cheap labor. Internal colonialism adapted the model within a nation, as in our case of Chicanos in barrios under the management, supervision, and administration of a host of Anglos. We are the labor, and, daily, we travel out of the barrio to work for whites at cheap wages in their areas and return at night. Whites come into the barrio daily to police, teach, sell, pick up domestics, and day laborers, and leave by nightfall to their suburban homes. Only the police remain at night to protect us from us, they say. The model of internal colonialism came under severe criticism from many quarters, and academics who had employed the analytical framework abandoned it by the 1980s as not applicable or viable.

Dallas, for example, by the 1990s had a black mayor, a Hispanic city manager, a black police chief, a brown fire chief, a white woman city attorney, and ethnic and racial minorities on the city council. The glaring exception was the police force. More white males than minorities get hired as cops. Some say this is because the city lost its Affirmative Action plan in court in 1998. They point to a federal appellate court ruling that opined race could no longer be used as a primary factor in hiring and promotion. Whites had sued the city after only ten years of Affirmative Action, claiming enough was enough to remedy past discrimination and exclusion. And, the federal courts agreed with them that we have had enough AA!

The result of this ruling was felt by 2000 when 65 white police officers were hired and only 25 blacks and only 19 Hispanics. White women cops are still being counted as minorities, though. In the years between 1988 and 2000, more white than Hispanic men were hired and admitted into the police academy, if we do not add in the white women. In 1993, for example, 8 white and 11 Hispanic males were hired. If we add white women to the white category rather than the woman category, then 15 whites got hired. In 1994, utilizing the same method of computation, 23 white and 26 Hispanic males were hired, but add women and the total figure becomes 34 whites to 30 Hispanics. In 1996 and 1997, the city hired 26 and 22 white males, compared to 38 and 36 Hispanic males, respectively. Add the white female cops hired and sent to the academy for training and you have 50 and 46 whites to 46 and 38 Hispanics hired, respectively. This is Affirmative Action for White Cops! Internal colonialism is still alive and well in Dallas in 2002.

(See Dave Michaels, "White Men Gain More Police Jobs," *The Dallas Morning News,* November 13, 2000, p. 1A, with chart on statistics on p. 6A.)

46. Who Defines Wins

In school we learn that Columbus discovered America and named the natives Indians. Subsequent voyagers to the Americas called this the New World. In reading the chronicles, letters, and diaries written by Columbus, Hernán Cortés, and other *conquistadores*, the reports of various priests that accompanied the many *conquistadores*, beginning with Cortés, it is clear that the *indios* discovered Colón in their bay on October 12, 1492. It is clear from these writings that the *conquistadores* and the priests realized the Americas were actually an Old World, not new. The Aztec, Maya, Inca, Toltec, Quechua, Mapuche, Tonanac, Otomí, Anazasi, and Zapotec civilizations had been in existence longer and in important respects were more advanced than those in Europe at the time.

47. *Laura sí, Oprah no*

Laura en América is the new 2001 show from *Telemundo* that has kicked *Cristina* (Saralegui) over at *Univisión* out of the Raza family television room. *Cristina* was moved to a new time slot. Later, she quit television altogether. Laura Bozzo actually out-polled Oprah on the Nielsen Station Index. Laura commands top slot among talk shows in either language. Laura is also known as *la abogadita*, the lawyer.

Also in the news are Benicio del Toro for *Traffic* and Martin Sheen of "The West Wing," for being the first Hispanics to receive Golden Globe awards. Benicio played an honest Mexican cop in *Traffic,* and Sheen was President of the United States in *The West Wing.* Can you imagine a brown president? And Jennifer López became the highest-paid Latina in film. Her career took off with starring in *Selena*.

(See *El Hispano News*, January 24, 2001, *Entretenimiento Latino*, p. 1, and *The Dallas Morning News*, January 27, 2001, p. 36A.)

48. Becas Para Aztlán, Part II

Back in the early 1970s, I met with President Luis Echevarría Álvarez of Mexico and asked him for scholarships for Raza. He offered me a total of fifty, and with those, began the Becas Para Aztlán scholarship program. Later, President José López Portillo increased the number of *becas* per year. We focused the program on the training of medical doctors.

Several persons helped with this program: Luz Bazán Gutiérrez, Irma Mireles, Carlos Guerra, Francisco "Pancho" Velásquez, Abel Amaya, Reies López Tijerina, Ed Morga, and Ed Peña. While at the University of Houston, together with Dr. Tatcho Mindiola and Dr. Armando Gutiérrez, I got another graduate program going with the Colegio de México. This summer program was an intensive study of Mexico and how it works. Helping me start and maintain these programs were many Mexicans, including Jorge Bustamante, María Becerril de Brun, Graciela Orozco, Roger de Cossío, various directors at CONACYT, administrators of the Secretaries of Labor and Public Works, and aids to various presidents, for example. This *becas* program came under severe criticism. Georgie Ann Geyer, the right-wing U.S. columnist, attacked me and the program as being treasonous. Riordan Roett, a Latin American expert at Johns Hopkins University, said we were disloyal for establishing such links with Mexico. Medical schools in the U.S. refused transfer to our medical students. The U.S. medical schools would not accept any course taken in Mexican universities for credit. The *becas* program ended when Mexico was in an economic slump during the Miguel de la Madrid administration.

During a junket to Cuba in 2001 with the Hispanic Congressional Caucus, U.S. Representative Ciro Rodríguez (D-San Antonio) drew criticism for accepting Fidel Castro's offer to train 500 Chicano doctors in Cuba. I doubt any U.S. medical school will permit transfer or extend credit for course work done in Havana, much less allow Cuban-trained doctors to take the medical boards in the U.S. and practice medicine.

If you want to go to Cuba and study to become a medical doctor, you must be under twenty-five years of age, without a criminal record, have a high school diploma, and commit to stay and study for six years. You can go straight from high school to a medical degree. There is a Spanish-language course for twelve weeks for those in need of a refresher with the mother tongue, then hit the books and lectures *en español cubano.* Cuba will pay for tuition, books, living expenses, but not travel costs. When you return with degree in hand from this Becas Para Aztlán, you must take three exams (medical boards), enter a residency program in the U.S., and complete it successfully. Good luck with the exams and in finding a residency program.

(See Alfredo Corchado and Christopher Lee, "Congressman Assailed for Backing Castro Offer," *The Dallas Morning News,* December 27, 2001, p. 13A.)

49. Stickers for la Raza *and La Lupe*

During the heyday of La Raza Unida Party in the 1970s, the *partido* expanded into nineteen states and the District of Columbia. To promote the party, we had political buttons and bumper stickers with the *partido* name and logo, as well as posters, T-shirts, banners, flags, and the like. Every Chicana and Chicano *partido* militant proudly wore buttons of *la causa* as medals earned in battle. Our *carruchas* and *ranflas* were plastered with bumper stickers on Chicano causes: "*¡Raza sí, Migra no!*" "*Chale con el* Draft," and "Free *Los Siete.*" And we also had bumper stickers with slogans like "Chicano Power," "Southwest: Occupied Mexico," or "*Aztlán está en mi corazón.*"

The current generation of youth is reviving the use of stickers. The hottest rage among *razita* practitioners of pop culture are not bumper sticker but stickers to affix on lockers, books, clothing, boom boxes, tote bags, and skateboards. They buy the stickers from vending machines usually found at grocery stores and arcades. I buy my Homies, *M'ijos, M'ijas,* and Lil' *Locos* at such vending machines and occasionally a sticker or two for my girls at home.

Miguel Alfaro of Fifth Sun/Aztlán Graphics in Chico, California, came up with this idea for the vending machines. He has a line of Latino religious mini-stickers featuring La Virgen de Guadalupe, Jesús, Mary, the Madonna, and low-rider cars. He also has a sticker of La Raza Unida. Good *onda*, Miguel!

50. Scholarships for La Raza

The favorite activity of Chicano nonprofit groups, among others, is to raise money for scholarships. This activity is favored over direct political action because it is safe, noncontroversial, educational, clean, conscience-soothing, and detached. Now, even the major corporations are getting into the picture. The college football game between the Texas Tech Red Raiders (Lubbock) and the University of New Mexico Lobos (Albuquerque) is billed as the Transamerica Hispanic College Fund Classic. Tickets to the 2000 bowl game sold for $35 each, and 42,238 were sold out of 50,000 seats possible at Jones SBC Stadium. It is a good chunk of change for Raza from Transamerica and a little or a lot of pocket change also for Texas Tech, depending on how much they cream off the top of the receipts for administration and management of the scholarship fund and the expense of putting on the game.

51. The Chicano Mayor

President Bill Clinton went to Africa in the last months (late August 2000) of his administration and invited Dallas mayor Ron Kirk, an African American, to accompany him. During this same time, Mexican President-elect Vicente Fox Quezada visited Dallas to meet with presidential candidate George W. Bush, Jr. In the absence of the mayor, the Mayor Pro Tempore Chicano Steve Salazar took over. He had the duty of officially greeting the Mexican President-to-be. It pays to have at least two Chicanos on the Dallas city council. It pays off even more if one of them is the mayor pro tempore.

52. Do It Yourself

José O. Mata from Cristal City, Texas, said, "When I got into politics, I did it because I wanted to make my contribution. I wanted to make a change. I wanted something positive to come out of my efforts. And I think I did well. I am satisfied with myself."

Shortly after discharge from the military and a tour in Vietnam, Mr. Mata joined Ciudadanos Unidos, the community-based organization supporting the Raza Unida Party in Crystal City, Texas. He worked on political goals with such passion and fervor that he was elected president of the organization, elected to the school board, elected to the city council, and elected mayor of the city. He was a *partido* delegate to various conventions, state and national.

"After I got out of politics, being involved directly as a candidate or as an officer in board meetings and in boards, I decided that I wanted to make a last contribution. And I wanted it to be a family effort for our community. So, my wife supported me in that idea that we were going to build a gazebo downtown in Cristal City. We, as a family, were going to undertake that project, which we did. We started making fundraisers. My wife, myself, my sons, my daughter, we started making fundraisers to gain the money to start building the gazebo. We made dances. We made tacos. We made all sorts of plates until we finally reached the amount of money we needed to build the gazebo."

The Mata family had approached the city council, the school board, and the county commissioners for funding, but only the county contributed a token amount. Regardless, they got the gazebo built.

"To this date, you can see the elderly meet at that gazebo. Every morning, they will be sitting there drinking coffee. And that was the spot that we decided that we wanted to build it in because that's where the elderly would meet every morning and socialize. But there was nothing there but a bench. Now, they have this gazebo where they can sit in and chat and drink coffee. And that's something that I feel proud of because that was our project; that was our family project that has made that happen."

(See Interview with José O. Mata, General Libraries, Special Collections, University of Texas at Arlington, Arlington, Texas, p. 38.)

53. A Chicano Legacy

Bidal and Olga Agüero have published *El Editor* newspaper for more than twenty-five years in Lubbock, Texas. They were not the founders of that newspaper, however; Nephtalí De León was. When Nephtalí and Bidal were in high school, they conceptualized a Chicano newspaper. Almost every Mexican-American Youth Organization chapter across Texas had a local newspaper, as did every Chicano organization in the country. It was the thing to do.

"We were all young people, high-schoolers. We were still in high school and already fighting the establishment, already fighting the system, presenting cases."

The newspaper *La Voz del Llano* was in print for nine years before De León sold it to his assistant, Bidal Agüero, who renamed it *El Editor*.

(See Interview with Nephtalí De León, General Libraries, Special Collections, University of Texas at Arlington, Arlington, Texas, p. 33.)

54. Eleventh-Hour Appointments

Lydia Camarillo, former regional director of the Southwest Voter Registration and Education Project and chief executive officer for the Democratic National Convention of 2000, tells a fascinating story of how Federico Peña got to be Secretary of Energy during the second Clinton administration: "So, when we met with Erskine Bowles and the Vice President . . . Well, the President has nothing to lose. And the Vice President has everything to win. And so that is why strategically we did that. And we got at the last, and it was truly at the eleventh hour, and I mean truly at the eleventh hour, Federico Peña getting Energy [cabinet post] because all of a sudden all the appointments are occurring, including Aida Álvarez and [Bill] Richardson. At eleven o'clock . . . about eight o'clock, I would say, Henry [Cisneros] goes to talk to . . . to speak to the President. He outright tells him all hell is going to break loose if there is not another appointment at the cabinet level. Then, word gets to the vice president through the President, of course. And then Xavier Becerra, the congressman who is going to be the next caucus chair for the His-panic Congressional Caucus, meets and has a two-hour debate and discussion and negotiation meeting with the Vice President. And the question is, at that moment, what position is left that I haven't prom-ised yet; and, second, who could possibly at this late hour pass the FBI test, if you will, without worrying about whether or not they are going to pass it? Federico Peña. Energy. At eleven o'clock, they called Federico and he says, "I need to talk to my wife." At midnight or so, Federico accepts.

"*The Washington Post* was totally convinced that it was going to be this white woman that didn't get it. And *The Washington Post* prides itself with . . . I think I should have stated it before . . . prides itself with never being wrong. And being wrong and for the first time. CNN takes note that it was the Latinos who made this happen. Since then, though, we have made numerous recommendations for sub-cabinet posts and, yes, they have made appointments here and there, but when it comes to key, core positions that require Senate confirmation in the new era, we are nowhere to be seen."

(See Interview with Lydia Camarillo, General Libraries, Special Collections, University of Texas at Arlington, Arlington, Texas.)

55. Women Belong in the House . . . and Senate

The first woman state senator in Texas was Judith Pappas Zaf-firini from Laredo, Texas. Prior to being in elective office, she toiled within the Democratic Party of Texas. That paid and volunteer work earned her points with many Democrats during those years. And one point, she was a college professor and administrator in Laredo. Her higher-education experience left much to be desired. She is part of what I call the walking wounded. We are the survivors of battles in the academy.

Senator Zaffirini believed she was discriminated against for many, many years by the university president on the basis of sex. When she finally tired of it, she got a lawyer and filed suit. This is her statement: "One of the major examples of his sex discrimination, for example, when he was named president, I believe it was in 1974, he promoted me to Director of Communications and what he told me was, 'I wish that I could name you my administrative assistant. You are the one who has the skills that I need, but I can't have a woman.' He said, 'I can't travel with a woman. I have to have someone who can travel with me.' So he said, 'So I am going to name this other man as my administrative assistant, but I am going to look to you to do the work. You will do the work for me, but he will have the position.' Well, he was also paid several thousand dollars more than I was, and, basically, the reason that I got to the office at five o'clock in the morning was that I was doing my job and a lot of his. I would do the reading for the president; I would brief him; I would write his speeches; I would write his reports. So, I was doing basically my job and the job of administrative assistant, to a large extent. I don't recall his ever changing one word, one comma in any report or any speech that I wrote for him. Ever. He read what I gave him, and then not only would I read for him, I would summarize for him. It was just amazing. But there was a lot of discrimination in terms of sex, and I experienced it. And I not only filed a lawsuit, I also filed an EEOC complaint, and their finding was that the discrimination was not only evident, but it was blatant and malicious. So, that's why we won."

What did Faulkner write? "Hell Has No Fury Like That of a Woman Scorned." Judith was worse than scorned; she was harassed and abused.

(See Interview with Judith Zaffirini, General Libraries, Special Collections, University of Texas at Arlington, Arlington, Texas, pp. 34–35.)

56. On-Line Latinos

The Association of Hispanic Advertising Agencies commissioned a study to determine the extent of Internet usage among U.S. Hispanics and found that 38 percent of us, age 16 and older, use the Internet on a regular basis. According to AHAA, the typical Latino Internet user is 28 years old, male, unmarried, and speaks Spanish, mostly at home. Internet radio *en español* is one of the big pastimes of the typical Latino user on the Net, some 15 hours per week. And the profile above of the Latino Net surfer also revealed that about one-third of us have done on-line shopping, mostly for CDs, airline tickets, electronics.

In my case, all of the above are correct, plus car rental, hotel bookings, book purchases, and other gifts.

Because of our growing numbers and increased purchases of computers, there are many e-businesses hosting websites for us. The National Association of Hispanic Real Estate Professionals has promoted a website in Houston, Texas, for persons wanting to buy a house on-line called "Buscar Casa." Check it out. (See www.HAR.com.)

57. The Jukebox *o, mejor dicho, La pianola*

The jukebox, *la pianola*, has been around for many decades. The jukebox brought music to the working people at a bar, pool hall, dance hall, restaurant, and arcade, at the drop of a coin, now a dollar at most outlets. The jukebox also created fortunes for Chicano entrepreneurs like Arnoldo Marroquín of Alice, Texas; Richard Telles of El Paso, Texas, and Arturo Velásquez of Chicago. Marroquín took his jukebox business and developed a record industry, Falcon Records. Telles used his jukebox network to build a political machine. Velásquez used his first jukebox, bought by his mother, to build a $2-million business in the Chicago area. Today, at age 85, Velásquez has more than 2,500 jukeboxes, video games, and pool tables in some 500 outlets in the Chicago area. Like others in the business, the Velásquez Automatic Music Company has had to weather the technological changes that threatened his business time and again, such as the switch from 78 rpm records to 45s, later to CDs, and now the Internet, music videos and DVDs.

Literally, these entrepreneurs have taken the nickels, dimes, and quarters of Raza and made businesses worth millions of dollars. The same is true of many other vending-machine operators. Nickels, dimes, and quarters do add up to millions of dollars over time.

58. Tiger Woods, Golf Champion

The U.S. golf media proclaim him the greatest athlete in the world today. And a lot of people agree because he wins more often than he loses, but he does lose. He lost the 2002 British Open by lots of strokes. Woods finished even on the course with a 284.

Sergio García, an emerging champion, beat Woods with a 280; that is four under par for the British Open course.

Lest we forget, there have been other Raza golf champions in years past. Lee Treviño from El Paso won back-to-back British Open championships in 1971 and 1972. Seve Ballesteros, *el español*, won it in 1984 and again in 1988. Anybody remember Chi Chi Rodríguez?

59. *Chicanólogos*

Don't the words sound funny: *chicanología, chicanólogos?* Maybe the words sound funny to some, but it is very serious business to others. The Mexican Secretary of Foreign Affairs has a Chicano desk. The Mexican Presidency has had various on-call *chicanólogos,* beginning with Jorge Bustamante during the Echevarría administration (1970s). *Chicanología* or, more formally, Estudios Chicanos have been part of the curriculum at the Universidad Nacional Autónoma de México (UNAM) since 1988. UNAM had an interest in Mexicanizing Chicanos since 1984, when it established a satellite campus in San Antonio, Texas, and held annual conferences (*Encuentro Chicano)* and seminars (*Seminario Permanente de Estudios Chicanos y Fronterizos*), beginning in 1982.

Mexican authors are writing books about Chicanos. Early works include Gilberto López y Rivas, *Los Chicanos: Una minoría nacional explotada* (México, D.F.: Editorial Nuestro Tiempo, S.A., 1971); Ettore Pierri, *Chicanos: El poder mestizo* (México, D.F.: Editores Mexicanos Unidos, S.A., 1979); and, more recently, Roger Díaz de Cossío, Graciela Orozcoé y Esther González, *Los mexicanos en Estados Unidos* (México, D.F.: Sistemas Técnicos de Edición, S.A. de C.V., 1997). The Mexican programs study Chicanos to understand us. The Chicano Studies programs in the U.S. study us to find our roots and explain us to ourselves and others.

On both sides of the border, we have it going on. The task, it seems, is keeping it going on as it was and not dilute or overreach into Ethnic Studies, Race and Gender Studies, or Latino Studies.

60. The Well Connected: Mexican Restaurant Owners

Recently, I had lunch at Jovita's, a Mexican restaurant in Austin, Texas, located on South 2nd Street, and owned by Mr. and Mrs. Mayo Prado. Jovita is the mother's and daughter's name. Mayo, who looks like an authentic *indio meshica* with a long ponytail, told me a story about a *Univisión* (TV station) salesperson who came to sell advertising. The salesman had a glossy-print information packet about the station and all kinds of demographics on the growing Latino community and the "facts" about their viewing audience. Mayo turned him away without a sale.

Mayo explained to me that his restaurant caters to Anglos, not Mexicans, that he serves Mexican food for the Anglo taste, and that his nightly entertainment is for Anglos that like Americanized Mexican music. Jovita's does not need to advertise to the Latino community; it needs to keep its Anglo customers. And Mayo knows most of his clients personally. Mayo is well connected. Mayo contributes to many local community causes and is active with the Mexican-American Democrats of Texas.

In the late 1950s, another restauranteur, Félix Tijerina of Félix Mexican Restaurants in Houston, was well connected. He was the national LULAC president for four terms, 1956 to 1960. As such, he began the highly acclaimed and successful preschool, bilingual program, the Little School of 400, and was also a leader in the Viva Kennedy campaign. There is an elementary school named after him in Houston, Texas. It helps to have money and do volunteer work in the community.

In 1953, Félix and Janie Tijerina decided to adopt a child from Mexico and applied to the INS for the naturalization of Félix, Jr. The application was denied because INS argued that Félix was not a U.S. citizen, but a Mexican citizen. The INS produced a Mexican birth certificate used in the 1940s by Félix to gain entry into the U.S. that showed he was born on April 29, 1905, in the village of General Escobedo in Nuevo León, Mexico. The FBI got involved in this attempt to commit fraud with public documents and the naturalization process. Felix hired another lawyer right away, an Anglo one. He hired William J. Knight, a prominent lawyer and River Oaks resident who ate at his restaurant on the maid's weekly night off.

Tijerina sued the U.S. Attorney General Herbert Brownell, Jr., *et. al.* and produced in open court a birth certificate that showed he had been born in Fort Bend County, Texas (Sugar Land).

Federal District Judge Joe Ingraham finally heard the case in May 1956. Judge Ingraham listened to the testimony of the Tijerinas and that of Fort Bend County Judge C.L. Dutton, who testified to how well and long he had known Félix Tijerina. The federal judge carefully examined both birth certificates. Judge Ingraham ruled in favor of Félix Tijerina. Case closed.

Federal District Judge Ingraham and County Judge Dutton and attorneys Phil Montalbo and William J. Knight all had one other thing in common, other than the Tijerina case. They all ate at Félix Mexican Restaurant. Because of this clientele, Félix had money to hire good, effective lawyers.

(See Thomas H. Kreneck, *Mexican American Odyssey: Félix Tijerina, Entrepreneur & Civic Leader, 1905–1965*. College Station: Texas A&M University Press, 2001.)

61. Who Is Louis Kossuth?

I don't know, either, but I do know there is a statue of his likeness in Algona, Iowa, and a book entitled *How and Why Iowans Named Kossuth County in 1851*, by Rezso (Ralph) Gracza (Beaver's Pond Press, 2001). Reportedly, Kossuth was a Hungarian Freedom Fighter in the 1850s.

What about the hundreds of thousands of Mexicans who worked, and still work, in the sugar-beet fields of the Red River Valley in Minnesota? Will a migrant ever have a statue dedicated to her in a Minnesota town? Maybe Lalo Zavala with the Minnesota Migrant Council will get on this project. Maybe you will e-mail the Immigration History Research Center (IHRC) and suggest such a statue and offer a nomination: ihrc@umn.edu. I nominate Griselda Flores López, formerly from Crystal City, who worked in those fields with her older sisters and brothers. She and her husband were sprayed with dangerous pesticides while working in the fields, like countless other farm workers have been over the years. She and

Alfred, her husband, sued and settled with the grower for that airplane douche.

How about a king-size statue of Ignacio Zaragoza, the hero of the battle of Puebla on Cinco de Mayo, in the center of town in Goliad, Texas. That is his hometown.

Maybe you will submit a photograph to the IHRC of a Mexican immigrant for inclusion in its website. The IHRC is one of many organizations benefiting from National Park Service grants, "Save America's Treasures." These grants propose to save heritage.

Our migrant and immigrant experience is heritage. If you don't toot your own horn, who will?

(See www.umn.edu/ihrc/news.htm or call 612-625-4800.)

62. My Spanish Name: Gutiérrez, Part I

When learning of Malcolm X, I was most intrigued by the X. I read with great interest how the Nation of Islam suggested to its converts that they rename themselves shedding the slave owners' names. Since the chain of ancestry had been broken by centuries of slavery, African Americans do not know their real tribal origins and family names. American genealogy does not and cannot track African names as easily as that of Anglo whites and other European whites. Records of slave names were not kept by slavers. They kept numbers but not names. Present-day names in Spanish, English, Portuguese, Dutch, French, Italian, and German are those of former slave owners and those trafficking in slavery.

Then I thought of the origin of our names, my name: Gutiérrez. If relatively few *españoles* came across the Atlantic from 1492 to the immediate post-conquest period in 1535, and some died, then how can it be that we are mostly of Spanish origin? The *españoles* that came for the conquest were also mixed bloods themselves, including lots of Moors from North Africa and other slaves. The *españoles* and more African slaves that came after 1535 were mostly males. These immigrants did not include Spanish women, except for a few notables who imported wives and future-wives from Spain, the Canary Islands, and other Spanish-held territories at the time, such as Cape Verde. I estimate it was not until about 150 years from 1492 that

Spanish women began to cross the Atlantic in significant numbers. How can we be mostly Spanish?

The truth is we are not. Our surnames are Spanish for the very same reason African names in the Americas are English, French, Spanish, Dutch, German, Italian, and Portuguese. Our names are the surnames of *conquistadores* who mated with *indias* and made them their property. The *africanos* who came with the conquistadors and subsequent waves already had Spanish surnames, and they also mated with *indias* and passed on those names as if they were their own.

(See *Recovering History Constructing Race: The Indian, Black, and White Roots of Mexican Americans,* by Martha Menchaca. Austin: University of Texas Press, 2001.)

63. My Spanish Name: Gutiérrez, Part II

Genealogists can produce reports on the origin of Spanish surnames and even furnish a coat of arms for that family name. The Gutiérrez one, for example, is a colorful insignia in bright gold and royal blue with a castle tower at center base and a knight head in armor at center top just above the castle tower. On the edges are *fleur de lis*-like decorations and vine-looking coils ending in tassels. It is pretty to look at. It is also fascinating to read that the name can be traced to the times of the Visigoths in the Asturias region.

The story goes like this. Around 3000 B.C., the land area known as Spain today attracted Iberians from northeast Africa. The Celts came from the area now known as Europe around 1400 B.C. and settled in what is called Galicia and Portugal today. Traders from the western Mediterranean area came to Spain from 1200 B.C. to 700 B.C.: Greeks, Phoenicians, Carthaginians, and Punicians. The second Punic War in 219 B.C. destroyed Carthage and gave the Romans control of Spain. It took 200 years to subjugate and control the various fierce tribes and clans in the Iberian Peninsula. The Romans forced acceptance of Latin as the official language and Roman customs on these mixed peoples. Rome's last emperor was a Hispano-Roman, Theodosius.

The Roman Empire fell in the fifth century A.D., and the Visigoths took control of the peninsula. In 711, the Moors invaded, took control of the southern half of Spain by 718, and eventually, all but portions of the very northern provinces of Castilla, Aragón, and some of Asturias. By 950 A.D., the Christians had fought back against the Islamic forces to recapture León and all of Castilla. By the thirteenth century, the Catholic kings, Isabela and Fernando, had reconquered all of Spain, except for Granada, which fell in 1492.

The first recorded use of "Gutiérrez" was found in a royal court document in Asturias in 835 A.D. The signature of the witness on the document was Nunus Gutiérrez.

The Gutiérrez name spread from there. In history books that chronicle the conquest of the Americas by the Spanish, you can find that Elvira Gutiérrez married Juan Montalvo, a *conquistador* of Bogotá, Colombia. Felipe Gutiérrez was with Francisco Pizarro during the conquest of Peru. Francisco Gutiérrez de Murcia participated in the conquest of New Granada in 1530. Hernán Gutiérrez and his wife, Leonor, came to Florida in 1563. Inés Gutiérrez came to Hispaniola (Dominican Republic and Haiti, today) in 1565. My grandmother, Marcelina Crespo from Racines, Asturias, Spain, was sent to marry José Gutiérrez in Matamoros, Tamaulipas, Mexico, in 1880. Her son, Angel Gutiérrez, was born there in 1887. This is my dad. My name is a combination of both grandfather and father and mother, José Angel Gutiérrez Fuentes.

Of my mother's side, Concepción Fuentes, I know little. My grandmother was María del Refugio Casas. She was from Villa de Santiago, Nuevo León, Mexico. My grandfather was Ignacio Fuentes. He was from another hamlet near Villa de Santiago; both are on the outskirts of present-day Monterrey, Nuevo León, Mexico. My grandparents migrated north into the San Antonio area by Natalia, Texas, at the outbreak of the Mexican Revolution in 1910. My mother was born in San Antonio, Texas. My father migrated north into the Rio Grande Valley in the late 1920s as a political exile and then, to the Crystal City area. As mayor of Torreón, Coahuila, my father had countered political initiatives by Plutarco Elías Calles, the strongman who became president of Mexico at that time.

My mother was given to my father in an arranged marriage. She did not like this at all. After ten years of marriage and no way out for my mother, I was born in Crystal City in 1944, an only child.

All of us have multiple identities and some we know little about. All of us choose which identities make sense to us, and we fiercely hold them dear. Surnames, religion, language, culture, and gender make for cement-like symbols within our personas. It is who we choose to be. I did not know who I was during my early years, as most children do not until they are told. I chose to be Chicano in my formative to adult years. Now I think of myself more as a *mexicano,* never really having felt welcome or part of being an *americano,* as a white male of the United States.

64. My Spanish Name: Gutiérrez, Part III

The owner of Tejaztlán Books in Houston, Texas, is a Chicana from Alice, Texas. A project she started, among many, is the mailing of books to Chicano prisoners. In Texas, family or friends cannot just place a book or magazine in the mail for delivery to a *carnal* in the state penitentiary. The book or publication can only come directly from a publisher or book retailer. She is also an amateur genealogist. While doing research as a visiting scholar with the Mexican-American Studies Program and the University of Houston in 1998, I attended a conference and met her. She was enthusiastic about her search for her family roots. She had books, maps, notes, names galore. She traveled to South Texas, Mexico, Spain, and the Canary Islands in search of further information. If she ever wanted to wallpaper her house, the family charts she already had would have done half the job.

When I applied to recover my Mexican nationality, it was necessary to produce a birth certificate for my father. I knew he was born in Matamoros, Tamaulipas, Mexico, to José Gutiérrez and Marcelina Crespo, but little else. Irene Estrada helped me with critical dates, locations of possible relations, and information on the names Crespo and Gutiérrez. With that information, I obtained the birth certificate with the help of the Dallas Mexican consul, Luis Ortiz Monasterio, now Mexico's ambassador to Colombia.

(See George Ryskamp. *Finding Your Hispanic Roots,* Baltimore: Genealogical Publishing Company, 1997, for an introduction to the area of genealogy de la raza. See also www.tejaztlan.com.)

65. Pass the Ketchup and *chile*

I was flabbergasted to learn a few years back that ketchup sales in the U.S. had been surpassed by those of hot *chile* sauce (or *salsa*). I use the real thing, *chiles serranos molidos en molcajete con ajo, cebolla, tomate, y poquito de comino,* or sometimes I'll roast a *jalapeño* or two and eat those *toreados*. When that is not available or impractical to make, given time, I go for Pace's hot *chile* sauce, formerly Anglo-owned and made in San Antonio, but now based in New York.

Now there are *s*alsas galore, the latest of which are Bronco Bob's Wild Cherry Berry Chipotle and Tangy Apricot Chipotle sauces. The rage among Anglos and Hispanics is to add hot chile to fruit flavors. Bronco Bob has a four-bottle set of sauces, including Roasted Raspberry Chipotle and Smoked Bacon Chipotle. Go figure.

Don't look for it at the store. Make your own sauce and go peddle it. Or do what Jesús Gutiérrez, a Dallas resident, has tried to do: Invent a label and paste it on another brand. Food processors and bakeries and tortilla makers (especially chips) and restaurants and many others will for a fee gladly put your label on their product and sell it to you for resale. It is all about money.

66. *Tejano* Music Purists?

Mario Tarradell, like Ramiro Burr, is a Tejano music critic who is paid somewhat well for his informed opinion by newspapers and related outlets for his written work. He has a great job doing what he likes: getting free tickets, going backstage and into dressing rooms, attending pre- and post-performance parties with the artists, and getting the inside scoop on industry *chisme*.

One of the many issues he raises about Tejano artists is the very same one raised by those critical of the Hispanic generation, including the N, Y, and X generations. In short, the question of Tejano artists and of Hispanics is, how Chicano are you? Where is the Chicanismo in what you do?

Tarradell raised that question with regard to a hot band, Los Kumbia Kings. Abraham, Jr., is the leader of the band. He is the late

Selena Quintanilla Pérez's brother. She was the *reina de la onda chicana.* A.B is . . . I don't know what he is. I don't know what his music is. But whatever it is, as Tarradell writes, it is one that "merges Tejano's infectious cumbia rhythm with street-savvy R&B, old-school soul, dance-hall reggae, sizzling salsa, and trippy, loopy funk." The Kings' 2001 CD *Shhh!* sold more than 500,000 units for EMI/Latin. The CD remains in the top 20 of *Billboard's* Latin albums chart. That is something.

The Kumbia Kings were front and center stage at the State Fair of Texas on October 6, 2002. They were something else.

If it ain't *Onda* music and it ain't *Chicano* music, and it ain't *Tejano*, what's the next term for what we like?

67. Salma as Frida?

The hit movie at the Telluride Film Festival, held in Colorado annually over the Labor Day weekend, was *Frida*, starring Salma Hayek as the Mexican painter with the one eyebrow all the way across her face. Frida also was the spouse to Diego Rivera, the internationally recognized Mexican muralist. Alfredo Molina plays Diego in the film. Antonio Banderas is in the film somewhere, as are a lot of *gringos*. The movie is directed, after all, by Julie Taymor, also known for her work with *The Lion King*.

It is a positive step that more and more Latino actors are being cast to play Latinas and Latinos. It is a positive step that more and more movies are being made about us. And the concept of "us" is getting expansive when you see Antonio Banderas, the Spaniard, playing Pancho Villa in a movie soon to be made. Maybe we'll see a movie made on the air heroics of the *Escuadrón de México* during World War II. I'm tired of all those gringo war movies without Raza as if we have not been serving in all wars, from the Revolutionary War to the Persian Gulf War.

(See *Telemudo's* documentary *Soldados* and, of course, *Frida*, when it is released to the public. If ever at the National Archives in D.C., check out the film footage on the Mexican air squadron that flew combat missions over Europe in the 1940s.)

68. Tafolla, *la prima de Gabe de Uvalde*

Carmen Tafolla is the cousin of my former college buddy and housemate at Texas A&I. He died at an early age, but not before leaving his mark on Chicano politics at A&I and Uvalde. An alternative school in Uvalde is named in his honor. Carmen is a lot like Gabe in her commitment to social change. Dr. Carmen Tafolla is an educator (Ph.D. from the University of Texas at Austin, 1982), writer, artist, and wonderful Chicana. In 1987, she won the National Chicano Literature Prize (University of California at Irvine).

I ran into Dr. Tafolla at the Hispanic Women's Network of Texas annual conference held in Fort Worth, Texas, in early October 2002. She made two presentations at the conference: one a lecture on the state of Chicano arts and letters, the other a dramatization of characters in Chicano life. She was excellent in both. Carmen acted out various characters: Tere, La Dot, Leona, and La Tía. She poked fun at the conference planners for failing to note the embarrassing typographical error in an advertisement in the program book. Spellcheck did not catch this error as it is a legitimate word. The ad had "Pubic Relations" instead of "Public Relations."

She also had her 2001 book *Sonnets and Salsa* (San Antonio: Wings Press), for sale. At the moment she is working on a novel, her autobiography, and a biography of Emma Tenayuca, an early Chicana labor leader. (See www.wingspress.com.)

69. Reading Clubs: Nuestra Palabra

The concept of *primera voz,* first voice, is simple: we should all have our own voices and not have others speak for us. Anthropologists and liberals share this trait and character fault; historically, they have sought to be the voices, agents, interpreters, and presenters of oppressed peoples and groups. They would research and write about *la raza,* us, and speak for us to others. In their eyes, we were part of the broad category of global oppressed peoples and groups that needed an agent, a representative, an interpreter, a speaker. Over time, we have cast aside such pseudo-representatives and emerged with our own voices, representations, interpretations, creations, visions, goals, and narrations. We do not need ventriloquists.

Fortunately, there are now so many, many Chicano published authors and even more non-Chicanos that write about us, no one can read them all. And someone has to tell us of a great book they just read. Consequently, Chicano reading clubs have begun to emerge across the country.

In Houston, a small circle of friends of Chicano literature began Nuestra Palabra, a reading club, just a few years back. They were spawned from the Mexican-American Studies Program at the University of Houston. Tony Díaz, then a visiting scholar with the Chicano Studies program, started the effort. Today, the meetings, held every last Wednesday of the month draw hundreds of interested readers to meet the author(s), discuss and buy their books.

In Dallas, a similar project, Primera Voz, began in March 2001, with a handful of charter members. Today, members are reading and meeting Chicano authors every other month on the first Friday.

70. ¡Qué Sebo!

Sebo in Spanish is fat, like fat from animals. Dr. Norma Williams, author of *The Mexican American Family* and a Chicana from Kingsville, Texas, told me she was going to write a Chicano humor book one day and title it, *¡Qué Sebo!* In the Chicano culture, *qué sebo* is used basically to note how stupid a person can be, how dumb, how lacking in common sense he is, and how much of a jerk a person can be. The narrator of such a story usually places it in a humorous envelope.

When Norma gets around to writing the book, I will nominate the story of Gloria Garza, now Cantú, and Gary Bigger, both residing in Kingsville, Texas. Gloria and Gary were college mates of mine at Texas A&I University in the mid-1960s. Gloria was the epitome of what I imagine an Aztec princess to have looked like. She was tall and leggy, had jet-black hair down to her bottom, had high cheekbones, slanted-almost-Asian almond eyes, and a skin color of rich, dark coffee. She walked gracefully about the campus with an air about her that discouraged uninvited come-ons. She was strikingly beautiful and the object of desire of every Chicano male I knew, me included.

Gloria would have none of us. She only had eyes for Gary Bigger, the blond, blue-eyed, kind of hippie artist who either had a cigarette in his mouth or was slurping a cup of coffee. When Gary and Gloria decided to marry, neither family was pleased. Her family wanted a Mexican son-in-law, not a *gringo*. His family certainly did not want some Mexican girl to give birth to dark-skinned, half-breed children named Bigger. When Gloria took Gary home to be introduced, the Garza clan resigned themselves to the choice. He treated her well. When Gary took Gloria to his family in Corpus Christi, Texas, his mom quizzed her immediately about Gloria's skills in the kitchen. She did not want her son to not be fed well. She asked Gloria if she could cook American food. Gloria replied, "Anybody can make a tuna sandwich."

¡Qué sebo!

71. Playing the Stock Market

The working poor of Raza do not buy stocks as an investment. They have no spare money. If they do have some stock, it is probably in some corporate-sponsored pension plan or 401(k), like that of their middle-class brethren. Let's hope that in the wake of the blatant and scandalous display of corporate greed by major CEOs and other high-level corporate stand-ins for rich stockholders, our people did not lose the little wealth they had accumulated.

Partly to blame for these white-collar crimes was the regulatory commission asleep on the job or looking in the other direction. Thank goodness, no Chicana was sitting on the Securities and Exchange Commission (SEC) when these scandals began to unravel and be reported in the press in early 2001. She might have been accused of covering up for the President when, as a candidate, he wrongfully reported (by not reporting timely as required by law) his stock dealings in the wake of disaster for other stockholders and a huge loss of value for the corporation right after he bailed out.

Well, not anymore. The SEC is getting a Chicano, Roel Campos, from Harlingen, Texas. He will serve a three-year term. Watch the corporate crooks, Roel, and especially watch Cheney and Dubya

Bush. You never know, literally, you never know from looking at the cooked corporate books, certified audits from crooked CPAs, and SEC filings.

72. Astronaut or Execunaut?

Ellen Castro is the execunaut (I made up the word), while Ellen Ochoa is the astronaut. Ellen Castro is from San Antonio, Texas, and was among the first Chicanas to obtain a master's degree in public administration at Southern Methodist University (SMU at Dallas, Texas). Upon graduation in 1975, she was snapped up by Exxon Corporation, and by the age of twenty-nine, she was a senior executive, with millions in budget and thousands of employees under her supervision. By the mid-1980s, she was burned out after eleven grueling years at Exxon, making cracks in the glass ceiling there. She had given her executive career all she had to give. The white, male corporate bastion was formidable. Ellen was alienated from herself, her Chicano roots, her *familia*, and her life.

Being the smart woman that she is, she quit Exxon and took off to Harvard for another degree in education. She turned her life around and is most happy now with herself and her life. She is now on the faculty of the Business Leadership Center at SMU. She earns thousands, teaching white male corporate types about leadership. She hires out to corporations for training sessions, just like the Stephen Covey leadership business machine. She writes, lectures, trains, consults, and teaches about leadership.

Read her 1998 book, *Spirited Leadership: 52 Ways to Build Trust on the Job,* Allen, Texas: Thomas More, or go to the website: www.rclweb.com. E-mail her at ellen@ellencastro.com.

73. Bless Me Forever, *Última*

Rudolfo Anaya, our eminent Chicano writer from New Mexico, couldn't be happier. There is a trend emerging across the country dealing with reading. In such cities as Austin and Tucson, the entire community is being encouraged to read the same book, and then start a dialogue about the content.

In Austin, the Chicano mayor, Gus García, said he wanted everyone to read and discuss Anaya's *Bless Me Última*. Tucson has adopted for community reading the same book. I am sure that as the copies fly off the bookshelves, Anaya and his agents are saying, "Bless us forever, *Última*." Way to go, Anaya, García, Austin, Tucson. . . . Maybe a book of mine will be chosen somewhere, sometime. . . .

The seed has been planted.

PART III

COMPLEX POWER STRUCTURE
AND LEVEL OF POWER

1. "We'll Be Back!"

In the 1970s, Rosie Castro ran for a spot on the San Antonio City Council and lost. At a press conference the day after the loss, she was quoted in one of the local newspapers as saying, "We'll be back." Rosie started her electoral activism while an undergraduate student at Our Lady of the Lake College as president of the Young Democrats. Soon, she joined the Mexican-American Youth Organization, and later, the Raza Unida Party. She became a *partido* stalwart and leader in the city, county, region, and state.

After the defeat, life went on for Rosie, and she continued to dedicate much of her time to political and electoral causes. She worked tirelessly for unionization of city employees and worked on María Antonietta Berriozábal's mayoral race, which was nearly won in the 1990s. She also had to hold down a full-time job. Like many Chicana leaders, she had to be both mother and father to her twin boys, Julián and Joaquín. There never was enough money in the Castro household. The boys managed to graduate from Jefferson High School and went off to Stanford University with generous financial aid given because of their academic records. They both excelled at Stanford. Both boys then enrolled at Harvard Law School and again excelled. They came home and got jobs as lawyers with a big corporate law firm at very good salaries. They started helping Rosie financially. It was time to pay back mom for all her sacrifice. But they were also doing political and electoral work.

Julián ran for the city council in the 2001 elections, held May 5. He won. He is the council member for District 7. Joaquín ran for the state legislature in the 2002 elections and won.

The transfer of Chicano power from one generation to another is completed in this case. I guess that is why Rosie said, "We'll be back" and not "I'll be back" some thirty years ago.

(See the Rosie Castro videotaped interview in Special Collections of the University of Texas-Arlington and Cecilia Balli, "Twins Peak," in *Texas Monthly*, October 2002, pp. 100–03, 153–58, or www.texasmonthly.com.)

2. The Plumbers' Unit

The FBI and the CIA have college-trained, advanced-degree personnel in an investigative unit called the plumbers. Their job is to capture fecal material and other disgusting fluids from "targets" to evaluate their health and lifestyles. These federal employees intercept hotel and apartment plumbing lines, pry into septic tanks, look in garbage cans, and do rerouting of regular sewer lines from residences; hence, the name, plumbers' unit. The goodies captured can provide DNA, evidence of disease, what the person has recently digested, and traces of drugs, alcohol, blood, etc. This is a very important intelligence-gathering activity, especially if the FBI, DEA, INS, or NSA is targeting a head of state or drug lord or political dissident.

The local Chicano scammers are not interested in all of these goodies. They will not intercept your sewer line or pry into a septic tank. They go after your garbage can. The ugly can you place out on the street or curb for the collectors to come by on a given day is their goldmine. The scammers are interested in your credit card and bank statement or cancelled checks and phone bill or catalog-order receipt and other bills you threw out. They are even observing you at gas stations or stores when you pay the cashier with a credit card and discard the receipt as you walk out. Beware of what you throw away in the street or place in the garbage can. These bills and receipts contain valuable information that scammers can use to develop a profile on you that can cost you thousands of dollars in charges made by them on your cards and numbers. Better to shred or tear up receipts and bills and place them in two different trash cans. Make it more difficult for scammers to find your important papers and glue them back together.

3. ¡Gooooooooool!

How do you say *gooooooooool* in English? You know, the scoring of a goal in soccer?

We don't need to know. It's the same in either language; besides, you can see the goal being made unless you are in line buying beer or leaving recycled beer you rented during the game.

Soccer, or *fútbol*, has become the hottest sport in the United

States. On October 20, 2002, Radio Única, a national Spanish-language network, will broadcast the MLS Cup 2002 championship game to be held in Foxboro, Massachusetts. The radio network cut a deal with Major League Soccer to broadcast the games, host a one-hour MLS news show, *Única en Deportes*, and recap the *fútbol* games around the world on Sundays, *Únicamente MLS*.

A couple of problems are on the horizon for soccer in the United States. First, there are few facilities in U.S. cities to practice and play soccer. There are plenty of golf courses, however. There is money to be made here. Second, there are *movidas* in the making to bar Raza referees, leagues, games, championships, marketing, and so on with a simple age-old *gringo* trick called credentialing. The *gringos* insist on credentials they recognize, not our credentials of knowing the game, the rules, playing for decades, being in leagues, etc. What credentials are these? The ones they recognize because they own the credentialing process and issue the certificates. Got it?

4. Curling: An Olympic Sport?

You've seen the event on TV. Two guys are racing down an ice-capped alley-like chute sweeping in front of a rock with a handle on top. That is curling, an Olympic sport. The game began somewhere in the Dark Ages in a land with big rocks everywhere and where there was lots of ice on the ground, probably Sweden or Iceland. It has a lot of popularity in Canada and some northern U.S. states. A curling team called a rink consists of four players that take turns sliding a "rock" toward a target across 146 feet of ice. The scoring area or target is twelve feet in diameter and called a house. One player flings the rock over the ice toward the house, while two team members sweep in front of the rock. The fourth team member is behind the house with another broom that serves as the guide for the rock shooter. Each team gets eight shots during a turn, and when both teams are done, it is called the end. It takes 16 rocks to play a regular match called a *bonspiel* that can last more than two hours because each team gets eight ends. In a championship game, there are ten ends. You score by placing your rock in the house, by not getting knocked out of it by the opponent, and by knocking the opponent's rock out of the house with your rock. Got it?

This is not a cheap sport. These granite rocks weigh 42 pounds and cost about $250 a piece. And, can you believe that David Villegas from Dallas, Texas, dreams of building a team to compete in curling at the 2010 Olympics. Pray tell, what sport will be left that whites will be able to play?

(Check this sport out in your local area or at www.dallascurling.com or www.uswca.org [women] or www.usacurl.org [United States] or www.icing.org [international].)

5. Sunday: The Most Racially Polarized Day in America

Someone claimed that Sunday is the most racist day of the week because everyone wakes up in their segregated neighborhood and turns on the Sunday television news programs to see their favorite white commentators, usually all with right-wing opinions and discussing topics of interest to white America. Each family then goes to its segregated church for Christian services and eats lunch out at a segregated restaurant, where the help is Latino but not the customers. Back home, the men watch sports played by black and Latino players directed by white coaches and owners. The women go to the mall near a suburb where the customers are predominantly white.

I forgot the newspaper. If you look at the Sunday comics, as most of our Raza children do when we read the adult stuff, notice that all the strips are about white people or some animal.

Only recently has a Chicano comic strip, "Baldo," been syndicated in enough newspapers to be considered a national strip. "Baldo" was created by Héctor Cantú of *The Dallas Morning News* and *Hispanic Business*. (See www.baldocomics.com.)

6. *El Águila Azteca*

The United States has its Medal of Freedom Award bestowed upon citizens (nonmilitary) for exemplary service to the nation. Some Chicanos have received the Freedom Medal in years past. President Reagan gave one to Héctor P. García, founder of the American G.I. Forum, and President Clinton gave one to Mario Obledo, former general counsel of the Mexican-American Legal Defense and Education Fund (MALDEF) and national president of LULAC, among other accomplishments. But the number of Raza recipients can still be counted on one hand.

Mexico also has an award for exemplary service to Mexico and Mexicans awarded to non-Mexican nationals, El Águila Azteca. This award, established in 1933 by President Manuel Ávila Camacho, is usually presented by the Mexican president at a formal ceremony. The award is presented to persons recommended by the Secretary of Foreign Relations.

The first Chicano I know of who received this award was Porfirio Salinas, the artist. He painted bluebonnet landscapes. President Adolfo López Mateos loved his paintings and bought some, so he gave him the award. Next, President Carlos Salinas de Gortari during the 1990s gave the award almost exclusively to Chicanos/as. I was present at one ceremony in 1991 when some of the recipients were: Antonia Hernández, head of MALDEF; Luis Leal, outstanding academic; and Blandina "Bambi" Cárdenas, dean at the University of Texas at San Antonio. The ceremony took place on December 11, 1991, at Los Pinos, the official residence for Mexican presidents. Lunch was at Tlatelolco, the site of the Aztec main square and the offices of the foreign secretary. A reception was held later that evening at the Sala de Arte Público Siqueiros, where an exhibit of Chicano poster art was on display. The Chicano posters were on loan from the University of California at Santa Barbara's collection, the California Ethnic and Multicultural Archives, featuring twenty-nine artists from Self-Help Graphics and Arts, Inc. (1972). Some of these artists were Samuel A. Baray, Yreina Cervántez, Leo Limón, Diane Gamboa, Dolores Guerrero-Cruz, Gilbert "Magu" Luján, and Victor Ochoa.

We are recognized and honored more by Mexican presidents than U.S. presidents.

7. One Mexico?

There is a professor at the University of New Mexico (Albuquerque), Charles Truxillo, who has caused the anti-immigrant lobby in the United States and other right-wing zealots grave concern. Dr. Truxillo proclaimed that the southwestern states and the northern Mexican states should secede and form the Republic of Aztlán. Dr. Truxillo is quoted in Patrick Buchanan's latest book, *The Death of the West* (New York: St. Martin's Press, 2002).

There are others who are continuing my work on building closer collaboration between Chicanos and Mexicans. Rare is the family in Mexico that does not have a relative living in the United States.

There is a working relationship between agencies of the Mexican government and U.S. organizations. One such relationship is that of NCLR and the Secretaría de Educación Pública (SEP). This specific relationship was practically cemented when Ernesto Zedillo was the secretary of this cabinet position and then became president. As secretary, he began a program headed by Roger Díaz de Cossío of contact and collaboration with U.S.-based Mexican organizations. At NCLR's annual convention on July 19, 1994, a special workshop was held, "An Encounter: NCLR Affiliates and Mexican Organizations in the United States." More than twenty-five leaders of Mexican organizations in the United States attended, as did scores of representatives of NCLR affiliates. The dialogue was spirited, provocative, highly charged, emotional, and visionary: Aztlán? *¿México? ¿La Reconquista?* Babies and Ballots, Not Bullets! Paint the White House Brown! *Somos los mismos.*

"Houston, we have contact," the NASA officials usually say after a successful launch and communication is established. I say, *"Tenemos contacto: ¡Somos un sólo México!"*

8. Hispanic Radio in the United States

I recently spoke at the eleventh national conference of HIRE in Houston, Texas. HIRE is the organization of Hispanic Internal Revenue Employees. Yes, Raza are in the IRS; some are the tax collectors. In another session, a handout was provided, "Hispanic Radio in the United States," which was prepared by the National Communications Division of HIRE. Here are some select "radio factoids" from the handout:

- Currently, there are more than 13,000 radio stations—more than 600 of these are Hispanic-format stations.
- Spanish-language radio is one of the most important media reaching Hispanics today, largely because Hispanics listen to the radio 20 to 30 percent more than the general population.
- Radio reaches 96 percent of all Hispanics every week.
- In some markets, Spanish-format stations lead the audience ratings.
- Hispanic men spend more time listening than any other group.
- Hispanic women 65+ spend more time listening than any other female group.
- Mexican regional is the most-listened-to radio programming in the East, North, Central, Pacific, Mountain, and Central Regions.
- Most Mexican regional listeners make $25,000 or less.

9. More on Smoking

Oklahoma has the highest per-capita consumption of tobacco use in the Southwest: 109 packs per person, per year. By comparison, Texans smoke 69.3 packs a year, while those in Arizona suck up 58.5 packs and New Mexicans do 53.8 packs annually.

And where do large numbers of Raza live and smoke? Duh!

10. Political Cartoons

Caricaturists are found busy at work at theme parks, regular parks, busy sidewalks, and movie studios. These are the talented people who in minutes can draw your features in an exaggerated likeness. Political cartoonists, on the other hand, are those who can draw a simple picture that conveys a powerful political message. They are usually found working their talent for newspapers and newsmagazines. In all of the Spanish-speaking countries of the world, you will find Raza cartoonists and caricaturists working away, making life more humorous for us all. Some Chicanos from the 1960s will remember the Mexican political comic books by Rius.

We have some Chicanos at work here as illustrators, cartoonists, and caricaturists today. Lalo Alcaraz, for example, teamed up with Ilan Stavans to illustrate the book *Latino USA: A Cartoon History* (New York: Basic Books, 2000). And at *The Los Angeles Times*, the top editorial cartoonist is none other than Michael Ramírez. He is very, very good. Regularly, his cartoons gig and lampoon the mighty politicians in the country. Yeah, a Chicano-Japonés is doing it and getting paid good bucks to do it! "Only in America," the right-wingers would remind us.

(E-mail him at Michael.Ramirez@latimes.com and buy a cartoon or two from him to frame for your wall. He is a Pulitzer-prize-winner and has two Sigma Delta Chi awards from the Society of Profession Journalism.)

11. *Amigos de México de Plano*

This is an organization based in Plano, Texas, pronounced Plain-Oh, not *Plan No* in Spanish. The U.S. Border Patrol is the federal agency paid to hunt Mexicans. The *Amigos de México* hunts for lost Mexicans the Border Patrol missed. The hunts are for different reasons. The Border Patrol wants to deport Mexicans. The *Amigos* want to find Mexicans and assure family members in Mexico that their relative is safe. The issue is the thousands of missing persons and deaths reported annually for Mexicans crossing into the United States. As of this writing, some 905 Mexican nationals out of 1,358 reported missing have been found by the Mexican government.

The job of finding missing Mexican nationals rests with the Mexican Secretary of Foreign Affairs (read consular offices), but they only find some in the easy places, such as jails, hospitals, morgues, and at work. They find others under assumed names and living another life, usually when they come into a consular office seeking some assistance or paperwork. This year so far, the Mexican government has received more than 1,000 reports of missing persons.

The real crisis is in the 2,189 unidentified bodies found since 1995, presumed to be Mexicans, found in the desert, in truck trailers, drowned, murdered, and otherwise mutilated and decomposing, most often along the border in the Southwest, but not always. For example, this past June 2002, some seventy corpses were found in the deserts of California and Arizona or floating in the Rio Grande along the Texas border with Mexico. *The Dallas Morning News* reported July 28, 2002, on two Mexican immigrants found dead in a truck trailer in Anna, Texas, north of Dallas. And forty others were found wandering aimlessly near a truck stop in southern Dallas that same day, suffering from heat exhaustion and dehydration. For more than twelve hours, they had been in a closed truck trailer traveling from Sante Fe, New Mexico.

The Mexican government used to count unidentified bodies in their gross numbers of missing Mexicans, but not anymore. In this manner, the official Mexican figures show progress in the numbers found and identified and an overall lessening of the crisis.

The Amigos are picking up the slack in the effort to find missing Mexicans. When they get a request to find a missing person, they put out an all-points bulletin via the Internet to all their contacts across the country. They call on local Spanish-language media to air as a public service announcement the notice of the missing person's origin, last known destination, physical description, and the Amigos' phone number: 972-964-0385. Amigos also have e-mail at amigos-demexico@hotmail.com. Amigos's volunteers process the requests and handle the calls with information. They find people.

12. Operation TIPS

Some of us have utilized the Freedom of Information Act (FOIA) to obtain federal government records of surveillance on Chicano leaders and organizations. State and local governments have also engaged in domestic surveillance of Chicano groups and leaders, particularly during the Chicano Movement and in decades prior to that era. I have done extensive research and gathering of documents on the subject and can assure the reader that the U.S. government has been at war with us since the 1920s. I say "at war" because we have been the targets of surveillance during every decade of the last century because our political activity was viewed as suspect and we had the potential to be enemies of the U.S. government.

Again, in 2002, the federal government is at war with us. We still have the potential to become enemies of the state, and our political activity, particularly dissent and protest, will be viewed as suspicious.

I recommend you write or call your member of Congress and ask for a copy of the Patriot Act, which is now the supreme law of the land. Meanwhile, let me tell you about Operation TIPS being carried out by agents of the Department of Justice (DOJ) under the direction of the U.S. Attorney General John Ashcroft. The acronym TIPS stands for Terrorism, Information and Prevention System. President Bush wants this program in place and operational at all costs as soon as possible.

In essence, TIPS provides for the establishment of a clearinghouse to handle information provided to the DOJ by millions of persons reporting suspicious activity. All of us are being asked to help win the war against terrorism by reporting persons engaged in suspicious activity. You had better be nice to your neighbor. You had better not complain or criticize the government, the president, or anything "American," especially the flag. You could become a TIPS suspect.

The Fourth Amendment to the U.S. Constitution prohibits unreasonable searches and seizures and establishes the right of the people to be secure in their persons, houses, papers, and effects, while the First Amendment protects not only speech and association but also direct action and public protest. TIPS seeks to make an end-run around both the First and Fourth Amendments. You see, the FBI or any other law-enforcement official must not gain entry into your home, search and interrogate you, for example, without proper legal authority, such as a search warrant or legal counsel present. Under TIPS, the cable guy, the girlfriend, the neighbor, or the fireman can gain entry into your home, and search and interrogate you without any authority or permission. In fact, you probably will have let them in voluntarily and willingly.

And, the cable guy, your girlfriend, the neighbor, and the fireman now have a duty to inform and report any suspicious activity. What is suspicious activity? Your local bigots and religious-right zealots can answer that in a swift second, and they will. Your local *vigilantes* (yes, it is a word lifted from Spanish) and other busybodies will be doing their American duty and informing on your activity. Cancel the evening backyard cookout. Cancel the *quinceañera* gathering to practice the processional. Forget the speech on immigrant rights you were going to give. Do not check out any book from the library on Cuba or Islam. Stop payment on your tanning sessions; in fact, stay out of the sun and lighten up. Speak English as much as you can and Americanize your name to any extent possible. (See my work "Surveillance from 1920 to the present," in Renato Rosaldo Monograph, University of Arizona, 1986. See also Ernesto Vigil, *Crusade for Justice: The Government War on Dissent* [Madison: University of Wisconsin, 1999] and *St. Louis Post-Dispatch*, July 20, 2002.)

13. FAIR or NOT FAIR?

There are several websites readers should familiarize themselves with because they affect your future. See www.americanpatrol.org or www.uniteamerica.org or www.fairus.org. The latter site is that of the Federation for American Immigration Reform. FAIR is stridently anti-immigrant and especially anti-Mexican. It opposes any and all immigration legislation except that which would close the U.S. borders and deport undocumented persons immediately. In its view, any discussion of legalization by U.S. officials and other such influentials stimulates illegal immigration by people who hope to be in the U.S. in time to take advantage of such legislation. How would a dirt farmer in Michoacán, Mexico, or Iztalcolco, El Salvador, learn that Minority Leader Dick Gephardt (D-Missouri) discussed his immigration legislation at the National Council of La Raza's (NCLR) annual convention? Where would he read or hear that the Democrats propose that permanent residency be made available to undocumented persons who have been in the United States for at least five years and held jobs for at least two years, provided they passed a criminal background check? Pulleze . . .

14. *Un nuevo Plan de Aztlán*

During the heyday of the Chicano Movement, the *Plan de Aztlán* was written, proclaimed, and adopted by thousands of Chicano

Movement activists as the guiding truth toward liberation as a people. Those of us who toiled in electoral work as a liberating tool built the Raza Unida Party and took political control over several jurisdictions. We won seats on city councils, school boards, and county governments across the country. Frank Shafer Corona got elected to the Adams-Morgan School Board in Washington, D.C., for example. Others in Cucamonga and Parlier, California, got elected to school boards and municipal government. In Texas, we also got elected to many public offices. I was elected to both a school board and a county judgeship in Zavala County, Texas, during the 1970s. In our view, with these initial victories, we were building a Chicano nation: Aztlán. Then in the 1980s, we lost elections, ballot status, and political party affiliation, and there went the Chicano nation.

Roberto Rodríguez, a journalist/columnist, has proposed a *nuevo plan* in his recent *amoxtli* (*Náhuatl* for book). He simply posits that we not wait for a physical victory over the lost territory, but instead proclaim individual Raza sovereignty. Just do it, one by one. Say it, believe it, do it, and it will happen.

This is a new ideology, a spiritual irredentist movement, to proclaim *una América*.

(See *Codex Tamuanchan: On Becoming Human*, self-published by Rodríguez, [Albuquerque, New Mexico, 1998] or contact him at xcolumn@aol.com.)

15. Babies and Ballots

The National Council of La Raza (NCLR) has several publications available on various subjects. The most recent one released during the summer 2002 was on Hispanic voting power and issues.

The report said Raza votes could increase from 5.7 million cast in 2002 to 7.9 million in 2004 because our voter registration and voter turnout rates are increasing. The number of our registered voters has grown from 2.5 million in 1972 to 7.6 million in 2000. The reader will notice that our numbers decrease greatly between those that register to vote and those that actually vote. Approximately 79 percent of Raza registered voters turned out to vote in 2000. The comparable rates for black voter turnout was 84 percent and 86 percent for whites. The reader can see why, given our lower voter turnout rate, we are not considered as important and necessary as black or white voters. But the figures are changing rapidly and dramatically.

Recently, I gave a commencement speech for the Chicano Caucus at Princeton University and used the metaphor of a basketball playoff game to illustrate the points being made above. I said that in a televised basketball game, the home viewer can see the entire team on the bench and on the court, including the coaching staff. All the "players" involved with either team are on the court or on and near the bench. All the action is there to be seen. And, I said, they are either black or white; rare is the Latino or Asian basketball player, but there are some. No player, however, can foul out or get hurt. No player can quit or leave the court. No coach can do much about what players he has to play. All you see on the court and on the bench is all they have. They have present power. And that scenario is very close to our presence in the United States.

We are not on the court and we are not on the bench. We certainly are not the coaches. We are the potential power in reserve, yet to come. When a white person dies, there is no replacement. The white population is a declining population. When a black person dies, there may be a substitute. The black population is not growing, either; it is also declining, but not as rapidly as that of the white population. The only future powers-to-be among all groups are the Asians and us. We are the immediate future, with Asians challenging us in and around 2050.

We are the populations with growth and have been responsible in decades past for the overwhelming rates of growth in all areas: population, consumer spending, business development, voting strength, students, homeowners, television viewers, and radio listeners.

16. Community Activism

We must be engaged and involved in community activities to make a difference. Dolores Huerta was the right hand of César Chávez in building the United Farm Workers of America union. She continued her labor-organizing work years past the death of Chávez. Over the course of the years, she gave birth to numerous children, but that never stopped her from continued organizing and public speaking. The police and other anti-union thugs beat her on various occasions, the last time quite severely. She now suffers from the results of those police-inflicted internal injuries. She was inducted into the National Women's Hall of Fame. She campaigned vigorously for several presidential candidates. She campaigned for Hillary Clinton in her successful pursuit of a U.S. senate seat. She recently received the César E. Chávez Spirit Award from the University of California in Los Angeles (UCLA) for improving the lives of farm workers and their families. She has been doing this for nearly fifty years.

You go, Dolores.

P.S.: Over the Labor Day weekend, 2002, she marched in Fresno, California, in support of the farm workers' demand that Governor Gray Davis sign the Agricultural Labor Relations Bill, with the proviso that growers negotiate in good faith with a set time limit after a unionization vote.

17. *The COINTELPRO Papers*

The book above (Cambridge, MA: South End Press, 2002) was written by Ward Churchill and Jim Vander Wall and is a revision of an earlier work published in 1990. It is about the secret war by the U.S. government aimed at U.S. citizens engaged in lawful First Amendment activities, namely politics. The government called these activities counterintelligence programs, e.g. COINTELPRO. The government's COINTELPROs were illegal activities. The documentary evidence compiled by the authors, and often photocopied in the book, is thousands of government files obtained under the Freedom of Information Act and other government sources. Regrettably, the only Latinos mentioned as government targets are those involved with the Puerto Rican Independence Movement of the 1960s. Raza, however, has been the target of U.S. government surveillance since time immemorial.

Mauricio Mazón uncovered documents of the FBI and military

intelligence targeting *pachucos*. I found documents of surveillance by the FBI on LULAC as early as the 1940s, as well as other documents on major Chicano organizations and leaders. Ernesto Vigil wrote a book about the government's war on Chicano dissidents in Denver. Rodolfo Acuña, our notable historian, in several editions of *Occupied America* named undercover agents in the Chicano Movement and pointed to similar illegal activity on the part of local police intelligence units in Los Angeles. Many of our critics labeled us as paranoid, conspiracy-hunters, anti-U.S. government, anti-law enforcement, etc., as many persons today label those who dare criticize the appointed U.S. President and his new domestic surveillance policy initiatives (TIPS) and law, e.g. the Patriot Act, 2002.

Now, we find out that the Denver police also engaged in similar illegal activity. And because of citizen pressure and media exposure, the city government has opened the files for sixty days to the public to request copies.

I am sure Ernesto Vigil and other crusaders are in line for copies.

18. *Todavía no se puede*

Our great Chicano leader César Chávez made popular a Chicano call for a public display of will combined with direct political action, *¡Sí se puede!* It is the converse of the title above. Chávez and his right-hand woman, Dolores Huerta, were undaunted and formed a national union of farm workers in the United States. They boycotted, they struck, they recruited, they organized, they educated consumers, they internationalized the struggle, they picketed, they sued, they registered voters, they voted, they pushed legislation, they lobbied, they made friends with important public figures (the Kennedys, Jesse Jackson, many movie stars and writers), and involved legions of volunteers worldwide. The unforeseen factors in the early 1960s of rapid mechanization and improved chemistry (pesticides) made for unfavorable farm-worker unionization. The human factor of sheer will and determination, however, helped Chávez and Huerta, their members, and volunteers win labor-union elections all over California and Arizona.

The problem, yet unresolved despite the presence of the Congressional Hispanic Caucus and Black Congressional Caucus, is that the National Labor Relations Act does not cover farm workers. Never did and still doesn't. Chávez and his union members successfully lobbied and passed a state law, the Agricultural Labor Relations Act, in 1975, when Jerry Brown was governor of California. Under this law, farm workers have a right to unionize and bargain collectively. The United Farm Workers of America, since 1975, have won 428 elections to unionize, but have only bargained collectively on 185 signed contracts. In other words, the UFW wins the unionization election but the grower does not negotiate a subsequent labor contract in good faith. A vegetable grower in particular, D'Arrigo Brothers of Salinas, California, despite years of negotiations since 1975, has yet to sign a contract with the 1,400 workers. That is more than a quarter century of waiting while paying union dues *pa' nada!*

As it turns out, Chávez *no pudo* and died still trying to have farm workers prevail over farm owners in labor negotiations after winning union elections. Under subsequent leadership, Antonio Rodríguez, Chávez's son-in-law and the new UFW president, together with union members and scores of volunteers, successfully lobbied the California legislature to amend the Labor Relations Act. The bill (SB1736) passed by the legislature and sent to Governor Gray Davis calls for binding arbitration after a favorable union vote. Governor Davis is a Democrat and is seeking reelection. The California agricultural industry opposes the bill. Agribusiness in California is big business: $27 billion a year in sales.

Governor Gray Davis finally signed the bill on October 1, 2002. (See *The New York Times,* August 9, 2002, p. A10.)

19. Top Cities for Hispanics

I was a migrant for some years of my early life and had no choice of where to live. My mother and I went to work where we could find it. I lived and worked in various states: Wisconsin, Illinois, Minnesota, California, and Oregon. I worked in agriculture-related endeavors, mostly. In decades past, need, accident, circumstance, violence, government abuse, and luck usually determined where you were born and lived. Today, your birthplace is still determined in the very same way. Your living situation, however, can now be a matter of choice.

Annually, *Hispanic* magazine publishes a list of the Top 10 cities for Hispanics to live in. In the August 2002 issue, the magazine listed in ranked order: San Diego, Austin, Miami, San Antonio, El Paso-Las Cruces, Albuquerque, Tucson, Los Angeles, New York, and at number 10, Raleigh-Durham-Chapel Hill, North Carolina. Yes! Raleigh-Durham-Chapel Hill in North Carolina is a better place to live than Denver, San Jose, Laredo, San Francisco, Chicago, McAllen, Tampa, Houston, St. Louis, Dallas, Milwaukee, or St. Paul-Minneapolis. Ouch!

The list-maker for *Hispanic*, Gigi Anders, explained her methodology and analysis as including political representation, Spanish-language use, Latino cultural vibrancy, and "hipness," not just Hispanic population numbers.

Bueno, bye, see ya in Chapel Hill, North Carolina.

20. Distance Learning

La Tec de Monterrey, as in Nuevo León, México, is the Technological Institute of Monterrey that is collaborating with the Mexican government to provide distance education and learning to rural Mexico via computer centers with Internet connection.

The Internet is making nation-state borders an obsolete concept. The Internet crosses international boundaries with a click of Enter or Send.

In Miami, Houston, and Dallas, *La Tec de Monterrey*, the Mexican government via its consular offices, and local expatriates organized as nonprofit groups in the U.S., such as *Familia Nuevo León* in Dallas at 1630 Prudential Drive off Mockingbird Lane (214-631-2783), have teamed up in a collaborative project. The tri-organizational project is now reaching local Mexican nationals within the United States with the high-tech speed and capability of computer centers. The distance learning and education computer centers in these three cities are teaching Spanish, English, and computer skills classes to those interested. In the works are classes on health, business development, and other group-specific interests.

This is teamwork. This is solid public-private collaboration. This is Chicano-Mexicano international relations. This is bridging the technological and information divide.

¡Adelante, raza!

21. The *Harper's* Index

Harper's is a magazine not readily found in Chicano homes. It is more than 150 years old and published out of 666 Broadway, New York, NY, 10012. But then, what mainstream products are aimed at us, anyway? It is changing slowly as we grow in consumer spending power. But *Harper's* can be a source of extraordinary information for us to use as talking points on just about any subject, particularly the section called the *Harper's* Index.

Here's some stuff I call talking points from recent Index items:

- March 21, 1995, is the date the state of Mississippi ratified the Thirteenth Amendment to the U.S. Constitution, abolishing slavery.

  This is great news now that Raza are relocating to Mississippi and other southeastern states.

- In 2001, the Pentagon could not account for expenditures in the amount of $22 billion.

  After WorldCom, Haliburton, Tyco, ImClone, Lucent, Enron, and other businesses allegedly cooked their books to show greater profits than they had in reality, can we audit the branches of the government and affiliated agencies?

- The average number of Americans killed by prescription drugs is 1,900 each week!

  When I read stuff like this, sometimes I am glad we can neither afford health care nor be covered by health insurance.

- Exxon Corporation was ordered in 1994 to pay $5 billion in punitive damages for the *Valdez* Alaskan oil spill in 1989. Exxon has paid zero.

  It's great to have friends in high places who can keep the collectors away. I should be so lucky.

- Every presidential year (that is every four, next one being

2004) since 1972, there has either been a Bush or a Dole on the Republican ticket.

Talk about the American Revolution against George III and the fiction of royalty in America! And, now we are into sons, brothers, and wives of Bushes and Doles in U.S. politics. Elizabeth Dole is the Republican nominee for U.S. Senator in North Carolina, Jeb Bush is seeking reelection as governor of Florida, and George Dubya, the appointed president, will invariably seek another term as president. *Harper's* Index will again read, "Last year in which neither a Dole nor a Bush has appeared on the Republican presidential ticket: 1972."

And, if all goes well for Jeb and Lizzy, *Harper's* Index in 2008 or 2012 could read exactly the same.

Raza, let's paint the White House brown!

22. Mickey Mouse Is a Rat!

"Mickey Mouse is a rat!" declared Roberto Alonzo, Texas state representative, at a press conference called in Dallas, Texas, to denounce the attempted implementation of Proposition 187 in California, a virulent anti-immigrant public initiative aimed at hurting Mexicans in that state. Representative Alonzo had just learned via the news media that Disney Corporation was reported to be, among others, a contributor of significant dollars in support of Proposition 187.

The measure passed on November 8, 1994, under the rubric of Save Our State. Many people and entities contributed financially to promote passage by voters of this proposition. Such contributors and entities not only must report the contribution to the state, but also the Secretary of State must make available to the public the list of such persons and organizations. This is also true of almost all candidates for public office in the United States. They must file reports with some government office, local or state or national, as to who gave them money, how much, when, and the report is open to the public.

Because we have Chicano Studies programs in many colleges and universities across the United States, albeit not enough of them, research is undertaken by scholars associated with these programs on topics of the day. Proposition 187 was studied and continues to be studied by students to this day, but few look into who funded the initiative and made money from working on its passage. The Chicanos at the University of California-Riverside did and found some interesting entries in the voluminous pages of the reports. For example, Rick Oltman, who listed an address of 714 C Street, Suite 209, in San Rafael, CA 94901, received a salary of $3,000 for the period of 10-1 through 10-22, basically $1,000 per week, to work for the committee "Yes on 187—Save Our State" in favor of the proposition. Sue Gilliam, listed as treasurer for this committee, also worked on the road for passage. She traveled and billed for 1,255 miles at 28 cents per mile or $351.40 plus $175.33 in expenses for parking, meals, copies, bridge tolls, and the like during the same period in October as Rick. Her salary was $500 per week. Her address was the same as Rick's. It was the office.

The California Republican Party (ID# 810163), with a listed address of 1903 Magnolia Blvd., Burbank, CA 91506, contributed $20,000 in support of the measure, plus $76,513.89 as in-kind contributions for postage and list rental and another in-kind contribution of $10,164.20 for absentee ballot mailing.

Among the big six-figure moneymakers were Kiley & Associates, 5208 Vista Montana, Yorba Linda, CA 92686, which earned $51,000 for its work on behalf of 187, and American Petition Consultants, 11280 Trade Center Drive #100, Rancho Cordova, CA 95742, for gathering signatures from April 1, 1994, to June 30, 1994.

(See pp. 14-15 of Schedule F, California 1994 Form 419, for this committee's report, I.D. number 941975, for the period 10-1-94 through 10-22-94, on file with the California Secretary of State for Oltman and Gilliam; Citizens for Immigration Reform/Save Our State, Schedule A, California 1993 Form 419, ID Number 931819, p. 52, for the state Republican Party and Schedule C, California 1994 Form 419, ID Number 931818, p. 40; Schedule F, California 1993 Form 419, p. 61, for those mentioned as making a six-figure income from their work on behalf of the proposition.)

23. Dataveillance

We used to call the political intelligence gathering on Chicanos by the government just plain ol' surveillance. Now, with computers, credit cards, use of social security numbers for identification, and all sorts of electronic gizmos that track and clock number entries, it is best to call this political intelligence gathering "dataveillance."

Imagine for a minute that you set the security alarm as you leave home, drive to the nearest gas station for a fill-up and pay with a credit card, go to the bank and make a withdrawal from the ATM machine, stop at the grocery store for some items and pay with the credit card again, then proceed to the gated parking lot of your company or work site and gain entry with your employee card, and clock in for work at the site. You have just left a paper trail of no less than six transactions, maybe more if you passed traffic surveillance cameras on the road, at the ATM machine, grocery-store parking lot, at the job-site parking lot, entrance, hallways, and bathroom, if you use one.

Beginning on July 1, 2002, the four major credit bureaus in the U.S. (Equifax, Transunion, Experien, Inovus) are allowed to release credit-card information, mailing addresses, phone numbers, and other pertinent information contained in your history to anyone who requests it.

You can stop it!

The procedure, as outlined by Lynne Ayala, is complicated and tricky, but reliable: Dial 1-888-567-8688. Once the recorded message begins and prompts you to push a button, push #2 even though option #1 refers to the subject matter of this notice (it will say "e-mail"). Listen carefully, then push #3 because the first part of the recording is an option to stop the release of your information for a two-year period. The third option opts you out of this service forever. The recording will ask for more information. Within a couple of weeks, you should get confirmation in writing that you have opted out of the service.

Do it today!

Pass this on to others because every one of us, individually, has a credit history.

24. Cuban Remittances

The money earned by Mexicans residing in the U.S. and amounts sent to relatives still in Mexico runs in the billions of dollars annually. The same is true of Central Americans in the U.S. sending money home to relatives. In most cases, the remittances outpace or equal the money spent by tourists in those countries, including Mexico. Remittances save U.S. taxpayers money in that less foreign aid is spent on these countries.

What about Cuba?

This is a reverse scenario. Given that Cubans were paid to come to the United States beginning in the 1960s by this government, they number in the millions. About 84 percent of Cubans here are white. Only with the advent of the Mariel boatlift in the late 1980s did some *cubanos negros* begin to arrive. *Cubanos* in the United States also send dollars to *cubanos* on the island, some $700 to $800 million annually. The benefit is primarily among white Cubans, not *cubanos negros*. According to the Central Intelligence Agency, black Cubans are 11 percent of the island's population, 37 percent are white, 1 percent are Chinese, and a whopping 51 percent are mixed black and white.

In 1993, the Cuban government legalized possession of dollars. The result is the enrichment of white Cubans and the continued impoverishment of *cubanos negros* on the island nation.

(See Alberto de la Fuente, *A Nation for All: Race, Inequality, and Politics in Twentieth-Century Cuba*.)

25. *La Migra*

As persons of Mexican ancestry, we hold the dubious honor of having our own dedicated federal police force. The U.S. Border Patrol, *la migra*, is our very own federal cop agency. They are paid to hunt us and process us. We are the reason for their existence and continued prosperity. In 1970, *la migra*'s budget was a mere $70 million. In 1997, *la migra*'s budget reached $1.7 billion, and under the U.S. Patriot Act of 2002, the agency is expected to grow by tripling the number of agents on the payroll. I say "paid to hunt us" because in March 2002, there were 9,094 Border Patrol agents on duty along the four southwestern states of Arizona (1,932), California (2,533), New Mexico (521), and Texas (4,108), according to the U.S. Office of Personnel Management. On the Canadian border at the same time there were only 346 agents on duty! That is 26 times as many *migra* agents on the Mexican border as on the Canadian border! And one of the terrorists involved in the World Trade Center and Pentagon airplane suicide missions of September 11, 2001, entered via the Canadian border. Not one terrorist has ever been apprehended on the Mexican border. There are 260 Border Patrol agents in other states, particularly the Southeast; South Carolina has 50 and Florida has 62, for example.

Another fact as to why I say "paid to hunt us": The U.S.-Mexico border is 2,000 miles long. The U.S.-Canadian border is 5,525 miles long. If you take the number of agents at each border, you'll find a Border Patrol agent every .20 miles of the U.S.-Mexico border. That is a distance close enough to wave and say "Howdy," without adding in the military personnel (400 soldiers) from Joint Task Force Six on duty at the same border from Ft. Bliss in El Paso.

The good news is that under the U.S. Patriot Act and its tripling-of-agents provision, the force will be more evenly distributed between the borders. I doubt it.

The good news is that *la migra* duty is so miserable and hot and dusty and boring that Border Patrol agents are deserting the agency for service in the newly created Air Marshal Corps. Why? The Air Marshals offer a $20,000 signing bonus and greater salary to fly in air-conditioned comfort and sit in padded seats, pretending to be a normal passenger.

26. The Book of Hispanic Firsts

A book of *Hispanic Firsts* has been written. Nicolás Kanellos did that in 1997 for Visible Ink Press, a division of Gale Research. It is a splendid book that covers 500 years of achievement, one that no home library should be without. Similarly, Elizabeth "Betita" Martínez compiled the *500 Years of Chicano History* via photographs and commentary.

Basic research is imperative. It builds a foundation. No house can stand too long without a foundation.

27. *La mera, mera* Chabela

I am writing about Isabel de Castilla (1451–1504), also known as the "Crusading Warrior Queen." She married Fenando de Aragón in 1469. With the two houses, Castilla and Aragón, united in marriage and finances, she moved rapidly to expel the Islamic Moors. She launched crusade after crusade. She also sought the expulsion of the Jews from her area of influence. Against the heretical Christians, she imposed the deadly Inquisition. Of course, she also was the financial patron behind the various voyages of Cristóbal Colón.

Why is she in this book?

If *La Chabela* had not married Fernando, and as Queen of Spain, funded Colón, launched crusades to expel the Moors and remove the Jews, imposed the Inquisition before she died, and sent the colonizers to the New World, we would not be here reading this book.

28. Secession or Incorporation?

The quest for political power by Chicanos and other Latinos continues unabated. The opposition to Latino political power also continues unabated. Every decade of struggle by Latinos in the electoral arena has been met with ingenious counterstrategies, such as the poll tax, White Primary, literacy tests, citizenship and residency requirements, run-off elections, at-large districts, even delayed implementation of the 1965 Voting Rights Act until 1975. Gerrymandering remains a favorite ploy of incumbents intent on keeping Latinos out of public office.

The least-tried Latino strategy is secession or incorporation. At the beginning of this century, residents in sprawling Los Angeles began pushing for breaking up the city into smaller cities. They did not call this secession. They called this incorporation.

Raza should support these efforts. The two rules of thumb for getting more Latino political power at this juncture· are: smaller jurisdictions and a greater number of seats on governing bodies, especially those elected from single-member districts.

La Raza Unida Party (LRUP) in Los Angeles sought incorporation of East Los Angeles in the 1970s. Such a move had been tried before in 1961 and 1963 by others. LRUP began a campaign in 1974 to incorporate East Los Angeles and obtained ballot status for the measure. LRUP simultaneously recruited and placed in nomination five candidates for the governing city council of East Los Angeles in the event the voters approved the measure. The LRUP candidates were George García, Celia Rodríguez, Raúl Ruiz, Arturo Sánchez, and Daniel Zapata. They won, but the measure lost by a mere 1,941 votes. Raúl Ruiz, the mayor without a city, was the top vote-getter-with 2,240. The other RUP candidates placed seventh through fourteenth.

We are a highly urbanized community across the country. It is to our advantage to break up governing units to smaller size, particularly school districts and cities.

If at first you don't succeed, try, try again.

29. Community Needs and Needs Assessments

First, you do an assessment of needs to determine the obvious: What are the needs in the community? Then comes the hard part: once identified, meeting the needs of the community.

Several Mexican groups in Dallas, eleven immigrant groups to be exact, joined with other Latino organizations in 2000 to formulate a needs-assessment instrument and conduct survey research. Once the study was concluded, the group designed a strategy to meet the needs identified. The first thing the group has done is to incorporate the various groups into an umbrella agency: the Centro Communitario Mexicano. Next, they identified resources to meet needs and designed a website: www.dallasinternational.com/CentroCommunitarioMexicano/CCN.htm.

Now, anyone with a need can find the path to gratification on the website—for example, the Guide to Low Cost Medical Services (*en español*), more than 100 classes in North Texas for ESL (English as a Second Language), and links to major community resources. The group inaugurated a Saturday school in October 2002, to teach Spanish and Latino culture to younger children.

See, ideas never die, they just dance themselves from one decade to the next.

30. The Blame Game, Part II

"Voodoo economics" was the charge leveled by Republicans against Democrats in the 1996 presidential election on the use of statistics to make a case for continued prosperity under Clinton. The "black box" was the euphemism used by candidate Bush against candidate Gore in the 2000 presidential election to dismiss the years of economic prosperity under the Clinton-Gore administrations. Then came the corporate scandals of the twenty-first century involving unbelievable and insatiable greed on the part of various chief executive officers and other top corporate officials. These executives cooked the books or had them cooked by willing and compliant underlings.

This is not news. We have had political and corporate graft, corruption, theft, fraud, and scandal, since time immemorial. How did Bush get to be President? It is: dog eat dog, King of the Mountain, bigger is better, and more is never enough. It's a capitalist system, you say? The U.S. Supreme Court ruled, you say?

But shouldn't we expect more from educational leaders? Education should not be about making money or turning a profit, or should it? The contracts to privatize education, such as with the Edison School Project, and the transfer of millions more tax dollars to the ill-prepared charter schools are scandals in the making.

But what about the drop-out rates? Do the school officials cook the books? Yes, they do!

First of all, individual states use different methods to quantify who is in school and who drops out. The true measure is a quantifying model that begins with entering class in the first grade and ends with awarding a diploma upon completion of the twelfth grade. No state employs that method. Each one has arguments galore as to why not: students move, students transfer, students fail, students die, students don't enroll in a timely manner, students change names, and some students are migrants, including military brats.

The federal government counts drop-outs only among those who start the ninth grade and finish the twelfth grade in the various states. Some states, however, start their count at the earlier grade level of sixth or seventh grades. Starting the drop-out counting in earlier grades lowers the overall drop-out rate because most states have a mandatory school-attendance requirement up to age 16 or 17, which is past junior high school age.

According to the National Center for Education Statistics, the worst offenders with severe drop-out problems for 1999–2000, the most recent figures available for the largest twenty school districts in the nation are: Chicago with a 15.8 percent push-out rate, Philadelphia with 11.5 percent push-outs, Houston with 11.2 percent push-outs, Baltimore City with a 10.5 percent rate, Milwaukee with 10.4 percent, New Orleans with 9.9 percent, San Antonio with 9.6 percent rate, Albuquerque with an 8.8 percent push-out rate, and Fort Worth with a 9 percent rate of drop-outs. These are annual rates! In other words, multiply the rate by four to get the total rate for the high school years.

Look at a map. Where are these school districts located? Figure out which kids are being pushed out of school and by whom. Are these school districts Anglo-dominated or Latino-led?

(California, Florida, and New York did not report their data. If they did, it would be worse than some others above.)

31. Taped Interviews: Another Form of Writing

I started working on an interview project in 1994. At first, I was unsure of the direction to take in terms of interview subjects. I knew I wanted to establish a large collection of interviews to form a conspicuous and notable body of knowledge, but of whom? I was torn between two groups of significant public figures. *Músicos* and *políticos*. I started with *músicos* and ended with *políticos*. The political figures were easier to find, more numerous, and the subject matter, leadership, was of greater interest to me than music. I am, after all, a lifelong student of politics.

The project ended, for the time being, in early 2002. All research has to end in order to write; otherwise, it goes on and on and on without a written product. You have to know when to stop. Sometimes ongoing research becomes the excuse for not writing.

I completed and stopped at 157 interviews of public figures, all Texas-based persons of Mexican ancestry, except for three. The transcribed interviews and videotape(s) of each are found in the Special Collections Department of the General Libraries of the University of Texas at Arlington. Currently, these interviews are being digitized for placement on the World Wide Web at http://libraries.uta.edu/tejanovoices/.

This collection is the largest of its kind in the nation.

Maybe tomorrow someone will begin work on establishing a Center for Chicano Biography.

32. Jane Long, the Mother of Texas?

White male-written history claims Jane Long to be the Mother of Texas. White people are this way. When they arrive, they benchmark that date as THE discovery and BEGINNING of time. *¡Están locos!*

The Mothers of Texas were the hundreds of thousands of Indian women already in Texas possible as early as 11,000 years ago.

The Mothers of Texas were the eight Spanish women who first came to Texas in the 1716 with the Diego Ramón expedition: Ana María Longoria, Antonia de la Cerda, Antonia Vidales, María Antonia Ximénez, Ana María Ximénez de Valdez, Juana de San Miguel, Josefa Sánchez, and Ana Guerra. Guerra was the only single woman, a *señorita*.

In 1779, three of the top ten cattle owners in the present-day San Antonio area were women: María Ana Curbelo, Leonor Delgado, and María del Carmen Calvillo. The latter was the owner of Rancho de las Cabras, the largest goat-and-cattle ranch in the area of today's Wilson County, Texas. She was born in Bexar (San Antonio) on July 9, 1756, and died on January 15, 1856. She lived to be almost 100 years old.

The Mothers of Texas were the Mexican women who lived through the Texas revolt against Spain, against Mexico, against *gringos,* and the Confederacy—not Jane Long, who had a baby girl in

1821 at Bolivar, near Galveston Island.

(See Donald E. Chipman and Harriett Denise Joseph, *Notable Men and Women of Spanish Texas* [Austin: University of Texas, 1999], pp. 250–277.)

33. Mariano Medina, Father of Nebraska or Montana?

Mariano Medina was born in Taos, New Mexico, in 1812. His father was Antonio Medina from Spain, and his mother was María Hurtado from New Mexico. Perhaps Mariano was the first *mestizo* to venture into Nebraska and Montana. By 1844, Medina had been a trapper in Utah's Snake River, Montana's Missouri River and Nebraska. He acquired a Shoshoni or Flathead Indian woman as a wife with the name of Tacanecy or Kansey. They had a son named Antonio Medina, like his grandfather; for sure, he was the first Chicano to be born in Montana. In 1856, Mariano was operating a ferry across the Sweetwater River, Wyoming. By 1857, Mariano was back in Utah and a daughter, Marcelina, was born there. In Utah, Medina did battle with U.S. troops against the Mormons until 1860, when he relocated to Miraval (Miraville in Colorado records) near the Denver area. Miraval, Colorado, was founded by José de Mirabal, born in 1812 in Mexico and resettled in the Rocky Mountain area by 1858. Industrious and visionary, Medina built a ferry and bridge on his land across the Big Thompson River near Miraval. The bridge was called Mariano's Crossing, and later it became known as Marianne's Crossing and Marianna's Town. He charged from a dollar to fifty cents to cross via the bridge or his ferry. According to some, he never charged any Mexican to cross.

As business increased, Mariano added a saloon/trading post, a stable and corral, lodging quarters, and a cemetery. The buildings all faced an open area on three sides, just like a *plaza*. By 1874, Mariano was head of the potato cooperative in the area that supplied food and livestock to Denver residents. The Medina family grew with more children, Martín and Rosita.

When his wife died in 1874, Mariano married an Anglo woman, Susan Carter Howard, and she gave him another son, Rafaelito. Mariano Medina died on June 28, 1878. *The Denver Daily Times* carried the notice on page one. *The Fort Collins Courier*, on July 18, 1878, also carried the obituary, but changed his name to Mariano Modena.

In 1956, what remained of Medina's complex on the *plaza* was torn down. The bridge was relocated at least twice. The remains in the Medina cemetery were removed to Namaqua Park in 1959. And Zethyl Gates, a librarian in Loveland, Colorado, aware of Mariano Medina's legacy to the Rocky Mountain area stretching from New Mexico to Colorado, Nebraska, Wyoming, Montana, and Utah, researched and wrote his biography.

We have to write our own stories or wait for someone else to take an interest and write them for us.

(See *Mariano Medina: Colorado Mountain Man* [Boulder: Johnson Publishing Company, 1981].)

34. *Reales* or Dollars or Pieces of Eight?

As a child, I heard older Spanish-speaking family members refer to *dos reales* as the price for some goods or commodities. To me, in my emerging English-speaking world, that was 25 cents or a quarter. A half-dollar or a 50-cent piece was *cuatro reales*. I always thought then that the Spanish equivalent for value of coins was too complicated. You had to do math and figure times tables in your head. I thought then, "Why is it that everything in English is simpler and better? Why is it so complicated and difficult in Spanish?" The dollar was better than the *peso duro*. I was learning to favor English over Spanish, the Anglo over the Mexican. I was learning to hate my culture and myself in the process.

In my college years, I finally learned from books on U.S., Spanish, and Mexican history that the Continental Congress under the Articles of Confederation for the United States mandated the use of the pieces of eight as standard currency, as did the English pirates for prior decades. I learned that the *peso duro en plata* was divided into eight pieces by the Spanish and similarly by the Mexicans. And every country in Central and South American and the Caribbean followed the practice of cutting the *peso duro en plata* into eight pieces for trading in lesser value than a dollar, *un peso de ocho reales*. In other words, eight pieces equal in size and weighing *un peso duro de plata*, one hard complete silver coin, made a dollar.

Then it clicked, of course, that if there are eight pieces total to a coin then *dos reales* has to be a quarter of a coin and *ocho reales* is half of that coin, half a dollar, half of a *peso duro*. The *peso duro de plata* was the forerunner of the dollar and our current U.S. system of coin value. When this clicked for me, I then thought, "We invented the system of currency." I felt good about my discovery. I felt good about the ownership of this part of my heritage.

35. Manifest Destiny Included Cuba?

While the United States was engaged in the war against Mexico to steal as much as possible of its northern border (the present U.S. Southwest), members of the Club de la Havana, a cabal of Cuba's wealthiest moguls, were meeting. Their plan was to offer to reimburse the U.S. up to $100 million dollars if the U.S. would purchase Cuba from Spain. President James Polk wanted to finish with Mexico before he took up Cuba. After the war against Mexico and signing of the treaty, returning U.S. troops were being offered mercenary duty in Cuba at good pay by the Cuban supporters of the Havana Club plan, with a new twist: annex Cuba to the United States. On May 30, 1848, President Polk discussed the plan with his cabinet, but no action was taken. On June 9, 1848, when the Mexican Congress approved the peace treaty with the United States, Polk ordered his Secretary of State to offer Spain $100 million for Cuba. Almost within a month's time, on July 23, 1848, Narciso López, leader of the anti-Spanish insurrectionists in Cuba, arrived in Bristol, Rhode Island, seeking political asylum. He quickly set about organizing a corps of *filibusteros* in the U.S. He relocated to New Orleans and found more public support and money for his campaign to invade Cuba. He raised a small army and hired ships, the *Georgiana, Susan Loud,* and the *Creole* to transport his men to Contoy Island off the coast of Yucatan, Mexico. From there, he invaded Cuba on May 19, 1850. He failed and fled back to the safety of the United States, where he was charged with violating the Neutrality Act of 1818, but he was never tried. He organized another invasion on August 12, 1851, and failed again. He met his death on September 1, 1851.

In 1898, another Cuban, José Martí, assisted by U.S. troops, did succeed in rallying the forces to topple the Spanish's four-hundred-year rule over Cuba. Ironically, the same flag, the one star inside the white triangle, with red-and-blue bars, was used by Narciso López, José Martí, and Fidel Castro's Republic of Cuba to fly over the island nation.

Why is one man a hero and the other a traitor? Is it that losers are the bad guys and winners are the good guys? Is it that U.S. interests in the long run determine who should be the winner and loser in history? Was Lorenzo De Zavala of Mexico in the Texas Revolt of the 1830s the role model for Narciso López?

(See Tom Chaffin, *Fatal Glory: Narciso López and the First Clandestine U.S. War against Cuba* [Charlottesville: University of Virginia, 1996].)

36. Class-Action Lawsuits

Lawyers for Raza car buyers in Illinois filed a suit, then withdrew the case, against the Ford Motor Credit Company for discrimination. The plaintiffs alleged Ford Credit urged their sales representatives to increase the credit rate on car loans for Hispanics, as opposed to other buyers. The plaintiffs quit the case because a Chicago federal judge refused to certify them as class representatives for a national civil action. The plaintiffs alleged this rate increase *movida* was going on nationally. Obtaining the class-action go-ahead would have meant they could get national data from Ford Credit instead of proving their allegations on a case-by-case basis for each plaintiff. Class-action status also means more money for the lawyers in fees and more responsibility to clients spread across the country.

In the case of Raza farmers in Fresno, California, they were able to obtain class-action status in their lawsuit against the U.S. Department of Agriculture's Farmer's Home Administration for loan denials and poor loan assistance counseling to small Raza farmers. They got certified as a class and promptly settled their case for $1.2 billion dollars. Not bad, *¿qué no?* Ask Gloria Palacios Morales at 409-222-2222 how she put the whole effort together.

37. Political Espionage

This is not how to get and keep a job. This behavior is blatantly illegal, grossly unethical, and not to be condoned. I am raving about the antics of political espionage by Juanita Yvette Lozano. By Juanita's own admission in federal court proceedings, she is a lifelong Democrat. Yet, she took a job with George Dubya's media campaign consultant, Maverick Media in Austin, Texas, during the 2000 presidential campaign. Juanita had been a babysitter for Mark McKinnon for years. Mark McKinnon also worked at Maverick Media and got her the job.

A task assigned to Maverick Media was the preparation of George Dubya for the debates with Al Gore. While on the job, Juanita stole a briefing book, a practice videotape, and other related papers from the Maverick Media office, put them in a package and mailed them in September 2000, to U.S. Representative Tom Downey (D-NY), who was advising Al Gore in preparation for the first presidential debate. An alarmed Downey turned the stuff over to the FBI. He was not going to be set up by some Republican trick like this. Nixon Republicans were notorious for dirty tricks.

The FBI checked with the U.S. Postal Service, which in turn checked with its postal branch in downtown Austin and asked for the videotape of counter transactions for the postmark day. The replay of the videotape for that day revealed who mailed the package. The FBI had their woman on videotape. Maverick Media confirmed it was their material and, more importantly, that Juanita Lozano was their employee.

When confronted, Juanita said she was returning some mail-order dress slacks her boss had ordered from The Gap. "Not true," said the boss. Juanita then said she was just mailing stuff for the office and had no idea who Representative Downey was. Not true. Her home computer revealed that she had Internet searches for Mr. Downey's home address. The FBI had gone into her home with a search warrant. She also lied under oath to the federal grand jury investigating the matter.

Almost a year later, Juanita Lozano finally pled guilty to mail fraud and perjury and was sentenced on August 31, 2001. Federal

District Judge Sam Sparks sentenced her to a year in prison, a $3,200 fine and costs. She will also have a three-year post-release probationary period during which she cannot regain her right to vote.

Don't get caught on candid camera. Surveillance cameras are everywhere. Look for them. Don't you use and have stuff on your computer, particularly at work, that you don't want anyone else to see. You do not erase work in a hard drive just by pressing delete. It is there until professionally removed. Don't lie to investigators, much less while under oath before a grand jury. Just don't do illegal things! And, don't betray the people who help you with a job!

38. Who Is on Welfare?

It seems that daily someone maligns Raza as undeserving welfare recipients. I was on the Bill O'Reilly show, "The Pulse," a national summer program on Fox News, and he made the assertion that "29 percent of all illegal aliens from Mexico are on welfare." Boy, did I get hot!

Let me tell you about who is on welfare.

The single largest welfare program is Social Security. The overwhelming number of persons on Social Security Insurance and its companion programs, such as Medicaid, Medicare, College Benefits for Dependents, widow's benefits, for example, are white. They will continue to be white in the near future, another three decades, until about 2035—until the last widow and dependent child of the last one of the Baby Boom generation dies. The ones who collect least from Social Security are Raza. We are the ones paying in to support white welfare.

The next largest welfare program is agricultural subsidies. According to the last agricultural census taken in 1997, there were 1,911,859 farms in the United States. A total of 685,029 of these farms were on agricultural subsidy, e.g. welfare for farmers. Texas is the largest farm state in the nation in number of farms. Texas has 41,537 farmers on government subsidy; 21 percent of all Texan farmers are on the take, out of 194,301 farms.

The top ten states receiving agricultural government subsidies were in 1997:

- North Dakota with 79 percent of its farmers, 24,185 of them on welfare.
- Iowa with 75 percent of its farmers, 67,795 of them on welfare.
- South Dakota with 70 percent of its farmers, 22,037 of them on welfare.
- Nebraska with 69 percent of its farmers, 35,367 of them on welfare.
- Illinois with 65 percent of its farmers, 47,711 of them on welfare.
- Kansas with 65 percent of its farmers, 39,735 of them on welfare.
- Minnesota with 64 percent of its farmers, 46,977 of them on welfare.
- Wisconsin with 56 percent of its farmers, 36,946 of them on welfare.
- Indiana with 52 percent of its farmers, 30,295 of them on welfare.
- Montana with 50 percent of its farmers, 12,008 of them on welfare.

Raza, we are in the wrong business! Raza needs to farm and get to growing crops on the subsidy list: corn, barley, sorghum, oats, wheat, rice, and upland cotton, for example. Between 1985 and 1994, the U.S. government doled out $108.9 billion in welfare checks to farmers growing these crops. Then, there are at least two other welfare programs for farmers: a soil conservation program to keep land out of production and a subsidy not to plant certain crops. Neat, huh? They get paid not to farm and not to plant; plus, they get paid for certain crops they do plant. And they get paid this by the county; some farms are in more than one county. And this does not count money paid for flooding or other disaster relief.

In Uvalde County, Texas, the Chicano tradition dating to the days of the *movimiento* of maintaining a community newspaper are being upheld by Alfredo Santos. He publishes *La Voz de Uvalde County*. In the May 15, 2002, issue, he listed by name, location, and dollar amount, the 103 *gringo* farmers on welfare in the county. These are the biggies. There were 427 welfare recipients in Uvalde County, Texas, on agricultural subsidy from 1996 to 2001, and they took in an astounding sum of our tax dollars: $32,822,371! This is one group of *gringo* farmers in one county! The average payment was $76,390. The biggest welfare queen in Uvalde County was the Cole Farms & Ranch; she pulled down $753,639.79 in welfare dollars from our tax coffers!

You did read the figure above for the nation from 1982 to 1994: $108.9 billion!

A last kick in the pants: These farmers do not live on the farm usually; they are city slickers. The welfare checks mailed by the U.S. government go to city addresses in large urban centers.

Keep exposing the welfare queens of the twenty-first century and of all past centuries: the *gringo* farmer!

(Contact Alfredo288@aol.com and call 830-278-7183 for subscription service, or fax 830-278-8678 and letters to Box 5334, Uvalde, TX 78802.)

39. Education Is Big Business

Higher education is big business. The budgets are huge. Public education, pre-K to twelfth grade, in most cities across the nation is just as big, if not bigger. In fact, the payroll of the local school district(s), colleges, universities, and technical schools usually place them way up there on the list of large employers. Check out your district's payroll and number of employees. Look at the budget. This is public information.

40. Making Babies

Demographers supply the data that academics, policy-makers, journalists, and political pundits, to name a few, utilize to make projections about the population make-up of the future. The spin doctors among these professionals then use select portions of the statistics produced by the demographers to create scenarios that promote sensationalism, mass hysteria, immigrant bashing, and fear.

Population projections are a complex matter, but basically, you start with the reported figure of the last census. Then, for the year following, demographers count the numbers of live births, subtract the deaths, subtract persons leaving, and add persons entering a given locale, such as a state or nation, but it could be a city or county. The total of that math is the population growth for that year, compared to the previous year. With several of these annual estimates, a demographer begins to see a rate of growth. At one end of the extreme, a demographer can find zero growth or, at the other end, a dramatic rate of growth, say 10-percent annual rate of growth. Most states have an official demographer charged with the duty to analyze decennial population data and make projections so that the legislators and other policy-makers can with some accuracy and confidence make plans for the future needs of that population—say schools, hospitals, roads, airports, colleges, cemeteries, job creation, housing starts, jails and prisons, and recreational areas. Most states report an annual growth; however, the eastern seaboard states and some central states have been losing population. Therefore, they have lost congressional seats that are apportioned among the states based on population.

Texas has an official demographer, Steve Murdock, based at Texas A&M University, College Station, Texas. He heads up the State Data Center (TXSDC). The TXSDC number is 979-845-5115 or texassdc@txsdcsun.tamu.edu.

Dr. Murdock has caused alarm in Texas among Anglos, worry among blacks, and joy among Raza because he projected as early as the mid-1990s that the Raza population would become the majority of the state's population in 2015, assuming a continued 1-percent rate of growth. After the 2000 census data came out, he revised his estimates and projected an earlier date. In other words, we are growing faster than a 1-percent rate. We are serious about making babies. We practice diligently . . . often.

The TXSDC breaks out the data by county, metropolitan area, race, ethnicity, gender, age, and every conceivable way you can imagine. The website posts the presentations he makes across the state and nation. Each presentation is a gem of information.

Regardless of the Murdock calendar date and its accuracy, the fact that the Raza will become the majority is inevitable. This is the important fact.

Are you ready for this?

Do you have a plan for this eventuality?

Are you ready to lead?

Have you a strategy between now and then?

41. Chicano Studies

Most *veteranos* and *veteranas* of the Chicano Movement will correctly peg the impetus for Chicano Studies to the *Plan de Santa Bárbara,* developed by young people involved with the *movimiento* back when. When exactly the call extended to high schools is unclear, but it did. Few heeded the call, unlike Irene Hernández teaching in the Denver Public Schools. She wrote a grant proposal and got funding with which to write a curriculum on the Raza Unida Party, which she called "El Alma de la Raza Series."

When I was in Denver once, she gave me a copy and asked for my critique of the various curriculum units. I promised to comment, but never did. Later, when I did finish reading the 468-plus pages, I found it to be excellent. I wish every Chicanita and Chicanito in the country could have access to this type of curriculum.

Someday.

In the meantime, it is written and being used in one place. It is a start, a big start. It is written.

42. A-Rod?

How do you go from Alejandro "Alex" Rodríguez to A-Rod? Only in *gringolandia*, I guess. Alex is with the Texas Rangers baseball team and is Puerto Rican, a cultural cousin of Chicanos. He is the highest-paid athlete in baseball at the moment. The rich guy owner of the team, Tom Hicks, does not fraternize with the players, but he does with A-Rod. They dine. They play golf. They visit over coffee. They chat on the telephone. He should. A-Rod cost him hundreds of millions of dollars to sign. And Tom Hicks does because A-Rod delivers.

Toward the end of the season and with the strike looming, Alex hit multiple home runs in single games, in consecutive games, time and again. He hit 40-plus home runs this season. He has gone error-less in more than 50 games. He led the American League in runs batted in (RBIs). He was a near miss for the third time at being named the Most Valuable Player. He lost that coveted title in 1998, 2000, and 2002, coming in second.

Alex earned $25 million dollars this year for playing baseball, not counting endorsements, commercials, speaking fees, and other income.

But, the players in the sport wanted to strike on August 30, 2002. Had the strike happened, A-Rod would have lost $98,360 per day of the strike!

The strike was postponed several times because of break-throughs in the negotiations. Would Alex have gone on strike? Would Alex have told Hicks, "I'm on strike?" You bet! Without mincing words or counting his dollars, A-Rod declared to the media weeks before the strike deadline, "My allegiance in this matter is to the Players' Association first." He even offered to return "30 to 40 percent" of his salary, if it would help the game. That is about $64 million of his 10-year $252-million contract.

End of story and lesson. This is solidarity!

You stand with those you share a community of interest with. Being *Raza* is being a member of one community of interest.

43. I Want to Be a Trustee!

When Iris Zamudio sought election to the Alamo Community College District (ACCD) board, she had no clue what she was get-ting into, or so she said. The annual budget for ACCD was $150 mil-lion in 2001–2002.

Iris Zamudio was an eleventh-hour candidate filing at the last minute on prompting by her buddy since high school, Eddie Metz. She is not a new kid on the block. Zamudio had done a stint as trustee for the Somerset Independent School Disrict, a rural commu-nity area south of San Antonio. Within a week of filing, she was being treated to a $20-plus dinner at Ruth's Chris Steak House by five "players" of ACCD politics and business deals. Over the course of dinner, Zamudio was assured by the "players" that she would have plenty of money for her campaign. They asked her to estimate her campaign budget. They also asked her to support an architectur-al contract, a land buy, and a bond issue. She balked. They balked two weeks later and withdrew their support for her candidacy. She withdrew from the May 4, 2002, race.

It was not over for Zamudio by simply withdrawing from the race. The press and other interests began digging into the restaurant affair because the "players" were Raúl Prado, a former city council-man and state representative candidate; Bobby Pérez, a city council-man and ACCD attorney; Robert Ramsay, the ACCD chancellor; Mark Sánchez, another ACCD lawyer; and Robert "Tinker" Garza, the former ACCD chair of the board. These men were not supposed to be there, discussing this topic, offering money in exchange for votes, and otherwise fixing deals for architects, land, and bonds. They said they were not there or were there but did not discuss such things as the $1.2-million contract for architect Louis Cruz.

It is great to have Raza in high public office, particularly in institutions of higher education. It is terrible that some Raza, like other public officials, become corrupt players of the game. I guess, with barrels of electoral success, come a few rotten apples.

(See lhood@express-news.net.)

44. Give Ourselves Awards

Don't wait for someone else to give you an award for distinction or meritorious service. Create an organization and honor our own. The Hispanic Women's Network of Texas, local chapter in Dallas, has started a Living Legend Award to honor a Latina Living Legend. How is that for a title of an award?

In Los Angeles, years back during the Chicano Movement, our actors and actresses got together and formed NOSOTROS and began giving themselves awards. They did not want to wait on the Academy Awards or the Tonys or the Golden Globes or the Grammies or the Emmies or whatever . . .

David Cruz received the 2002 Golden Eagle Award from NOSOTROS in late July. Cruz, a Chicano from the West Side of San Antonio, joins an impressive roster of recipients: Ricardo Montalbán, Jennifer López, Antonio Banderas, and José José, for example. Cruz began his entertainment career in 1972 in San Antonio, Texas, with station KWEX *en español.* Then, he moved to other stations in the same city: KSAT and KMOL, in English, before going to San Francisco. He now anchors the news in Los Angeles.

Yes, news anchors are entertainers. Just what did you think they were?

45. HANDS? Hands On!

HANDS, an acronym for Hispanic/Latino Action Network and

Leadership Development Summit, is a project of the National Latino Council on Alcohol and Tobacco Prevention (LCAT). The organization wants to stop young Latinos from smoking. Good idea. If we live longer, we may enjoy full political, economic, social, and psychological power in the United States. Tobacco and alcohol kill you.

Among Latinas in grades 9 through 12, in 1999 one in three smoked cigarettes. Ugh. They are not even kissable!

HANDS met in February 2002, and had 350 persons in attendance. Fifty-four Latinos signed up to be soldiers in the combat against tobacco use in their hometowns. The battles are many and the war is deadly. Money is a big weapon used against us. For example, the tobacco lobby since 1999, just four of the biggest companies, spent $44 million lobbying Congress. From January 2001 to April 2002, the tobacco industry contributed $4.3 million in soft money and PAC contributions to federal candidates, political parties, and political committees.

But we have the people! Power to the people! We are the future.

(See USDHHS, *Women and Smoking: A Report of the Surgeon General, 2001*. Visit www.nlcatp.org or e-mail them at lcat@nlcatp.org or call to get on the mailing list for their newsletter at 202-265-8054.)

46. CEO and President

Know that by 2005, one in every five women in the United States will be a Latina.

One of them is Irene Ibarra, CEO and president of O&I, Inc., a million-dollar business based in Whittier, California. It was not easy to get to this level, but Irene did it. And she did it the hard, hard way. Read on about this amazing Chicana from Santa Ana, California . . .

At age 16, she was pregnant. She was thrown out of her house. At 18, her brother (15 years old) died of a brain aneurysm. By age 20, she had three babies. That same year, another brother was killed in a drive-by shooting. Her husband beat her regularly. Once he broke three of her ribs and nose, cut her lips, and injured her internal organs to the point of hemorrhaging. He also gave her syphilis.

When she had enough, she left him and began building herself, empowering herself, reconditioning and reprogramming herself. She enrolled in classes at a junior college. She was hired by the city of Santa Ana at $12,000 a year. She became aware of government contracts. She became amazed at the dollar value of these contracts and vowed to learn the bidding process. She wanted some of that action. Teaming up with another Latina, they helped each other prepare their bid proposals to the Metropolitan Transportation Authority. They were awarded two contracts, and that was the beginning of her million-dollar empire.

What advice does she offer? "Well, life isn't fair, and you make your own breaks. Don't dwell on the negative or the past. By being proactive, you can make things happen."

(See Yasmín Davids-Garrido, *Empowering Latinas: Breaking Boundaries, Freeing Lives.* [Granite Bay, California: Penmarin Books, 2001, p. 206], or www.penmarin.com or www.EmpoweringLatinas.com.)

47. Vilma Martínez

Vilma Martínez was born in San Antonio, Texas. When it came time to graduate from high school, she began learning the art of argument because her father opposed her attending college. At the University of Texas, she did exceptionally well in her academic subjects and was accepted into law school at UT and at Columbia. She chose Columbia. She passed the New York and California bar exams, two of the toughest in the nation. Her first law job was with the National Association for the Advancement of Colored People's (NAACP) Legal Defense Fund. When the Mexican American Legal Defense and Educational Fund (MALDEF) was started in 1968, she served on the board of directors. In 1973, she became the head of MALDEF and remained until 1982. Under her tutelage, MALDEF's budget went from $800,000 to $2.6 million. Vilma knows the Eastern foundation world. She served on the MALDEF board again in 1992. She also served on the Board of Regents for the University of California System (1976–1990) and was the chair of that body from 1984 to 1986.

I forgot to mention that during this time, she gave birth to two boys, Carlos and Ricardo.

Not bad for a working mom now in private practice in Los Angeles.

(See "Vilma Martínez: Portrait of a Fighter," *Equal Opportunity Forum* [March, 1982]; Corinn Codye's *Vilma Martínez* [Austin: Steck-Vaughn Company, 1991]; Katrina M. Dewey's "Profile: Vilma S. Martínez, Partner, Munger, Tolles & Olsen," *Los Angeles Daily Journal* [January 9, 1992]; Sam Enríquez, "Vilma Martínez: *Regente con misión importante*/UC Policy-maker With a Mission: Vilma Martínez," *Los Angeles Times* [February 9, 1987]; Al Carlos Hernández, "*Vilma Martínez, una chicana ejemplar,*" *Nuestro* [August/September, 1981]; Dean Johnson, "Chair of the Board," *Nuestro* [September, 1985]; and Argentina Palacios, *Standing Tall: The Stories of Ten Hispanic Americans* [New York: Scholastic Inc., 1994].)

48. *El primo prieto: Samuel Betances*

The dude looks and talks like an African American from Chicago until he speaks *español y entonces es puro boricua.*

Dr. Betances is one of the top ten consultants of the Latino world. He earns thousands each year from speeches, consultant services, and his book sales. His motivational speeches are unforgettable. He is successful because he is imbued in *cultura, nuestra cultura.* His messages are inspirational and rooted in our *dichos* and *refranes.*

U.S. corporations pay him handsomely to explain the Latino culture to them. Schools pay him thousands to speak to students. They buy his books by the hundreds. And, when he is not on the road, he makes time to teach sociology to university students in Chicago.

Try one of his books: *Ten Steps to the Head of the Class: A Challenge to Students* (Chicago: New Century Forum Inc., 1998.)

49. Action Speaks Louder Than Words

When Jimmy Carter became President, he tapped Leonel Castillo, then comptroller of the City of Houston, to head the Immigration and Naturalization Service (INS), aka *la migra.* Can you imagine, a son of Mexicans leading the agency that hunts other Mexicans? Had he stayed on as comptroller, Castillo may have even been elected mayor of Houston in a subsequent election. Regardless, he went to D.C. and killed his political career.

Among other things he did as INS chief, he became the cheerleader for immigration reform. All of us, and I mean all of us, except Leonel, who was paid to do his job, opposed any restrictive and hurtful immigration proposal. Together, all the major national Chicano organizations—national programs, such as the Mexican American Legal Defense and Educational Fund and Project SER, and even the Socialist Worker's Party— joined the Raza Unida Party and successfully opposed every initiative. Finally, our loose-knit coalition lost on the 1986 Immigration Reform and Control Act (IRCA), but negotiated meaningful reform in the terms of amnesty, identification cards, and exemptions for agricultural workers and family unification.

Over the years and subsequent presidential administrations, immigration reform is always a legislative agenda because there are people in the United States who believe there are too many Mexicans in the country. Some business and agricultural interests feel they don't have enough Mexicans available for cheap labor. Other business sectors also want immigrants of any nationality if they can perform nursing duties and provide medical services, create computer programs, have engineering competencies, and other specialized services. We have won some battles and lost some. A major victory was in creating a new visa, H-1C, for special labor needs, such as nurses.

Another more recent victory was passage of the Legal Immigration and Family Equity Act of 2000 that opened a path through which an illegal immigrant could become a legal resident without leaving the United States. The estimate is that some 640,000 persons may be eligible. One provision under this act is the marriage paragraph. If an illegal person marries a U.S. citizen or legal immigrant, she or he can apply for protection under the act—if accepted and the proper paperwork is filed together with payment of an application fee of $225 and a $1,000 fine for entering the country illegally.

There were two problems with the process: (1) The April 30 deadline in 2001 was too short, and (2) applications for marriage licenses surged across the country. President Bush declined to extend the deadline by executive order, claiming no authority because it was a legislative initiative. Congress ran out of time and voted to extend the deadline. Then, the INS began beefing up the investigative activity to expose sham marriages. The penalty for marriage fraud is up to ten years in prison and a $260,000 fine.

At least we are learning how to create exemptions and special categories of laborers, just like the agricultural and business interests do.

50. Irma Mireles

In January 1977, Irma Mireles ran for a spot on the San Antonio River Authority (SARA), a multicounty water district. She ran as a candidate of the Raza Unida Party although this was a nonpartisan race. With a campaign war chest of about $98, she won the race. Irma beat an old, white male incumbent and became the first Chicana to win a countywide race in Bexar County, Texas (San Antonio). During her six-year term, she encountered multiple problems with her aging, white male colleagues on the SARA board and the executive director. But she hung in there and made history in more ways than one. She and her sidekick Anna Rojas made every meeting despite the fact that Irma does not own a car or drive. Anna does.

Later, Irma got burned out as the Raza Unida Party faded into oblivion. By then, she had a son, Gerardo, and both took off in April 1990, to find more fame and fortune in Alaska. Irma and her son braved the cold, snow, rain, wind, darkness, and loneliness for six long years in Juneau. Irma is a devout Catholic and activist Chicana. At church, she could not find La Virgen de Guadalupe, and old-timers in the parish told her they recalled a picture of the Mexican lady hanging in the church. She interrogated Bishop Kenney about the Virgen. He feigned ignorance. Soon, a new bishop was assigned, Michael Warfel, and he allowed Irma to search the church property for La Virgen. After extensive and exhausting rummaging in nooks and crannies and closets and attics, Irma found her in the basement of the cathedral. She dusted her off and hung her in a prominent display in the cathedral. Word spread and Raza came from all over Alaska to the cathedral to pay homage to La Virgen and to light candles. The Raza attendance at Mass doubled and then tripled, due, in part, to La Virgen being out in public again.

While in Juneau, Irma also made friends with the mayor's wife, Lupita, a Mexican, and got access to the mayor. He lent her his time to listen about her plans for projects and a job. Irma took over a radio program and hit the airwaves with messages to Raza about immigration, politics, cultural events, and organizational meetings until the station manager got wind of the partisan nature of her programming. Then, in April 1998, Irma and Gerardo returned to San Antonio, Texas. Irma had vested in her public service job in Alaska. She now works for the Mexican American Cultural Center (MACC), a Catholic educational organization, and is still active in city politics. Irma is also a grandmother now.

(See the video interview with Irma Mireles at the Special Collections Department of the University of Texas at Arlington.)

51. No Chicana Could Play Selena, and Buttsy Jennifer López Is No Selena

Selena Quintanilla Pérez, before her untimely death, had begun a line of clothing. Had she lived, that signature apparel line would have made her millions, along with her songs. Other Chicano and Latino artists are imitating Selena and producing product lines. Jerry García and his estate are going strong with a line of neckwear for men and *macho* women. Carlos Santana is also pushing clothes and aromas. You have already heard of Paloma and Carolina Herrera perfumes and Oscar de la Renta designer clothes and colognes, among other products by Latino personalities. Now, Jennifer López has teamed up with Andy Hilfiger, brother to Tommy, and is producing a clothing line under her moniker "J Lo."

Hopefully, this will catch on among Chicano stars and public figures. Maybe in a short time, we can buy a poster of Oscar De La Hoya in underwear at K Mart, designer lingerie by Daisy Fuentes at Victoria's Secret, or signature Wrangler jeans from Emilio Navaira at Wal-Mart, or pantyhose from Cameron Díaz at Walgreen's. How about tennis shoes from Eduardo Nájera, of the Mavericks, the only Mexican basketball player in the NBA?

I support this kind of brown capitalism: buy from your own. We already indirectly do when we buy CDs, go to movies, pay admissions, buy magazines, and watch television programs that feature Raza. They get a little bit of our dollar; the promoters get most of it.

52. Informed Opinion

"Fox becomes a new hero to immigrants," wrote Mercedes Olivera, a columnist for *The Dallas Morning News* on August 26, 2000 (p. 32A), about Vicente Fox Quezada. As Mexican president-elect, Fox came to Dallas, Texas and met with his compatriots, as well as with Anglo business owners and others. Fox drew the most applause when he said he would "create an office at the side of the presidency that will represent immigrants." Chicanos had made the demand for an office within the Mexican presidency or Secretary of Foreign Affairs to handle Chicano/Mexicano Affairs in 1971 during meetings with President Luis Echevarría Álvarez.

According to Ms. Olivera, "Mr. Fox also reminded the audience that he would govern 118 million Mexicans—100 million in Mexico, and another 18 million in the U.S."

I guess we now have two presidents. At least, the Mexican one claims us as his; I'm not so sure the U.S. one claims us in the same way. Fox was the first opposition candidate in 71 years to beat the Partido Revolucionario Institucional's (PRI) candidate since 1929. During the campaign, Fox's campaign consultant and adviser was, and continues to be, Rob Allyn of Allyn & Co. a Dallas-based media relations firm.

53. The Growing Electoral Power of Raza

According to the National Association of Latino Elected and Appointed Officials (NALEO), citing a U.S. Census report, "nearly 40 percent of Latinos said they were 'too busy to vote' in 1998." Yet, in 1998, some 500,000 more Latinos voted than in 1994. We are gaining in numbers even if some are not participating. Statistics on our numbers indicate that of the 20.3 million Latinos in the United States during the 1990s, 12.4 percent were eligible to register to vote, 6.8 percent actually registered to vote, and 4.1 percent voted in

1998. That was about a 33-percent turnout rate in a nonpresidential election year. The prediction for the 2000 presidential election was that 40 percent of Latinos would vote.

(See Mercedes Olivera's column, "Latinos can send message by voting," *The Dallas Morning News* [September 2, 2000, p. 44A].)

54. *Tequila, Tecate or Té?*

In order for it to be authentic, *tequila* must be from the Mexican state of Jalisco and made 100 percent from distilled juice of the *agave* pulp. If it is from Oaxaca, even if it has the worm, it is *mezcal*. In Chihuahua, it is called *sotol*. In many other places, the name is much simpler, it is just called *aguardiente* or burning water.

Currently, there are two problems with the *tequila* industry. First, the *agave* plant takes years to mature. It is in short supply, moreover, and supply has been getting shorter by the year; hence, the *tequila* on the market has gone up in price by about 300 percent, and *tequila* has been diluted. Most of the *tequila* bought today in the United States has a 49-percent *agave* base. Dilution is also the means by which the industry can make *tequila* affordable to the working-class person who imbibes regularly for medicinal purposes and practice sessions of *el grito*.

Here is a thought: If Mexico wants to continue to limit supply and output of *tequila* for export, it is a blessing in disguise. Why not begin to grow the *maguey* plant for its *agave* here in the Southwest? We can call it *Te Cae La*. We can sell futures on the commodities market. We can mix a bit with hemp or *sin semilla marijuana* and make it a liniment for arthritis.

55. You Are Part of the Problem If You Are Not Part of the Solution

Lauro Cruz, the first Chicano State Representative from Harris County (Houston) Texas in the 1960s, and his friend, Tony Padilla, former Director of Legislative Matters, Transportation & Communication Workers Union, met in 1988 for a visioning session. Some guys get together to drink beer, play poker, watch football, and the like; but Lauro and Tony got together to discuss the impact of Chicano demography by 2020 and the need for leadership development. "We said if they handed us the whole platter today, in 1988, we wouldn't be ready to take it. We wouldn't be ready to step in. Now, we need to train more leaders in the community . . . So, we went to the University of Texas [Austin], to the dean of the LBJ School of Public Affairs, and we told him what we wanted to do." The dean agreed and supported the idea with space and some amenities. Cruz and Padilla donated their time, put money out of their pocket, and used their personal computers to generate the training material. The program runs for nine months (twelve sessions of three hours each) at a cost of $100 per person. The curriculum consists of parliamentary procedure, public policy process, local government, law enforcement, the judiciary, education, media, politics, holding public office, and campaigning. Guest lecturers, experts or practitioners in the field, are brought in to discuss the topics.

In ten years, the program has trained more than 300 persons, mostly Hispanics.

The longer-term goal is to establish the program as part of the LBJ School of Public Affairs and hire a full-time director.

(See Interview with Lauro Cruz, General Library, Special Collections, University of Texas-Arlington, Arlington, Texas, pp. 55–58.)

56. Paths to Power

Gus García is an honest certified public accountant in Austin, Texas. He left an Anglo-owned CPA firm to start his own in 1965 and became successful. Around 1967, he joined others at city hall to protest the exclusion of Chicanos from the newly formed Human Relations Commission. The city council had appointed four blacks and one Chicano (Danny Ruiz) out of 21 such appointees. García had never been to city hall. Once there, he got into the face of a councilman, Dick Nichols, about the token Chicano appointment. Buckling under pressure, the council members decided to increase the total number to 25, and Nichols asked García to serve. He got appointed.

The Human Relations Commission took its job seriously and recommended measures that the city council posed to the voters in a referendum, including an open-housing ordinance. The voters defeated the measure and voted out of office its proponents. The new council members removed García and others from the Human Relations Commission and appointed more pro-business members, such as Milton Smith, owner of Economy Furniture.

Chicano workers were on strike against the Economy Furniture Company. García joined in support of the strike. This labor strike, much like the melon workers' strike against La Casita Farms in the Rio Grande Valley earlier in the 1960s, galvanized the Chicano community not only in Austin but also statewide. Many Chicano activists cut their teeth on these strikes and attendant protests and marches. Gilbert Martínez ran for the Austin School Board in 1968 and lost. He was the first Chicano to do so. Edna Canino ran in 1970 and lost. Richard Moya ran for a county commissioner post and won, the first Chicano officeholder in Travis County. Later, Gus García ran for the school board and won. He ran for the city council and won. In 2001, he ran for mayor of Austin and won, the first Chicano to do so.

(See Interview with Gus García, General Libraries, Special Collections, University of Texas at Arlington, Arlington, Texas, pp. 13–20.)

57. Gerrymandering and Redistricting in the 1990s

Elbridge Gerry was one of the Constitutional Convention delegates who refused to sign the Articles of Confederation. Later, as governor of Massachusettes in 1812, he invented the trickery of drawing political district boundary lines to exclude his enemies and include his supporters. The practice became known as "gerrymandering." Religiously, incumbents practice gerrymandering, beginning the odd year after the census enumeration of the population is taken. And, just as religiously, lawyers sue government entities, trying to increase representation and defeat gerrymandering.

Diana Orozco made history in Dallas County, Texas, in the 1990s. Others had sued the City of Dallas under the Voting Rights Act of 1975, as amended. The litigation was acrimonious and protracted. Dallas county commissioners saw a better way to resolve the redistricting issues than drawn-out and costly litigation; they offered to settle by creating two Chicano Justice of the Peace districts and one Constable district. Usually, someone in opposition to Chicano representation will holler that the Chicano seats are taken at the expense of blacks. This is a variant of the time-worn divide-and-conquer routine. This time, better minds prevailed, and blacks and browns came together on the plan. Raza got two judges and a constable, all positions won by Chicanos and one Chicana, Diana Orozco.

She had been co-counsel on the litigation, obtained attorney's fees from the settlement, won election as the first Chicana Justice of the Peace for Dallas County, Texas, in 1992, and subsequently, married the lead counsel on the case, William Garrett.

(See Interview with Diana Orozco, General Libraries, Special Collections, University of Texas at Arlington, Arlington, Texas, p. 3.)

58. The *Juan* and Only

His name is not Juan; it is Tony, and his surname is Garza. He is the son of a Texaco gasoline station operator and a stay-at-home mom with a college degree. He was born (1961) and raised in Brownsville, Texas, on the U.S.-Mexico border with Matamoros, Tamaulipas. He was sent to a private school for his education and ultimately obtained a law degree from Southern Methodist University. Even as a child he held conservative views. Incredibly, while living and practicing law in a border city and county where the Democratic Party historically has ruled the politics, he became a Republican. Incredibly, in 1988, he was elected county judge at age 27. By 1994, he had made friends with George W. Bush, Jr. And Governor Bush appointed him Secretary of State for Texas. From this post, he successfully sought the office of commissioner on the Texas Railroad Commission, a most powerful regulatory agency over the oil-and-gas industry. He was the only Hispanic elected to statewide office in 1998.

In 1980, another Republican Hispanic, Roy Barrera, Jr., almost beat the Democratic nominee for Texas Attorney General, Jim Mattox. Raza will vote for a Hispanic candidate, regardless of party affiliation.

Keep your eye on this Republican named Tony Garza, the *Juan and Only* Latino elected to statewide office at this writing. He has just been confirmed as the U.S. Ambassador to Mexico.

59. Digitize! Digitize! Digitize Everything!

The most current technology on copying is digitization. If you have Chicano archival material, movies, tape recordings, photographs, whatever, find a way to get the entire collection digitized. I did.

For the past six years, I conducted 153 (at this writing) ethnographic oral history interviews with public officials and other influentials in Texas, including musicians and entertainers. I had the interviews transcribed, copied on audio cassette, and on videotape. Some folks have told me that this is the largest collection on Chicano public figures in the nation.

The General Library's Special Collections Department Head, Dr. Gerald Saxon, and I discussed digitization of my work. He wrote a successful proposal for that, and his staff began to transfer the interviews to digital format. Now, this material, my work product, is available for the world to access via the Internet and our website.

Check it out: http://libraries.uta.edu/tejanovoices/. And, other entries in this collection referenced in this book may be found on the website, but not all my work has been digitized yet. It will get done soon.

60. Brown Political Power: Raza Elected Officials

The Joint Center for Political and Economic Studies, a black think tank, issues data on the number of black elected officials in federal, state, and local government. The Joint Center estimated black political power at approximately 9,040 elected officials in the country during the year 2000. There are elections all the time, and the number of black officials keeps increasing. For example, in 1990, the Joint Center calculated 7,370 blacks held public office.

Who does the counting for us?

The National Association of Latino Elected and Appointed Officials (NALEO) has been doing it since 1976, when it was founded. NALEO estimated there were 3,128 Latino elected officials in 1984; 4,966 in 1999; and, more than 5,400 in 2000. And, more to be elected in 2002! (See www.naleo.org.)

61. Kill the Computer Virus

Recently, during the early part of summer 2002, someone hacked into the electronic address book for the newly elected national president of LULAC, Hector Flores, and planted a virus. The virus via e-mail went to everyone on his e-mail address book. He has thousands, given his work with LULAC. I was one of them and I was furious. Checking for viruses before opening e-mail is like dental flossing after eating; you know you should but seldom, if ever, do it. I was wise enough to detect that the file had problems, so I just sent it back by forwarding it to him with a note to check his computer for viruses.

A better way to stop infected e-mail from getting into your address book is to make the very first entry in your address book a bogus one, such as AAAA for the name and Chingate@Aztlan.com for the e-mail address. The virus will come in to what is now your very first address and go out to cyberspace forever. When you get a failure notice in your e-mail, you'll know someone tried *y tú chingaste.*

62. *Latinobarómetro*

Polls are the staple of pundits, journalists, *políticos*, researchers, spin doctors, and happy-hour regulars. Poll results are quoted and cited to support argument and position with regularity by all.

Now, there is a Latin-American poll that reports on survey research done in the entire Spanish-speaking world of the Americas, from the Rio Grande in South Texas to Tierra del Fuego in South America. The polling outfit is called Latinobarómetro.

The Latin Barometer is a multicountry survey. It recently reported on attitudes of 18,526 people in 17 countries. The questions were all over the place, probing on politics, economics, democracy, culture, social behavior, and, the proverbial topic on the favorite *gringo* subject, corruption.

The margin of error was reported to be in the range of plus or minus 2.8 to 4.16 points.

Here are some findings:

On corruption: From 86 percent in 1996 to 80 percent in 2002, Latin Americans believed corruption has increased. And 27 percent of those polled in 2002 knew personally of an act of corruption. Those polled believed that out of 100 Latin American public officials, a whopping 71 percent were corrupt. This was a three percent increase in negative attitude on this question from 2001.

On democracy vs. authoritarianism: Fewer than last year, 2001, at 19 percent, in 2002, only 15 percent prefer authoritarianism over democracy, with 18 percent claiming it makes no difference, and 56 percent stating a preference for democracy.

On the source of problems in Latin America: Responding to the question of who is responsible for economic problems, those polled could check more than one source:

- 50 percent pointed to the government
- 24 percent blamed the lack of business initiative
- 19 percent blamed the lack of personal initiative
- 16 percent pointed to globalization, and the same number thought the lack of manufactured goods was the source of economic problems
- 15 percent blamed the International Monetary Fund (IMF)
- 14 percent blamed banks
- 8 percent blamed the World Trade Organization
- 9 percent gave no response. The famous. . . . "*Quién sabe. Yo no sé.*"

This business of survey research is a wide-open market for Raza. There is a lot of money to be made. There is a lot of information that interested parties want to know about us. Interested parties want to know how we will vote, what we buy, where we shop, who we are, what we think, what we want, and where we are.

There are a few Latinos in the business already and more seeking opportunity. At issue are the fundamental rules: Who is asking the questions? Who is responding? What language is used? How are the questions worded? Who codes and interprets the responses? When was the poll taken? Who paid for the poll? Who has the raw data and is it accessible to others?

The other fundamental issue is, who owns the polling business? If we are growing in importance, should we not be involved in more ways than just as subjects of survey research?

Contact Todd Robberson at trobberson@hotmail.com for more details on the poll. Better yet, go to the actual website: www.latino-barometro.org.

63. The Poor People's Banks

Exacerbating the problems of the poor *mexicano* and *centroamericano* is the issue of where they bank. Until recently, no bank would service their needs because of lack of an approved photo identification or valid driver's license. If a person has no legal documents for entry into the United States, he cannot get legitimate identification cards of any sort. This presents a problem when cashing payroll checks. This is also a problem when borrowing money. In an effort to reform the banking system's acceptance of immigrants, consulates have issued an I.D. card popularly called the *matrícula consular.*

But with or without the *matrícula consular*, the poor still go to pawn shops. Regardless of immigration status, race, ethnicity, gender, citizenship, national origin, or primary language, the poor go to pawn shops for money and to check-cashing entities to exchange payroll checks for cash. Both pawn shops and check-cashing services gouge the customer with high interest rates or fees for service.

Business has never been better for them. Cash America, a large chain of pawn shops, is making money hand over fist and expanding across the country. Ace Cash Express, Inc., another local business based in Irving, Texas, but with a national presence, is doing record business. At Ace Cashing, you can get cash for your payroll check minus 2.3 percent of the check's value. You can send money. You can buy a money order. You can get a short-term loan at high interest. With a signed car title as collateral, you can get a larger loan for a long term.

Ace has gone from $611,000 in net income in 2001 to $10.1 million in 2002, and at this writing, it still has a final quarter to go in the year. So far in 2002, it has made 1.8 million loans, compared to 1.4 million in 2001. That is a lot of money loaned and lots of interest earned. The face amount of checks cashed went from $4.5 billion last year to $4.8 billion now. Multiply that by 2.3 percent and figure the gross take. Check cashing constituted 51.9 percent of the company's revenue. Ace now is into franchising its outlets to investors. In 2002, Ace opened 40 stores and franchised 22 more. And as I wrote above, there are still three months left in the calendar year.

Contact araghunathan@dallasnews.com for more information.

64. Perales or Balderas?

On three occasions during October and November 2001, the plaintiff, Balderas, in the Mexican American Legal Defense and Educational Fund (MALDEF) lawsuit against the state of Texas, went to court. The plaintiff won, but lost. The ultimate goal was to create two new congressional districts with Mexican/Latino voter majorities in the state, one in Dallas and the other in the Rio Grande Valley. NOT! To this day MALDEF cannot collect attorney fees for the suit from the State of Texas. Even the incumbent Democrats, some Mexicans, opposed the MALDEF plan; they wanted to keep their seats. Raza in Dallas are tracked into three different congressional districts. In Houston, the Chicano seat is held by a white guy, Gene Green, and the remaining Raza are fractured into other congressional districts. And in the Rio Grande Valley, as in other congressional districts in South Texas and the border area to El Paso, Raza is packed into super-majority congressional districts to limit our chances in other districts.

Raza, watch out for the packing and tracking of our community that goes on during the redistricting process! While MALDEF lost on the congressional side, four new majority districts for Raza were nevertheless created for the state House of Representatives.

Call MALDEF in San Antonio, Texas, at 210-224-5476 or e-mail the regional director and lawyer in charge, Nina Perales: nperales@maldef.org. Nina, a *boricua*, is a cultural cousin and real whoop-ass attorney.

65. You *Can* Afford College

Yes, there are scholarships and loans available to attend college. The problem with these sources is that you may not get what you need. Another problem is that most applicants submit their applications for loans and grants and scholarships on the eve of enrolling. About $74 billion for federal financial aid is available annually.

I have friends who were denied financial aid for college even though they were unemployed and living off unemployment compensation. The denial was based on failure to file their income tax forms by the April 15 deadline. If you ask for an extension to do the IRS filing, you lose out on financial aid for that year. I have grown children who were denied financial aid because they worked and then wanted to attend school full-time. Another grown child was denied because of being claimed as a dependent by a parent. Many young persons are denied apartment leases, car loans, housing purchases, major appliance purchases, and education loans because they have no credit history. They need a co-signer with a good credit history, and those are hard to find.

The key is planning. Plan early. In fact, as soon as you have a first-born, begin planning. According to the College Board, the average cost of private college is $24,343 per year for tuition, books, supplies, and lodging. A public institution costs about $9,744 a year. The cost of tuition is rising about 6 percent a year at private institutions and as much as 25 percent at public institutions, but the future rate is anybody's guess. All costs are going up.

There are many sources of college investment accounts and tax credits for tuition. Individual colleges and universities have so much money in endowments that they will invest in your child, if she or he is their fit. Stanford University, for example, offers a full scholarship to those admitted. Money is not an issue if you have an acceptance letter from Stanford or Princeton or many other lesser-known institutions, such as Grinnell in Iowa. Other schools will make up the difference in costs to attend between an applicant's EFC and the total cost of attendance. The EFC is the expected family contribution, which is determined by income and assets. An asset not counted in the EFC is a retirement account, so save away for your own nest egg, as well as funding your children's education.

Under current federal and state law, a person is permitted to open a Coverdale Education Savings Account and/or a state-sponsored 529 College Savings Plan. You should do both. A Coverdale is open to anyone earning up to $110,000 annually or $220,000 jointly. The maximum a person can contribute to the Coverdale is $2,000. Any withdrawal and earnings of interest in this account are tax-free when used for educational purposes. The 529 state plans have no income requirements, but do cap at a $2,000 annual contribution. Some states limit total contributions to a 529 plan to $250,000 over the life of the account.

The tuition tax credits are available through Hope Scholarship Credit and the Lifetime Learning Credit. The Hope is worth up to $1,500 in tax credit per child for eligible expenses during the first two years of college. The Lifetime picks up after the Hope and offers tax credits for the remaining two years, another $2,000 beginning in 2003. The Texas Tomorrow Fund is a state plan that lets you pay for the cost of college in the future at today's prices. In other words, you lock in the price today and you pay as you go toward that day when your child seeks admission to a Texas school. If the child goes to another school elsewhere in the nation, the money follows him. It is not lost or forfeited, and it can even be transferred to another college-bound recipient.

(See www.campusconsultants.com and www.collegesavings.org for assistance in understanding these financial paths to higher education and to begin planning.)

66. Globalization and *las maquilas*

There is a movie you should rent, "Maquila." The film, available from New York's Cinema Guild, is directed by Saul Landau. The movie is about the *maquiladora* industry along the U.S.-Mexico border. In the late 1950s, the Mexican government began the PRONAF industrialization program on its side of the border. The United States did nothing. The U.S. was comfortable with the Bracero Progam that brought cheap Mexican labor to the U.S. beginning in 1942 as an emergency war measure but continued into peace time for decades until 1964. After that year, the U.S. was comfortable with the spillover effect of the program. Mexican labor continued to cross the border into the U.S. and work for cheap wages. This program fostered addiction to cheap labor and institutionalized the illegal condition of Mexican labor in the United States.

In Mexico a year after the Bracero Program ended, the first *maquila* opened in Ciudad Juárez, Chihuahua, across from El Paso, Texas. The *gringo maquila* owners hired Mexican supervisors and targeted young *mexicanas* to work in their plants. The internal migration from rural Mexico to the northern-most frontier of the country began. Southern states emptied as their populations flowed to the northern states, and women who could not find work in the *maquilas* mostly kept on migrating into the U.S. in search of work. Thousands and thousands of young women toiled in these sweat shops for decades.

In 1994 with passage of NAFTA, the *maquila* industry's rate of growth reached double digits. There were some 4,000 of these plants along the border in 2001. The annual exports, about $75 billion, from the *maquilas,* is Mexico's lifesaver. The *maquila* program was also a lifesaver for U.S. corporations. In addition to the cheap, gendered, and constantly renewed labor supply, U.S. corporations got huge tax breaks. They would ship raw material to their Mexican plants and return it as finished or partially assembled product duty-free. They brought across cars, trucks, trailers, engine parts, wood, plastics, electronics, and jet engines.

In early 2000, the bubble burst for the Mexican government and labor. The *maquilas* began to move to China for the very same reasons they had set up operations in Mexico: cheaper wages and controlled regulations, including labor. The cost of doing business in China and other Asian countries offset the trans-Pacific shipping costs and difficulties of long-distance management. Some 18 months ago, 500 plants began to relocate and have caused the loss of 250,000 or more jobs along the border. Mexican labor continues to pour into the border cities, but there are no jobs. What they heard about the *maquila* jobs was true, but no more. More plants are planning to shut down their Mexican operations. The Mexican state of Chihuahua has lost more than 100,000 jobs. This is the Mexican state that led the nation in employment in 1999.

With the advent of heavy security, post-9/11, the unemployed and hungry Mexican workers cannot cross the border into the U.S. as easily. There is a growing problem along the border. Hunger, drug use, prostitution, murder, crime are on the rise on the Mexican side.

I cannot do justice to this subject in these few lines; besides, graphics and audio are more powerful than the printed word. Watch the movie and learn about globalization.

P.S.: I have a collection of Homies. The last batch I bought, "Lil' Locsters," came in a box that read "Made in China."

67. Globalization and Welfare

How can this be, globalization and welfare? Easy! Read on.

As this is being written, the World Summit on Sustainable Development is being held in Johannesburg, South Africa. Representatives of 191 countries are present and talking. Every ten years, the rich and poor nations of the world gather to assess and discuss the state of the globe with regard to development. In 1992, the nations gathered in Rio de Janeiro, Brazil. The Kyoto Treaty on global warming came out of that Rio meeting. President Bill Clinton endorsed the treaty, and President George W. Bush pulled out of our commitment. Global warming is a big issue for industrial countries that want to continue polluting the environment and the nations that want responsible growth and development, but not at the expense of air pollution. The treaty seeks to cap air pollution at specific levels objectionable to Dubya Bush.

At the Johannesburg meeting, one issue was welfare for farmers, i.e., agricultural subsidies. The United States, European countries, and Japan sell the world cheap foodstuffs. They are cheap in price because growers get government subsidies. The poor farmers in developing countries simply cannot compete with the subsidized pricing schemes in the global marketplace. Their foodstuffs perish on the vine, in the barn, the bin, the cooler, wherever, because no one will buy a higher-priced item. The World Bank pegs the amount of agricultural subsidy by richer nations at $350 billion per year. And in the case of the United States, we also have the Overseas Protection Insurance Commission (OPIC) that buffers export losses. We also subsidize exporting. Poor nations want the rich countries to stop the agricultural subsidies. At this point, Dubya is thinking of cutting back $100 billion in farm subsidies by 2006.

Good beginning, the thinking part. Let's get to the doing part.

68. The Rule of 1, 2, 3

I teach political science courses at the University of Texas in Arlington. In the various classes that I teach, invariably the subjects of redistricting, voter participation, voter eligibility, and citizenship come up. I employ a concept called the Rule of 1,2,3 to explain the unique situation of Raza in the U.S. political system. I tell my students that of every 100 Latinos, only 60 are eligible to register to vote because 40 are too young. Our median age was 26 in 2000. I then tell them that of those 60, only 36 can register to vote because the other 24 are not citizens. And, I tell them that about 20 actually vote, and comprise about 6 percent of the national vote. Given the fact that all blacks and whites are citizens with very, very few exceptions, and that these two groups have a higher median age than Latinos (36 years of age for whites and 31 years of age for blacks), the turnout for them is higher. The black and white groups comprise higher percentages of the national vote than Latinos at this time.

In redistricting or in voting contests, you need 300 Latinos to roughly equal the voting capacity of whites. Blacks must number 200 to counter the turnout of 100 whites.

This is the rule of 1, 2, 3.

69. Paint the White House Brown!

You know that the popular vote means squat in electing the President. The vote that counts is by state, with the winner taking all the electoral votes for each state. Electoral votes are the key to victory;

270 of them are absolutely necessary to win the presidency.

We reside in significant numbers in ten states, and the electoral votes of those ten states equal 80 percent of the 270 needed to win the White House.

Which states are these? Colorado, Florida, Texas, California, Massachusetts, New Mexico, Illinois, New Jersey, Arizona, and New York.

(For current and timely reporting on Latino electoral activity, see www.naleo.org or call 323-720-1932 or 202-546-2536.)

70. Leveraged Politics

When I was organizing the Raza Unida Party and learned of negative criticism coming from Raza Democrats, I would look them up and try to reason with them. I did not succeed in most instances.

To my view, if we, the militants in the *partido*, would raise the issue or make the demand, the political leverage would be in the hands of the Raza Democrats. The conservative and moderate and liberal white office-holders and policy-makers would rather deal with Raza Democrats than us. To be sure, we would not get what we wanted, but it would be a gain from where we were and what we had before. I assumed that Raza Democrats would be effective negotiators once we opened the doors or initiated the dialogue with the powerful. NOT!

Raza Democrats, rather than practice leveraged politics, saw me as the enemy and practiced cannibalism. They ate me up. They did not go through the door of opportunity we had opened. They ran in our direction to fight us. They were proud to announce to the powerful that they did not support or endorse our views and that they wanted to see us destroyed. They set out to do just that. *¡Pendejos!*

Once we were destroyed, the powerful had no need for them.

71. The Judicial Appointment Process

An "Article II judge" refers to a federal judge because that is the section in the U.S. Constitution that deals with the judiciary. Federal judges are appointed by the President for life, after the U.S. Senate committee on the judiciary recommends them and the entire Senate votes for confirmation. Many nominees have been derailed because of their extreme views on hot-button subjects and topics such as abortion, death penalty, legalizing marijuana, prayer in the schools, and affirmative action, as revealed in published articles, court opinions, speeches, and the like. Partisan politics plays a big part in this process because sometimes the Republicans block the nominees of a Democratic President (Clinton) and sometimes the Democrats block the nominees of a Republican President (Bush). As this goes to press, Miguel Estrada, a Honduran immigrant, has been nominated by President Bush for a seat on the prestigious Court of Appeals in D.C., and grilled by the Democrats on the Senate Judiciary Committee. The Court of Appeals is the steppingstone to the U.S. Supreme Court. So, what's up with Estrada?

The problem is Estrada has not written much of anything. There is no written record to dig up. He has been operating behind the scenes. Moreover, he is not a typical Honduran immigrant. He is from the elite class of Hondurans who flew in, not walked over after a hurricane disaster. He attended private schools and is a Harvard graduate. His colleagues praise his competence and legal mind, and praise his conservative views. His political enemies claim his surname is the beginning and end of his connection to Raza. This is the crux of the problem. Opponents of the Estrada nomination include MALDEF, the Hispanic Congressional Caucus, and Professor Rudy Acuña. Supporters of his nomination include the U.S. Hispanic Chamber of Commerce, LULAC, and Fernando Oaxaca.

Should we as Raza blindly support any Latino because of ethnicity? Should we as Raza critically examine the policy position and philosophy of such nominees and candidates for public office?

In Dallas County, Texas, an Argentinean, Carlos López, has been appointed repeatedly to state and county courts. In 1996, he was appointed to the Dallas County Court at Law, No. 2, and lost in the Republican primary election. Judges in Texas are elected. Again in 2000, George W. Bush, as governor, appointed him to the 116th Judicial District Court bench. López is very conservative in his views. If you asked him whom he would like to have over for dinner, he would respond, "Jesus, his wife (Argentinean), his parents (also Argentineans), Ronald Reagan, George Washington, John Maynard Keynes, and General George Marshall." Not one of us is good enough to break bread with this Argentinean judge.

(See Dallas Bar Association, "Headnotes," an article by Kristen Castaneda on the judge, "Judical Profile: Judge Carlos Lopez," October 1, 2002, p. 7, and www.HispanicOnline.com of September 26, 2002, on the Estrada nomination.)

72. Let's Make a Movie

In 1971, I began to seek dialogue with the president of Mexico. I believed then, as I do now, that the Mexican president is to be held accountable by and responsible to those of us of Mexican ancestry residing in the United States. When I made contact and developed the relationship sufficiently, I asked President Luis Echevarría for money with which to make Chicano films. I asked Jesús Treviño, currently of "Resurrection Boulevard" fame, to make the first one, "Raíces de Sangre." Reies López Tijerina became the subject of another Mexican movie about the Chicano Movement, and it was called "Chicano."

During the same time, Efraín Gutiérrez was trying to make his own Chicano films with little money in San Antonio. He made three films in as many years in the late 1960s, but he did not enjoy the instant success of a Richard Rodríguez or the growing success of a Gregory Nava or a Moctezuma Esparza. In fact, Efraín got so burned out that he left the business for years and was very embittered. Efraín was the first Chicano filmmaker. The first pioneers usually pay a higher price than those that follow. As the apropos *dicho* states: *Nadie sabe por quién trabaja.* Efraín paved the way not only for the Treviños, Navas, Esparzas, and Rodriguezes of the industry, but also for the genre. He made Chicano films about Chicanos living the Chicano life when it was neither popular nor profitable.

Well, Efraín Gutierrez is back in 2001 with "Low Rider," a feature-length comedy about the low-rider culture in our midst.

73. Let's Make a Television Show

Chicanos and Chicanas watch as much television as the next person. The main difference is that other persons, usually white or black, watch themselves and programs about themselves on the screen. Whites are ubiquitous and blacks are becoming so. There is not a commercial, soap opera, documentary, comedy, feature film, or dance troupe on television that does not have scores of white actors and at least one black person in the clip. We are hard pressed to find ourselves in U.S. television shows or commercials. We are hard pressed to find ourselves in Spanish-language television as well. The Spanish television programs usually feature some exotic Latino or Latina from Uruguay, Venezuela, or Argentina, speaking with the appropriate natural accent. And these personalities do not look like us at all. The reason is that the ownership of the networks continues to elude Chicanos. The first and last of the big players in television was Danny Villanueva, the former Dallas Cowboy football kicker and former Los Angeles KMEX television executive. Now, our cultural cousins, the Cubans, are the big players in television out of Miami, along with other cousins: Venezuelans and Mexicans in Mexico (Emilio Escárraga). But we are not in the game, except as an occasional producer, director, or actor.

Jesús Treviño, the longtime Chicano filmmaker, has hit it big with "Resurrection Boulevard" on Showtime. He is the current occasional producer and director. The cast of the show is predominantly Chicano and is also making a statement. Casting whites and others as Chicano by outfitting them with brown contact lenses and tanning them is unnecessary because there is plenty of Chicano talent available. The ironies are twofold. One, Raza connected to cable are watching HBO, not Showtime. The viewers of "Resurrection Boulevard" are mostly Anglos and blacks. Two, the producers and directors, even when they are the Navas, Esparzas, and Rodriguezes, often cast non-Chicanos for the Chicano and Mexican roles. Think of J Lo in "Selena," Rubén Blades as a *manito* in "The Milagro Beanfield War," Antonio Banderas in "Spy Kids," and Benecio del Toro in "Traffic." Only Cheech Marin and Tony Plana have consistently played Chicanos in feature-length Anglo movies. And only two Chicanos, Anthony Quinn and Edward James Olmos, have consistently played non-Chicanos in feature-length Anglo movies.

Hey, let me not forget to mention that George López will start his second season on ABC with his comedy show, the first Chicano comedy program on national weekly television. If you want to watch movies, find or start a film festival like Frank Hernández of Dallas has done. He created a foundation in memory of his parents, and through that, he funds a nonprofit project, Vistas Film Festival, that annually previews Latino-themed movies.

74. A New Majority in California?

According to Census Bureau estimates released on August 30, 2000, whites are only 49.9 percent of the population of California. The state officially is now a majority minority state. California has about 33 million people. Hispanics are 10.5 million of that population and blacks are 2.2 million, with Asians/Pacific Islanders raising the numbers of the minorities to majority status.

Are you ready to lead? Have you even developed an action plan? A strategic plan? Any kind of plan?

75. The Web

The web used to mean the spider web or some intrigue, to folks my age, but now it means the World Wide Web of on-line participants. Most Raza cannot afford the hardware, software or the Internet cost of monthly service. Raza who live in rural areas may not even have it available to them, nor the medical services, dentists, hospital care, legal assistance, low-income housing, or year-round employment at a decent wage.

At this writing, 7.6 million Latinos accessed the Internet in June 2002—the third-largest group of participants, behind whites and blacks, in that order. The good news is that 6.1 million of us accessed the year prior. In other words, we grew by 13 percent of those connected. We are in the race of the Information Age and not running poorly.

In this race toward the future, of course, it is best to come in first, but it is far better to know how to come in. *Como dice la canción,* "El Rey": "*. . . como me dijo un arriero, no hay que llegar primero, pero hay que saber llegar . . .*"

Check the Nielsen/NetRatings on the Web to see how we are doing by the time you read this.

76. Net Worth

In the first pages of this book, I mentioned that *Hispanic Business* magazine (September 2002) published a list of "The Wealthiest Hispanics" by name and with a short, short biography of each one. Some are family groupings, and most are individual male listings, by and large. Together, they have a net worth of $11.4 billion. A few women are listed: Remedios Díaz Oliver & family, Irma B. Elder, Jennifer López, Cameron Díaz, Gloria Estefan and family, for example. Not bad.

Hopefully, they make regular gifts of cash, stock, or other wealth to Latino nonprofits and community organizations. Why pay taxes to Uncle Sam when they can get a deduction for tax-exempt contributions? Hopefully, they will prepare a will or trust and transfer wealth to their Latino offspring and relatives. Hopefully, they will employ and mentor and help other Latinos and Latinas to access capital and opportunity. Hopefully, they will contract with other Raza to be their lawyers, accountants, doctors, agents, dentists, architects, designers, therapists, planners, and lovers. Hopefully, each one of them will start a project or program to help other Raza, like a fund to help our people with the down payment for a home or the down payment for a business franchise.

Maybe . . .

Meanwhile, I suggest you just ask them for money for your project.

77. What Will I Be When I Grow Up?

This question nags us forever because we never know when we really have grown up. And when you realize you have, you are too old to want to try any new career path.

A smart way is to look at where the population is headed. In the case of the United States, it is an aging and dying white America and a growing and young Latino nation. A very good job would be nursing.

The Bureau of Health Professions predicted a nursing shortage of 6 percent for each year beginning in 2002 and the shortage jumping to 10 percent by 2010, 20 percent by 2015, 29 percent by 2020. The shortage will be five times what it is now. In Texas, the shortage in 2000 was 9 percent but expected to hit 26.3 percent by 2020. The report on this alarming catastrophe-in-the-making, "Projected Supply, Demand, and Shortages of Registered Nurses: 2000–2020," can be downloaded from www.bhpr.hrsa.gov/healthworkforce/rnproject/. In very similar fashion to the scarce production of certified bilingual and ESL teachers in the face of mounting demand, nurses are just not being produced. The total number of registered nursed has actually shrunk from 96,610 in 1995 to 71,475 in 2000. And the older nurses are leaving the profession, retiring, and dying. About one nurse in five is older than 40 years of age and beginning to think of retirement.

To my view, this means guaranteed employment at a premium wage in the location and working hours of your choice. Nursing is headed for a critical demand. And, Raza will need nurses who can talk *en español, en confianza*, and that understand us.

But when I walk the halls of the nursing school at the University of Texas-Arlington, where I teach, it is very, very white: students, faculty, administrators, and dean.

78. Covering Kids

The Robert Wood Johnson Foundation (www.rwif.org/index.jsp) initiated a program to insure children in the United States, Covering Kids. The foundation is promoting this effort because 5 million children in the United States do not have health insurance. According to the Urban Institute, about 1.1 million Texas children (those under 18 years of age) are uninsured. I bet they are mostly Chicanos and blacks.

A disease or injury can be deadly to the child without health insurance, and to the family and the greater community.

Instead of shouting as we once did, "*¡Viva la raza!,*" let us change that to "*¡Viva la raza viva!*" Get insurance. Apply to the Children's Health Insurance Program (CHIP) in Texas or get Medicaid. Let's start a sign-up campaign in every community to get our kids enrolled and covered.

79. Pay Taxes? Get Your Share of Federal Dollars

We all pay federal taxes, including those of us who are here without the proper documents to claim a refund. How many of us get our share of federal dollars back in the form of refunds, grants, contracts, loans, and program benefits? Not many.

Change this by going to www.cfda.gov/public/faprs.htm, which is the website for the Catalog of Federal Domestic Assistance. You will need to know the program numbers to access the information by department, so in that sense, it is chicken and egg, which comes first? You can order the book.

For this purpose, just access the website and punch in 14.592 in the "View Program" slot. Try 16.562 or 84.015, 84.021, 84.022 or 93.358 for nursing program assistance, or 84.063 for the Pell Grant or 27.006 for a summer job with the federal government.

Let me know how you did at JGutierrez@uta.edu.

80. Chicana Members of Congress in Mexico?

As part of the ongoing Chicano demands made of the government of Mexico over the years, another has come to fruition. For years, persons like Roberto Alonzo, Armando Navarro, María Jiménez, and me have asked for Mexico to allow Mexican eligible voters living outside the country to vote by mail or in person at consulates the world over. Our demand has been rejected over the years, but some reforms were made. In the 1994 presidential election, ballot boxes were placed along the border for U.S.-based Mexicans to go vote. In 2000, the Mexican government began the process of allowing Mexicans living abroad and seeking residency or citizenship in other countries to reclaim or keep their Mexican nationality. This was an important step because many Mexicans refused to seek residency or citizenship elsewhere out of intense feelings of loyalty to the mother country. They likened such a step as tantamount to treason and betrayal. This attitude among U.S.-based Mexicans made the Chicano efforts to make them citizens and join Chicano efforts next to impossible.

Now, the Mexican government has approved representation in its Congress for U.S.-based Mexicans or Chicanos and Chicanas who have recaptured their Mexican nationality. You have to acquire your Mexican nationality first, then seek nomination from a political party and get elected. Once elected, you will have an office in the United States within the district and another in Mexico City, D.F., a staff and budget to travel and carry out your responsibilities. Texas is slated to get five such representatives in the Mexican Congress; California and Illinois, a bunch; and New York, one.

I nominate María Jiménez of Houston, Texas, to be our nominee within the Partido Revolucionario Democratico (PRD) for Congress and recommend Armando Navarro from Riverside, California, to be part of that delegation.

81. He Had a Dream

Roberto Cruz was from *Corpitos* (Corpus Christi, Texas). He was a star football player but chose to become an academic instead. He obtained his Ph.D. from the University of California-Berkeley, and began to make a contribution. I recall when I lived in Oregon and worked on his campaign to become the national president of the National Association of Bilingual Educators (NABE). He put a *jalapeño* on his political buttons in that race. Later, he founded a university in Oakland, the National Hispanic University. Over the years, he built up that institution, accreditation by accreditation. He went through all the gates and roadblocks and got money for his students. As the university grew, he relocated to San Jose, California. He finally made the full-accreditation ranks of other universities. This was the first time this goal had been reached.

Historically, we have had other efforts: Colegio Jacinto Treviño (Weslaco, TX), Lincoln Juárez University (Austin, TX), DQ University (Davis, CA), and Colegio César Chávez (Mt. Angel, OR). They all achieved some level of success and functioned for a period, but ultimately failed.

Roberto "Bob" Cruz succeeded, and he died on September 4, 2002.

Bob had a dream and he pursued it to the end. Now, which leader will build on it?

Postscript

There is pressing need for us to explore and soothe the tensions that exist between us as Latinos, and between Latinos and African Americans, and between Latinos and Asians. We must approach our Latino cultural cousins and form alliances. We must negotiate reciprocity with each other. Latinos are the largest group in the U.S., outnumbering blacks. Asians are the fastest-growing group, faster than Latinos at this time. In Texas, for example, in 1980, Anglos were about two-thirds of all people in the state. By 2000, Anglos were just over half of the state's population. By 2040, Anglos will be less than 25 percent of the whole. Think about this dramatic shift in the population and the impact it will have on our lives and future. Will Anglos know how to behave as a minority? Will blacks accept playing second fiddle to us and later, third fiddle to Asians? Are we, as a community, ready to lead, govern, and take future responsibility for all generations in the making and to come?

The societal gains made by Latinos in the U.S. in the 1990s and in this early part of the twenty-first century have been at the expense of Chicano efforts of yesteryear. Mexican and Central American migrants arrived after the Chicano Movement and know little about our struggle. We must approach African Americans and Asians separately, and form coalitions. These communities can be our allies and working partners in the near future. Without them, at least one of them, we cannot take and hold political power.

Historically, the black community has wanted us to follow its lead and support its agendas. And, historically, we did. Blacks, by and large, believe they alone created and sustained the Civil Rights Movement in the United States. The black community remains ignorant about our struggle and our land claims. We need to ask it to support our agenda now and follow our lead. As we become the critical mass and largest minority, a position they once had, they should play a supporting role and not the most-favored minority role.

We need to learn about Asians quickly. The Asian communities will become the second-largest minority group in the U.S. by mid-century. They, too, will surpass the African-American community in numbers. We need to learn from Asians how to share this world. The first step is to recognize that, like Hispanics, the Asian community is comprised of many other communities, some of which are hostile to each other. There is a history there which we must learn and quickly.

Women will become the leaders of our community, as well as the communities of Anglos and blacks. There are more women graduating from professional schools and with advanced degrees than males, particularly so among blacks and Latinos. Our women will become the professional class in a decade or two. Our women will be the source of money in our local communities for the family, political campaigns, donations, business development, scholarships, and wealth. Latinas own about a third of all businesses in our communities. We will be woman-led, to be sure, in a couple of decades, if not sooner. But are we, as males, ready to follow? Are women ready to lead? Do they have a plan? Will women's leadership make any difference?

We will have representation in the Mexican Congress. Our political strategies and electoral plans will have to be binational and transnational. We are one people and are one Mexico, but the reality is that the border is there, and our separation must be bridged. Are you ready to act in a binational capacity? As Mexicans within the Latino milieu, we are about 60 percent of all Latinos, but the other 40 percent are a necessary part of our collective strength. Cubans who only numbered some 1.2 million in the last census cannot be ignored. I doubt Cubans will become social democrats in their political views or make us business partners anytime soon. The politics and economic clout of white Cubans can be isolated and neutralized, but only with the active collaboration of other groups, namely the black Cubans, younger generations of U.S.-born Cubans, and the 3.4 million Puerto Ricans or the 1.6 million Central Americans or the

1.3 million South Americans. The actual numbers of Central Americans and South Americans by nationality are not impressively significant: Dominicans numbered 764,945; Salvadorans numbered 655,165; Guatemalans numbered 372,487; Hondurans numbered 217,487; Columbians were the largest of the South Americans, numbering 470,684; Ecuadorians numbered 260,559; and Peruvians 233,926 in the 2000 Census. There are an additional 3.6 million Puerto Ricans on the island not included in these 2000 figures. We must push for statehood for Puerto Rico in order to increase our political power in the House and Senate of the United States and the Electoral College.

By 2020, we will have a critical mass of voters in Southwestern states and major U.S. cities. We will have the real possibility of electing persons of our choice to major public office. We will even be able to paint the White House brown. We will arrive at that stage, but we will also be susceptible to a divide-and-conquer attack from that moment on. As we become the majority, others will draw 5, 10 or 15 percent of our people to their causes in opposition. White Cubans already are in opposition. We must not only maintain solidarity and group cohesion but also learn persuasion, coalition- and, consensus-building, and keep our focus on the agenda. At the same time, we need to draw supporters for our agenda from the African-American, Asian, white, other Latino, and Native American populations.

Our agenda should be a poor people's agenda. Our agenda should be a woman's agenda. Our agenda should be a young person's agenda. The two most youthful groups in U.S. society, and coincidentally the two most numerous groups of Raza, Mexicans and Puerto Ricans, are also the youngest of Latinos. Mexicans had an average of 24.2 years of age in 2000, while Puerto Ricans aged 27.5. The Cubans were the oldest with a median of 41.3 years of age, even older than Anglos, aging 37.5 years on average. The comparisons in age are important to realize fully who is the future. Cubans and whites will die sooner and faster than the rest of us. Between now and then, what will they do to keep power and prevent us from getting more? This is the crucial question.

If those in power now do nothing different from what was done in years past, we are doomed to remain an underclass. We will not prosper, and they will fade into the dust bin of history, taking with them the legacy of a once great nation. If we are kept from information, education, health, increased income, decent housing, important and strategic employment, and political power, the nation will lose its global competitiveness. And we will lose. If those in power now are not approached and pressured to go about the business of public leadership in a different way, we are all doomed to second-class citizenship. If those in power now are not made to allocate resources in our direction for our well-being and made to reorder budget priorities with us at the top of the fiscal and monetary agendas, we will not have much of a glorious future. It will be a nightmare.

We cannot wait until we are positioned to reclaim our destiny as owners, governors, and leaders at the mid-century mark. The white nationalists such as Mortimer B. Zuckerman, editor-in-chief of *U.S. News & World Report*, are not waiting. This is not some right-wing nut or member of the Aryan Brotherhood; he is as mainstream as you can get among national media moguls. He is trumpeting a new call for reactionary immigration reform. He wants us to assimilate like other European immigrants of yesteryear. He wants family unification visas ended, and, instead, more immigrants with technology skills paid to come. He wants the processing of pending INS applications slowed down even more "until we can thoroughly assess how the children of today's immigrants will fare as adults." He believes, "The longer these new immigrants stay in the country, the worse they do in contrast to the upward mobility of earlier generations." (Read his entire diatribe in *U.S. News & World Report,* September 23, 2002, p. 118.)

Paraphrasing Elie Wiesel, I used this slogan when I ran for the U.S. Senate from Texas in 1993: If not now, then when? If not us, then who?

The time is now. The task is waiting. The ones to act are us. Now, not *mañana*.

Additional titles in our
Hispanic Civil Rights Series

Message to Aztlán
Rodolfo "Corky" Gonzales
ISBN 1-55885-331-6

A Gringo Manual on How to Handle Mexicans
José Angel Gutiérrez
ISBN 1-55885-326-X

Eyewitness: A Filmmaker's Memoir of the Chicano Movement
Jesús Salvador Treviño
ISBN 1-55885-349-9

Pioneros puertorriqueños en Nueva York, 1917–1947
Joaquín Colón
ISBN 1-55885-335-9

The American GI Forum: In Pursuit of the Dream, 1948–1983
Henry A. J. Ramos
Clothbound, ISBN 1-55885-261-1
Trade Paperback, ISBN 1-55885-262-X

Chicano! The History of the Mexican American Civil Rights Movement
F. Arturo Rosales
ISBN 1-55885-201-8

Testimonio: A Documentary History of the Mexican-American Struggle for Civil Rights
F. Arturo Rosales
ISBN 1-55885-299-9

They Called Me "King Tiger": My Struggle for the Land and Our Rights
Reies López Tijerina
ISBN 1-55885-302-2

Julian Nava: My Mexican-American Journey
Julian Nava
Clothbound, ISBN 1-55885-364-2
Trade Paperback, ISBN 1-55885-351-0

César Chávez: A Struggle for Justice / César Chávez: La lucha por la justicia
Richard Griswold del Castillo
ISBN 1-55885-364-2

Memoir of a Visionary: Antonia Pantoja
Antonia Pantoja
2002, 384 pages, Clothbound
ISBN 1-55885-365-0, $26.95

Black Cuban, Black American
Evelio Grillo
2000, 134 pages, Trade Paperback
ISBN 1-55885-293-X, $13.95